THE ECO-LIVING HANDBOOK

A COMPLETE GREEN GUIDE FOR YOUR HOME AND LIFE

SARAH CALLARD AND DIANE MILLIS

SEVENOAKS

CONTENTS

INTRODUCTION

Climate change has become an even more pressing concern since the first publication of this title in 2001. There is no longer any doubt that human actions are directly leading to global warming and unpredictable, extreme weather as a result. The United Nations Intergovernmental Panel on Climate Change (IPCC), which brings together the world's leading climate scientists and experts, has stated that there is now no question that the increase in these greenhouse gases is predominantly caused by human activity.

In 2006 the *Stern Review on the Economics of Climate Change* predicted that the overall costs and risks of climate change will be equivalent to losing between 5 per cent and 20 per cent of global GDP each year but that the costs of action – reducing greenhouse gas emissions to avoid the worst impacts of climate change – can be limited to around 1 per cent of global GDP each year. Despite this, however, government action is still frustratingly slow. For example, in the UK the government is exploring the idea of creating zero-carbon communities – Eco-towns – and looking into the idea of personal carbon trading or carbon rationing, while also backing airport and road expansion.

There have been bold attempts to raise awareness among people of their personal role in climate change. Take former US Vice President Al Gore's Oscar-winning movie *An Inconvenient Truth*, which exposes the myths and misconceptions surrounding global warming and argues that global warming is not just a political issue but a moral one – it has been seen by millions across the globe. There has also been the 2007 Live Earth event with more than 2 billion people watching 24 hours of music across seven continents marking the beginning of a "multi-year mass persuasion campaign" led by the Alliance for Climate Protection to move individuals, corporations and governments to take action.

RECENT STATISTICS

* The 2007 Arctic summer sea ice reached the lowest extent of perennial ice cover on record – 23 per cent less than the previous low in 2005. The amount of summer sea ice has decreased by 6 per cent over the past 20 years and Arctic temperatures have risen by 5°C (41°F) over the past hundred years. Scientists now predict a 60 per cent loss of summer sea ice by around 2050.
* Concentrations of carbon dioxide in the atmosphere are at their highest levels for at least 650,000 years.
* A study of six biodiversity-rich regions, representing 20 per cent of the Earth's land area, found that 15 to 37 per cent of all the species in these regions could be driven to extinction by the climate changes likely between now and 2050.
* Sea levels could rise by up to 1 meter (3¼ feet) by 2100 if ice sheets continue to melt as temperature rises.
* Snow cover has decreased in most regions, especially in spring. The maximum extent of frozen ground in the winter/spring season decreased by about 7 per cent in the northern hemisphere over the latter half of the twentieth century.

Despite this, there are still many who are either not convinced of the science or not prepared to change their behaviour. A recent UK poll found 56 per cent of people believed scientists were still questioning climate change and that terrorism, graffiti and crime were all of greater concern. While another poll found that 59 per cent of the British public is still doing very little to tackle climate change. In the US, just 36 per cent of children and young adults are worried about the environment compared to 75 per cent of Indonesian youngsters.

To truly tackle climate change actions are needed on several levels – personal and political. This book concentrates on the personal in the hope that it will lead you on to become active in a political sense as well. For most governments it is the economy that is their prime concern and you, as a "consumer", are a key player in the economy. Your purchasing choices will act as a signal to legislators and corporate enterprises that you want to see change.

But the planet will not be saved by shopping. It will need some intrinsic changes in the way we expect to live our lives. We must accept that flying and driving are luxuries that we should voluntarily ration, we must buy less, and we must take greater responsibility for our actions – whether it's leaving a phone charging all night or failing to take your own bags to the supermarket.

Unlike the first edition of this book, we are not asking you to make just one change. We are asking you to look at your entire carbon footprint and to use this book in order to do all that you can to reduce it.

The Need to Change

The main cause of this climate change is the shift in balance between carbon dioxide (CO_2) emissions and absorptions. Burning fossil fuels, such as peat, coal, oil and gas, to generate power results in the release of large amounts of CO_2. In less carbon-heavy times these emissions were absorbed by trees and plants, but they are no longer able to keep up, in part due to deforestation.

These emissions and others, such as methane from landfill sites, sit in our atmosphere, preventing the sun's radiation from escaping. The net result? The global average temperature is forecast to rise by up to 3°C (37°F) this century – a rise which has probably not been experienced in at least the last 10,000 years. Polar ice caps are melting, sea levels are rising and the natural balance of life is being altered as a result.

The loss of our planet's forests also has an impact on our climate and environment in other ways: rainfall in tropical areas is falling as there are no trees to provide the moisture that builds up in clouds above the forest canopy; soil is exposed to the drying effects of wind and sun and, without tree roots to hold it in place, is being eroded at a massive rate leading to landslides and drought; and many plants and animals are moving towards extinction as their habitat is destroyed. And this is all so you can have disposable nappies (diapers), garden furniture, burgers and envelopes!

ESSENTIAL CHANGES TO MAKE

✱ Decrease your reliance on fossil fuels: Save energy in the home, choose plant-based materials for decorating your interior, and avoid all petrochemicals in cleaning products, bodycare items and cosmetics.

✱ Reject all toxic pesticides: Buy organic food and practice organic gardening.

✱ Stop buying plastic: Most of it won't biodegrade, its manufacture is highly polluting and it can leach toxic chemicals into your food.

✱ Recycle as much as possible: Recycle as many items as you can, reject disposable products and use a composting system.

✱ Buy from sustainable sources: When buying timber or timber-derived products, such as paper, buy only from sustainable sources. Look for certification to prove this.

dumped from households and factories into our waterways and oceans. Fish and other aquatic life forms are soaking up these toxins, passing them on up the food chain and dying or becoming deformed or infertile in the process.

We are hoping that by reading further you will be left in no doubt as to just how important you are to the environmental equation and how much you stand to gain by making changes. The point of this book is to give you the confidence and knowledge to make informed choices in your daily life – be it in the do-it-yourself store, supermarket, clothes shop or electrical-goods store. If you should find that making eco-friendly choices in your home is both easier and more satisfying than you thought possible, then apply these ideas and principles to other areas in your life, such as eco holidays and charities. Hopefully this book will set you on a path that will take you to them and many other planet-friendly activities in the years to come.

It is not just deforestation that is effecting global biodiversity. Pollution is playing a huge part in the demise of plants, insects, animals and humans. Toxic chemicals are liberally sprayed over our crops, ending up in our food and the insects and animals that dare to nibble on them. Some of them will also leach into groundwater supplies joining the other chemicals that have been

BACK TO BASICS

Saving energy at home is one of the best ways we have of preventing further climate change and this is why how we heat our homes and power our appliances has never been so firmly in the spotlight. Simple changes such as increasing the insulation in our lofts, installing thermostats on radiators and switching to a green electricity supplier all have a significant impact on the amount of energy we use and, thus, the carbon dioxide emissions we produce. When we burn fossil fuels such as coal, oil, peat and gas, we are not only contributing to global warming, we are also adding to the depletion of non-renewable energy sources. However, concerns that carbon-based fuels are going to run out have been replaced with fears about what will happen if we keep burning fuel at the rate we currently are.

Until fairly recently renewable energy sources such as solar, wind and geothermal were not seen as a viable option by most people. However, today they are much more accessible and affordable – due to developments in technology and increased investment in renewable energy – and now green energy options for householders are a definite reality.

Before you look at what energy sources you plan to use to heat your home, consider how much insulation you have. Around half of heat loss in a typical home is through the walls and loft so they should be first on the list.

This is a fantastic way to save energy (and money) without first having to spend a lot of cash. Laying extra insulation in your loft is a job that most people can manage themselves and cavity wall insulation could prevent up to 35 per cent of all heat loss from your home.

Installing double glazing is another way of dramatically cutting energy loss in your home. Although it is a more expensive option, double glazing cuts heat lost through windows by half and, in the long term, saves you money on your heating bills.

The vast majority of energy we use in our homes goes on heating and lighting. In fact, heating is responsible for more than 75 per cent of the energy consumption of an average household.

Lighting our homes is another area where many people can make major savings in energy loss and utility bills. Standard incandescent light bulbs are incredibly inefficient and only convert around 5 per cent of the energy they use into light while the rest is lost as heat.

Converting to low-energy lightbulbs, switching lights off when you leave a room and changing to a green energy supplier such are all great ways to reduce energy consumption, CO_2 emissions and costs.

This opening chapter looks in detail at what steps we can take, on a very local level, to lessen our impact on the environment. Although our ultimate aim may be to replace our dependence on fossil fuels with renewable energy sources, there are easier and more immediate changes you can make today to save energy. So whether you live in a block of flats or a rambling farmhouse, go back to basics and make some energy-saving changes today!

RENEWABLE ENERGY

In order to repair some of the damage that has already been done and to prepare for the future, it is essential to look to renewable energy sources to provide heating and light. The phrase "renewable energy" covers a number of diverse technologies designed to produce heat and power in a sustainable way, including solar water heating, wind energy and hydropower. The easiest natural energy source to harness is solar power. Depending on your house and energy needs, there are various ways to use the sun's energy. Advances in technology are already making renewable energy sources, such as solar, a viable option for householders.

One of the simplest ways to make a difference is by choosing a green electricity tariff from your local supplier. Although it will cost you slightly more than a conventional tariff, lots of companies offer incentives for going green, such as a quota of low-energy light bulbs. Wind power, hydroelectricity and biomass are all forms of renewable energy that governments should be supporting to provide for our energy needs. We ought to be aware of these options and how they affect the planet – support any local initiatives for renewable energy schemes and arm yourself with knowledge so that you can inform others.

Solar power

Passive solar power design is a way of maximizing the energy that can be directly derived from the sun. It is most effective when a new building is being constructed, when decisions about which rooms should face which direction can be made. Most of us, however, live in housing that was not built to make the most of the sun's energy. Even so, it is still possible to employ passive solar power in our homes without any cost or inconvenience. There is nothing very new about it – over 10 per cent of the space heating in an average home comes via solar energy through walls and windows.

A good way to introduce passive solar energy into your existing home is to build a conservatory. This is an expensive option, but it does increase the value of your home by adding an extra living space that costs you nothing to heat. A conservatory will insulate your house and preheat the ventilation air, as well as providing direct solar heating to the intervening wall, which is then convected into the rest of the house. Other simple steps to utilize the power of the sun include opening your curtains wide to maximize the amount of sunlight in your home, cutting back any trees or hedges that block light and avoiding net curtains that diffuse sunlight.

Solar water heating

Using the sun to heat hot water for your home sounds like a rather impractical option at first, but there are a number of advances in this area that are making it more of a realistic option.

One of the best ways to use the sun's energy is to use solar energy to heat your water. Solar water-heating systems are not suitable for all properties and the type of system you choose will depend on various factors including the available area of south-facing roof, your existing water heating system and budget. A qualified installer will be able to advise you on the most suitable system for your property.

A solar water-heating system has few environmental impacts and those produced are generally a result of the processes involved in the manufacture of the solar panels, the most popular form of solar energy. There are different kinds of systems that can be used at home, so take a look at what is available and consider how best you can incorporate it into your particular living space.

There are different methods of solar water-heating systems: flat-plate collectors and evacuated-tube collectors. The flat-plate collectors are basically sheets of metal painted black to absorb the sun's energy. Water is fed through the panel in pipes attached to the sheet and picks up the heat in the metal. Look for pipes made from copper for better conductivity, and that contain non-toxic antifreeze for the winter. The metal sheet is embedded in an insulated box and then covered with glass or clear plastic. Flat-plate solar energy collectors should ideally be installed on a south-facing roof – if that is not possible then a roof facing south-west or east to south-east will do. The panels should be set at an angle of between 10° and 60°.

The evacuated-tube collector system is made up of a series of between 20 and 30 glass heat tubes grouped together. Tubes are insulated by a vacuum inside the glass and use a heat-transfer fluid instead of water. Like the flat-plate collector, this system needs to be situated on a southerly-facing roof in order to absorb the most heat.

Doing it yourself

Although it might not sound like it, a solar water-heating system involves simple technology, and making your own system is not nearly as hard as you might think. Do-it-yourself kit systems for solar water heating are, however, now available from the big DIY stores.

GETTING THE MOST FROM SOLAR ENERGY

- ✿ **The main glazed areas should face within 30° either side of south.**
- ✿ **Fit large windows in south-facing walls and smaller ones in north-facing rooms.**
- ✿ **Avoid overshadowing from trees and other buildings.**
- ✿ **Build a conservatory onto your home – try to make sure it is on a south- or west-facing site that is protected from the wind.**
- ✿ **Avoid using net curtains and keep curtains wide open during the day to allow the maximum amount of sunshine in.**
- ✿ **The building should be well insulated to reduce heat loss.**
- ✿ **Install a responsive heating system to reduce wasted heat.**

Solar water heating systems are not suitable for all properties and the type of system you choose will depend on various factors including the available area of south-facing roof, your existing water heating system and budget. A qualified installer will be able to advise you on the most suitable system for your property.

Solar photovoltaics

Photovoltaics (PV) is the use of solar energy to generate electricity directly in a clean, renewable way. PV technology is quite costly to install and it can take a long time to recoup the initial investment so they are generally considered too expensive for most domestic situations. However, solar-generated electricity can play a useful role in the home in the form of garden and security lighting among other devices.

The sun's energy is soaked up during the day and then provides light during the night. It will save you money as well, because once the device has been installed then the cost of the lighting is absolutely free. Another use for PV is to power a garden fountain – kits are available with installation instructions.

A solar water-heating system will reduce carbon monoxide emissions – one of the causes of global warming.

Solar water-heating systems can produce up to 100 per cent of our hot water needs during the summer months.

PV is used to charge leisure batteries such as those used in caravans (mobile homes).

Within half an hour, enough of the sun's energy is received by the earth to power all of mankind's activities for a year.

PV is already used to power a number of products, including calculators, watches, laptop computers, model cars and torches (flashlights).

The word photovoltaic originates from the Greek word for "light".

Green energy suppliers

Every time you flick a light switch or turn on the toaster, spare a thought for the huge amount of greenhouse gases emitted from power stations that produce the electricity. Each time you use electricity to turn on the television or microwave oven, another lump of coal goes up in smoke and carbon dioxide emissions are released into the atmosphere. The burning of fossil fuels to make electricity is the single biggest cause of climate change in the world today. Conventional electricity produces harmful emissions such as sulphur dioxide and carbon dioxide during the manufacturing process, and these pollutants contribute to climate change as well as to acid rain. One way to cut this is to switch to an energy supplier offering 100 per cent renewable energy from wind, hydro or solar power.

Green tariffs work in different ways. On some, for example, every unit of electricity bought by a consumer is generated from a renewable energy source. On others, the additional premium is invested into new renewable energy projects in the form of a fund, usually used for developing community-based renewable energy projects. It is hard to say which type of tariff is the greenest, however suppliers investing in new renewable energy projects argue that they are building an alternative infrastructure to fossil fuel-burning power stations. While the suppliers offering 100 per cent renewable tariffs insist they are building a customer base for renewables and providing a steady demand for existing renewable power sources.

A green energy tariff, particularly one offering 100 per cent renewable energy, costs slightly more than standard ones because of the limited supply of renewable energy. Suppliers offering a mixture of green and conventional power can usually charge less for their tariffs. For more details on green energy suppliers, see Resources on pages 244–6

Green tariffs are available in various countries around the world. Some countries are more active than others and some electricity suppliers more proactive than others. It is a case of contacting your national or regional energy supplier.

Wind power

There is a tremendous potential for certain countries with a suitable climate to use wind power as a source of sustainable energy. Electricity from wind can be produced at a cost comparable with electricity from conventional sources. Wind energy projects are simple, clean and cheap to maintain. Wind turbines are sited in the windiest areas, often offshore, and the electricity generated can be fed straight into the local grid. Wind power is one of the fastest-growing energy technologies in the world and already provides for at least some of the energy needs of nations. It is cheap to harness and use, but the main problem is that wind turbines themselves are large and some people consider them to be a blight on the landscape.

More people are considering the possibility of using wind turbines to provide some or all of their existing energy needs, and this has been boosted by recent moves among manufacturers and retailers to make the technology more affordable and accessible than ever before.

A small domestic turbine generates around 1.5 kilowatts of electricity and will provide around 30 per cent of the average household's energy needs. They are emission-free, cheap to install and will also save you money on your energy bills.

Wind turbines have a life expectancy of around 20 years and only require service checks every few years. However, they aren't suitable for every home. If you live in a built-up urban area it may be that you simply don't have enough wind — the output of a turbine will be virtually zero in wind speeds below 5 m (16 ft) per second. For information on suppliers and installation see Resources on pages 244–6.

Hydroelectricity

The energy potential of moving water has been employed by man for thousands of years. Traditionally, it was used to power wheels to drive mills and machinery. Large dam projects are currently in operation in many countries to provide electricity, but the potential of hydropower on a global scale is still largely untapped. The problem with hydroelectric schemes is that dams must be built, which can damage the environment by disturbing river ecosystems. There is also a high cost involved.

Recent improvements in small turbine and generator technology mean that micro hydro schemes are a very environmentally-friendly way of producing electricity even for domestic homes if they have access to a water source such as a stream.

Biomass

Biomass energy is created from wood products such as fast-growing trees like willow or from organic materials such as animal waste or from industrial and biodegradable products from food processing. As well as providing energy for local heating needs, biomass can be used in power stations to create electricity.

Energy from biomass is particularly beneficial for the environment because it is a carbon neutral process. This means that the CO_2 released when energy is generated is balanced by that absorbed during the fuel's production. It can also be used as part of a waste management strategy to prevent materials ending up on landfill sites.

Domestically, biomass can be used to heat your home and hot water. Either via a stand alone wood burner, which can heat a room very effectively, or by installing a special boiler connected to central heating and hot water systems which run on wood pellets, logs or chips. However, these boilers can be expensive to install, and then you have to pay for fuel on top.

Geothermal heating

True geothermal heating – obtaining heat from the earth's core – would require a bore hole several hundred metres deep or access to hot springs as in Iceland. What most people are referring to when they talk about geothermal heating are ground source heat pumps (GSHP) which use the solar energy absorbed by the earth to provide heating. To install a GSHP system a length of pipe is laid around 100–150 m (330–490 ft) deep, which is then filled with a mixture of water and antifreeze. The heat pump extracts the heat from the ground, which is then fed through to a distribution system of either under floor heating or radiators.

A GSHP system could reduce the CO_2 emissions created by heating your home by between 2 to 8 tonnes a year, depending on the type of fuel being replaced. And a well-designed system might be able to provide sufficient energy for heating and hot water requirements for a household, although some would need boosting with other heating sources. However, these systems can also be very expensive to install. Therefore, they are really recommended for new-build houses or for a house where the entire heating system needs to be replaced.

INSULATION

Around half of the heat loss in a typical home is through the walls and loft, so it's worth checking whether yours are adequately insulated. Making sure your home is properly insulated is crucial if you are serious about saving energy. By insulating your home well, you will be helping to reduce carbon dioxide emissions into the environment, and saving money as well as energy. A lot of the draughts that whip through our homes are a result of poor construction techniques, but there is still a lot most of us can do to reduce the amount of energy lost through walls, doors and windows. Start by checking that all your doors and windows are sealed properly and can be closed firmly against the wind, and look out for plaster shrinkage that can sometimes leave a gap between windows or doors and adjoining walls.

Insulating your home to its optimum may not be one of the most exciting things you have ever done, but it will pay dividends for you and the environment. It still amazes most people when they hear that the average domestic building is responsible for wasting huge amounts of energy as heat is lost through poor insulation. Do what you can to improve the insulation in your home, especially if it is an old building. Avoid synthetic materials and choose eco-friendly insulators derived from renewable natural vegetation instead. Lagging pipes and hot-water tanks are jobs that most of us can do successfully ourselves and these can make a lot of difference to the energy efficiency of our homes.

Loft insulation

This is one of the easiest and most cost-effective methods of insulating your home. Even if you already have insulation in your loft it is worth checking that it is thick enough – the general rule with insulation is that if you can make it thicker, do so. Loft insulation really needs to be at least 27 cm (10½ in) thick – this might sound excessive but it is worth it as insulation this deep could save you around 20 per cent of your heating costs.

There are different types of loft insulation, such as sheep's wool, cellulose fibre, hemp (burlap) and flax – most of which you can install yourself. The material with the lowest impact on the environment is blown-cellulose fibre, which has the added advantage of being able to fill all the air gaps that can sometimes be left by solid insulation materials such as glass fibre, making it the more efficient insulator. Wool- and paper-based insulation materials have the added attraction of being free from formaldehyde. Insulating your loft could save substantially on fuel bills and save around 1 tonne of carbon dioxide emissions.

* **Cover windows and doors with curtains to block out draughts.**
* **Choose renewable materials for insulation.**
* **If you cannot insulate your walls, then put in extra loft insulation.**
* **Make sure there are no gaps between floorboards and skirting boards (baseboards).**
* **Check for any gaps around pipes and loft hatches.**
* **Use stuffed-fabric draught-excluders to block draughts under doors.**
* **Create a buffer area between the interior of your home and the outside by adding a porch or conservatory.**

* Once your loft has been
insulated, make sure any pipes or tanks
are also well insulated to avoid the problem of
freezing in winter.

* Not all cavity walls can be insulated –
an installer will check whether your house is suitable.

* Once you have spent time, money and energy insulating your
loft, make sure you also draught-strip and insulate the loft hatch to
prevent heat loss through the opening.

* Add a newspaper layer beneath your carpet underlay for extra insulation.

* When draught-proofing, check the places where pipes enter your
home and seal up any gaps.

* Trickle vents in the window frame can provide
background ventilation and reduce the need to open
windows to prevent stuffiness.

* Make sure you close the door
behind you when you are leaving
or entering a room.

Tank and pipe insulation

Insulating your hot-water cylinder will cut heat loss by over 75 per cent, saving you energy and money. If it is already insulated, check that it is at least 75 mm (3 in) thick. If it is in the loft, do not insulate underneath the tank, so that warm air can rise up from the house and prevent it from freezing in winter. New water tanks generally have built-in insulation, but installing a ready-made jacket, available from most do-it-yourself stores, is easy to do. If this is beyond you, do not despair; you can always pay someone to do it for you.

You can also prevent loss of heat along the length of your hot-water pipes by insulating them. The most important pipes to cover are those between the boiler and the hot-water cylinder, as well as those in the loft to stop them freezing up in winter. This is quite easy to do yourself, but if you are paying a professional to install loft insulation, they should also lag your pipes at the same time. If you have a choice in the matter, keep the length of pipe between the hot-water cylinder and the most frequently used taps (faucets) as short as possible.

Wall insulation

Many people are surprised to discover that more heat is lost through walls than any other way. If they are not insulated, your walls could be responsible for up to 35 per cent of all heat loss. If your home was built after 1920 it probably has cavity walls, which means there is an inner and outer layer with a small air gap or "cavity" in between. Cavity-wall insulation is the most cost-effective method of home insulation after loft insulation, and can reduce heat loss through the wall by up to 60 per cent.

Insulating cavity walls is a fairly easy operation for a professional installer – they use specialized equipment to inject the insulating material into the cavity from outside by drilling small holes in the wall. If you are unsure about whether your house has cavity walls or not, you can usually tell by measuring how thick they are. Cavity walls are at least 30 cm (12 in) thick, whereas solid walls are normally only around 25 cm (10 in) thick.

Solid walls lose even more heat than cavity walls. Research has shown that a three-bedroom house could save almost 2.5 tonnes of carbon dioxide emissions a year by insulating solid walls. It is, however, more difficult and, therefore, more expensive than cavity wall insulation. The work should be done by a professional, who will apply a layer of render and cladding on the outside of your walls to provide insulation. This could be worth considering if your exterior walls need repairing or re-rendering. Another option is to insulate the interior of your walls when they need redecorating or repairing, but be prepared for upheaval, because it is a major job and involves removing all the skirting boards (baseboards), window surrounds and doors.

Windows and doors

Statistics show that around 23 per cent of heat loss from homes escapes through windows. One way of preventing this is by fitting double-glazing; in itself double-glazing is not very environmentally friendly. If possible, avoid using uPVC double-glazing – the energy needed and the toxic waste created during its manufacture and disposal make it an environmental no-no. One report by Greenpeace said that the production and disposal of all types of PVC release some of today's most damaging industrial pollutants.

Recycling uPVC windows is not viable, according to Greenpeace, because it degrades when recycled and so new products can only contain a small percentage of recycled material.

Timber-framed double-glazing not only looks good, it's also farmore environmentally friendly. Make sure the wood is certified by the Forest Stewardship Council (FSC) so you can ensure it has not been illegally logged. And check that frames are finished with breathable natural paints or water-borne preservatives, which will help to maintain them and have minimal environmental impact.

If double-glazing is not an option, then you could consider secondary glazing. This is where a second layer of glass or clear plastic is fitted inside an existing window but does not have an airtight seal and so, although it will reduce heat that would otherwise be lost from the inside of the building, it is not as effective as double glazing. However, this could be good option – along with a pair of heavy lined curtains or wooden shutters – if you can't afford timber framed double glazing.

To check for draughts, hold your palm up to a window or door to feel whether any cold air is coming in. Small gaps in windows and doors are responsible for around 20 per cent of heat loss and can be prevented by draught-proofing. Materials for do-it-yourself draught-proofing can be bought at most hardware stores and they are easy to install.

Insulating floors

The next time you decide you need to change your carpets or floorboards, think about floor insulation. If there are

gaps between the floor and skirting boards (baseboards) you can simply add wooden beading between them. By filling the gaps between floors and skirting boards you could save as much as 20 per cent of your annual fuel bills. There are plenty of types of tube sealants available, which can be used in the same way as you use a sealant around the edge of the bath. And if you can insulate under the floorboards on the ground floor, the room will feel warmer and you will save more money.

Natural materials for insulating flooring include Warmcel (a material made from surplus books, newspapers and telephone directories), sheep's wool and recycled rubber, which gives a softer surface to walk on, as well as providing soundproofing. Coconut fibreboard, made from the outer husks of coconuts, is a very durable and completely natural insulation material, with good thermal and sound insulation properties. These materials are available from environmentally friendly companies and builder's merchants.

Materials

Natural insulation products have environmental benefits over conventional materials. They are made from renewable plant or animal sources and their manufacturing processes use very little energy. Also, they are safe to handle and are re-usable or biodegradable at the end of a building's life. They have the added advantage of allowing the building to "breathe" because they can absorb airborne moisture and release it when the air is drier thus keeping humidity stable. A good example of a natural insulation material is flax, which can hold up to 25 per cent of its weight in water.

There are various materials available for insulating all areas of your home. Organic materials include cork, sheep's wool, cellulose and wood wool. There are also materials derived from naturally occurring minerals, such as mineral wool, which comes in different formats, such as quilt and loose fill.

As we become increasingly concerned about the materials used in our homes, a growing number of companies are developing innovative, environmentally friendly materials for use as insulation. Insulation material made from a recycled rubber such as Regupol is good for creating a softer surface underfoot when it is fitted underneath carpets, and it has the added advantage of offering effective soundproofing. Sheep's wool used for thermal insulation such as Thermafleece can absorb more than one-third of its own weight in moisture and therefore helps prevent timber from

rotting or from being attacked by mould or fungus, and prevents metal from rusting. Make sure the wool is from sheep that have not been dipped in pesticides; it should simply be washed and treated with borax to make it resistant to fire and insects. Sheep's wool insulation comes in a felted-quilt format and it can be cut with a pair of sharp scissors to fit exactly the area it is being used to insulate, so it is very easy to install.

Ventilation

Insulation does not mean that you have to seal up your home completely – ventilation is also very important if you are to avoid an unpleasant stuffy atmosphere. If you have a solid-fuel fire or gas appliances, ventilation is essential as a well-insulated house will trap vapours and gases that would escape from a less insulated home.

It is also important to keep the kitchen and bathroom well ventilated so as to prevent condensation and avoid wood rot. But how do you reach a balance between the two? If you do have a problem with condensation, consider fitting an extractor fan. If you have a solid-fuel fire make sure you have the chimney and air bricks checked for any blockages. A ceiling fan can also be good for circulating air in both the summer and winter.

ORGANIC INSULATING MATERIALS

* Cork, which comes in slabs, tiles or granular format.

* Expanded rubber for piping.

* Wood fibre as insulation board for walls.

* Sheep's wool, which is available in a
  felted-quilt format.

* Heraflax – felted flax quilts.

* Wood wool slabs.

* Cellulose loose-fill pellets.

LIGHTING

We could all save energy and money by being more careful about the way we light our homes. First, make sure that you are getting the most out of the natural daylight available to you and be aware of the amount of artificial lighting you use in your home. In the north hemisphere, a house designed to save energy would have large south-facing windows and skylights to make the most of the daylight. Try to arrange your living space around the natural light that is available throughout the day – in the morning use rooms that face south or east and in the afternoon and evening use those facing west. Rooms that have very limited light or face north should be used the least.

You can also remove any obstacles that block daylight getting into your home (within reason!) such as trees and bushes. Deciduous trees are a good way of keeping your house cool in the summer without blocking out light in winter. Make sure you can draw curtains and blinds completely away from windows to allow extra daylight in. You could also consider installing a skylight for dark attic rooms, hallways and stair areas that would otherwise require artificial lighting. If you are planning renovations, it might be a good idea to take the opportunity to install more windows in darker areas of the house.

Light bulbs

Of course we must all use some artificial light, but the choice of light bulb makes a huge difference in terms of how much energy we use to produce that light. By switching to energy-efficient light bulbs you will reduce energy consumption, save money and cut CO_2 emissions. Standard or incandescent filament light bulbs are extremely inefficient, because only around 5 per cent of the energy they use is turned into light; the rest is converted into heat.

Energy-efficient light bulbs, known as Compact Fluorescent Light (CFLs) bulbs, still cost more than standard bulbs but they last up to 12 times longer, saving you money as well as energy.

Compact fluorescent lights

Compact fluorescent lights work like standard tube fluorescent lights, only the tube is smaller and folded over to concentrate the light. The compact design allows them to be used in place of incandescent light bulbs. They can be a good way of introducing eco-friendly solutions into your home without causing a big disruption or incurring great expense. Although energy-efficient bulbs are more expensive than standard ones, they will save you money in the long run. Compact fluorescent light bulbs require less energy to produce the same amount of light as a conventional bulb because they convert much more of the energy to light – standard bulbs convert most of the energy to heat. They have a lifespan of up to 12 times longer than a standard bulb, so therefore save energy and raw materials during the manufacturing process and produce less waste.

It is a good idea to replace standard bulbs with compact fluorescent light bulbs in areas of your home where the lights are left on for long periods of time. Compact fluorescent light bulbs are available in most supermarkets, hardware and do-it-yourself stores, as well as by mail order from green companies. You have probably spotted them before and maybe you did not act because you thought they were too expensive and instead reached for the regular 40-watt bulb. If so, now is the time to think again.

Shape and size

As with standard bulbs, compact fluorescent bulbs come with both bayonet and screw fittings so they can be easily fitted into existing sockets. They are also available in a variety of shapes and sizes so you can choose the most appropriate for each lamp and fitting. It does not really matter what shape or size of bulb you use, but you will find that the "stick"-shaped bulbs give off a more rounded light, so they are good in central locations, whereas the flatter bulbs work better as wall lights, because they give off light from the top and bottom.

Compact fluorescent bulbs are available in a range of wattage, depending on how brightly you want an area to be lit. When replacing standard bulbs with low-energy equivalents start with rooms and areas most commonly used, as this will save more energy and money. Any lighting that is left on for long periods of time, such as outdoor security lighting, would be much more cost-effective if the bulbs were replaced with energy-saving ones, but it is worth noting that compact fluorescent bulbs do not usually work with dimmer switches, timers or sensors. If you are using a dimmer switch with standard bulbs, check with the manufacturer whether it is an energy-efficient appliance: some are, but others waste a lot of energy through heat generation – you can usually tell if this is likely to be the case because the switch will be warm to the touch.

Light emitting diodes

LEDs (Light Emitting Diodes) are a fairly recent development in the energy-efficient lighting sector and they are the eco-alternative to halogen spotlighting. LEDs use even less energy than CFL bulbs and can last up to 11 years, however, they are not yet widely available in retail outlets.

Although low-voltage spotlights, such as halogen, are more energy-efficient than incandescent bulbs, they can end up using more energy because, invariably, more spotlights are used to light the same space as one incandescent light.

Halogen lamps, a form of incandescent lighting, last up to eight times longer than conventional bulbs. They are often positioned where high light quality is needed and are commonly used in retail stores and commercial buildings. In terms of efficiency, halogen lamps fall between standard incandescent lighting and compact fluorescent lamps. They are, however, useful where light is needed in only a small area.

* Choose light fittings and shades that give a good amount of light.

* Use lamps to illuminate exactly the area you want.

* Decorate your walls in light colours to reflect the available light.

* Keep lights and windows clean to provide more light. Use natural light as much as you can during daylight hours.

* Replace your most frequently used light bulbs with energy-saving bulbs first as these will generate the most savings, in terms of both energy and money.

* Get into the habit of always turning off lights when you leave the room and nag everyone else in your home to do the same – after all, there is no point in lighting an empty space.

* If energy-saving bulbs are used outdoors make sure they are enclosed in a sealed unit to provide protection from cold-weather conditions.

* Use one higher wattage bulb rather than a few lower wattage bulbs in a multiple fitting; it will provide the same amount of light while using less energy.

* Use a combination of task lighting and general illumination.

* Use outdoor security lights with motion sensors to save energy and yet still discourage intruders.

HEATING AND HOT WATER

Heating and hot water are responsible for more than 75 per cent of the energy consumption of an average household and by controlling your heating you could save a substantial amount of money. Heating and hot water account for more than half the average fuel bill – even more if you live in an old building. There is no point spending time, money and energy on home insulation and draught-proofing if you do not heat your home efficiently. Having an overheated house can be as uncomfortable as a cold, draughty environment, so make sure you know how your heating system works.

Try turning the thermostat down a few notches – we often live in over-heated environments and expect to walk around in a T-shirt even if it is snowing outside. The thermostat should be set to around 19°C (66°F) for most people to feel comfortable without the room getting stuffy. Do what you can to make the most of the natural heating power of the sun and protect your home from cold prevailing winds if possible, as this will reduce the amount of energy you need to heat it. This is not always possible, however, so use techniques such as room thermostats, lining radiators and timer switches to cut down on wasted energy and to get the most out of your system.

Heating your home

Electricity is really the least energy-efficient way to heat your home and hot water because it is produced in incredibly inefficient power stations that burn huge amounts of coal or oil. When electricity is used for heating, around 90 per cent of the fuel's primary energy is lost due to inefficient transmission systems and electrical appliances.

Gas is the best energy source for heating your home and hot water, but there is great scope for the use of renewable energy such as solar power for purposes of domestic water heating (see Renewable Energy, pages 15–17). If you plan on moving house or you are considering carrying out major refurbishment work to your existing home, these are ideal times for exploring the renewable energy options available.

Reducing heat loss

There are a number of low-cost and even free steps that you can take to reduce your energy consumption levels. If possible, you should make sure radiators are placed on internal walls rather than on external ones, which has been the practice in the past. If you have no choice, then reduce the heat lost through external walls by pasting sheets of aluminium foil, shiny side in, on the external wall behind the radiator. Another idea is to place shelves (also with foil on the underside) above radiators to try and trap the heat. If you have enough room you could also consider creating a mezzanine level, which would make use of warm air near the ceiling.

One of the most effective ways of heating your home is to heat only the rooms that you are using, with different temperatures for different rooms depending on how much you use them. Our bodies lose heat through radiation – the transfer of heat from one object to another – so to reduce this it is advisable to use natural materials in your home such as wood and fabric, rather than glass and metal, which conduct heat more rapidly.

Central-heating systems

Have a look at your heating system to see how efficient it really is. There are a number of upgrades that can be made to central-heating systems to improve their efficiency, such as controls for room temperature and the temperature of stored water; on/off times for heating and hot water; and switching the boiler off when heating is no longer required. Thermostatic radiator valves also allow you to control individual room temperatures because they automatically turn off a radiator once the temperature has reached the desired level.

The key is flexibility, so that you can regulate the amount of space and hot water you want to heat without wasting any energy (or money). The controls of your heating system should react to changes in temperature. You should be able to switch your heating and hot water off and on whenever you want. Most modern systems are able to do this, but if you have an old heating system then its controls might be too simple. If this is the case, think about upgrading it and adding better controls. If you are thinking of updating your heating system and debating whether to add full or partial controls, you should consider the age of your central-heating system. If it is very old it might be wise to install the full range of controls, but if it is a fairly new system then it might benefit from simply adding thermostatic radiator valves.

Timers and thermostats

The time switch or programmer is one of the most useful of all heating controls because it turns your heating and hot water on and off automatically at pre-set times. Some will allow you to set timings for your hot water and heating separately. A room thermostat switches the heating off once the set temperature is reached, and then back on again if it drops below that level, giving you a constant temperature. The thermostat should be installed

HINTS FOR HEATING

✱ Save on your heating bills simply by
turning your thermostat down to 20°C (68°F).

✱ Instead of cranking up the central heating, consider
putting on a thicker sweater and socks.

✱ Have a hot-water bottle in bed rather than an electric blanket.

✱ Use thick, organic cotton sheets and a woollen blanket to make
the bed feel warmer and cosier.

✱ Make sure you heat only the areas of your home you need to.

✱ Turn the central heating down or off when you go out.
Alternatively install a programmable thermostat to maintain
the temperature only when you are there.

✱ Set your thermostat for heating water at around 60°C (140°F).
Don't have it scalding hot or you will have to run extra
cold water to cool it down.

✱ Make sure your boiler (or furnace) is serviced
regularly to maintain its safety and for
maximum efficiency.

on the wall of the most frequently used room, away from draughts, sunlight and other heat sources. It can be wired to your central-heating pump, but it will be more economical if it is fitted as part of a complete control system that switches off the boiler to prevent so-called "dry cycling", which is when the boiler fires up to keep itself hot even when it is not needed. You can also choose to have different heating "zones" in your house, so that you can heat certain areas individually.

Thermostatic radiator valves enable you to control the temperature of each room separately and can be useful in rooms that are inclined to overheat, such as the bathroom and kitchen. They work by reducing the flow of water to the radiator as the thermostat reaches its set temperature.

If you are installing a condensing boiler be aware that it will produce water vapour that is visible from the flue, known as the "pluming" effect. This can be unsightly and unpleasant, so to avoid irritating your neighbours, always site the flue away from windows and doors.

Most central-heating systems also heat your hot-water cylinder. One way of saving energy is to reduce the temperature of your stored hot water. If you have a pumped or gravity hot-water system then you can do this by fitting a thermostat to your hot-water cylinder and a motorized valve to the cylinder. Or you could fit a clamp-on cylinder thermostat as part of an integrated control system.

Boilers and furnaces

Most of us have had problems with boilers and furnaces at some point – there is nothing worse than waking up on a cold winter's day to discover that the boiler refuses to crank into action, leaving you without heating or hot water, possibly even both. Boilers generally have an efficient lifespan of around 15 years, after which they become a lot more expensive to run and far less energy efficient. Modern versions are, however, much more energy-efficient than older ones, so although investing in a new boiler is a major outlay, it will certainly save you money in the long run. Most manufacturers publish the seasonal efficiency of their boilers, so make sure you check out this information before investing. There are different ones for different jobs, so get advice on which is the best type for your living space. This is true of all central-heating systems – if you are installing a brand new system, look around for the one that best suits your specific needs.

Condensing boilers are the most efficient boilers available today. They convert around 88 per cent of fuel into heat, compared with the 72 per cent managed by most standard boilers. They can be wall-mounted or floor-standing and are suitable for any size home, but because they are more expensive than other boilers they are particularly good for larger houses where the initial cost will be recouped more quickly.

Other heat sources

Alternative methods of heating your home are gas fires, convector heaters, electric storage heaters and solid-fuel stoves. Electric storage heaters work by storing heat during off-peak periods when electricity is cheaper because there is less demand, and then releasing it the following day.

Although open-log fires are very appealing they are not very energy efficient and waste around 85 per cent of the fuel they burn. An open fire will use around 15 times the air content of the room it is situated in every hour. To compensate for this it sucks in air from gaps in windows and doors, creating draughts. Consider a wood-burning stove instead. If you run a stove alongside a central-heating system you could cut your fuel bills considerably, unlike an open-log fire, which is likely to push your fuel bills up. When choosing a stove, it is important to buy one that is not too big for the room because otherwise it will be underfiring and not performing at its best. Most stoves are made from cast iron, which is able to continue radiating stored heat well after the fire has gone out. They can be used for a number of functions, including direct space heating, hot-water heating and radiator heating. Some versions even have hot plates for warming up food.

*If you have a solid-fuel stove, save twigs and scraps of paper and newspaper to start it rather than using firelighters, which are created from paraffin and other flammable chemicals.

* Wood bought as fuel should come from a renewable source, such as a sustainably managed forestry system, or recovered wood waste.

* Look in the telephone directory or online for local tree surgeons and construction companies, who might be willing to give you waste material for fuel.

* Keep wood stacked outdoors, but under cover so it stays dry.

* Softwoods can be used for kindling as they burn very fast and hot.

* Invest in a "log maker", a device that makes logs from unwanted paper.

MATERIALS IN THE HOME

A look around the average household is enough to highlight the lack of natural materials we use in our homes. We are used to soft furnishings stuffed with synthetic fibres; floors covered in wall-to-wall carpet and walls finished with paints containing petrochemicals. By incorporating more natural materials, such as wood, clay, cork and hemp, you can reduce the amount of pollutants in your home and improve both the insulation and the quality of the atmosphere in your living space.

Using locally sourced natural materials is the best option in order to cut down on pollution caused by transportation. The average household suffers from the volatile organic compounds (VOCs) and other pollutants released by furniture made from composite boards, and synthetic fibres used in carpets and upholstery, as well as conventional paint and vinyl wallpaper. By seeking out more traditional materials, such as stone and timber, you will create a home that is more in sync with the environment and better for you and your family.

Avoid non-drip paints as they may contain polyurethane. Choose matt or satin finish paint over high-gloss versions, which contain many more solvents.

Problems with paint

The earliest paints were made using ochre – a clay-like earth material – and ground rocks to create pigments. Colourful pigments were created by grinding shells, stone and minerals to achieve a range of colours from red through to blue. Early oil paints contained linseed and hemp seed oil to dry and harden them. The creation of chemical synthetics meant that a whole new range of colours that had never been used before was introduced, and since then petrochemical synthetics have taken over from natural vegetable oil and resin bases for paints. Today, all paints, whether natural or synthetic, are either solvent or water based. Natural organic paints are made with solvents derived from plants such as citrus peel oil and other natural ingredients.

Synthetic paints are harmful to those involved in manufacturing them as well as using them, and they also pose a problem in terms of pollution. They contain solvents that give off volatile organic compounds (see above) during application of the paint, when it is drying and sometimes for years afterwards. Synthetic paints are also likely to contain fungicides and heavy metals such as cadmium. They can pose a major fire risk because once alight they will burn very quickly and emit toxic fumes.

According to research by the Centre for Alternative Technology, paint production is alarmingly inefficient in terms of energy usage, with the manufacture of 1 tonne of paint producing up to 10 tonnes of waste, much of which is toxic.

Natural paints are available for painting walls, plaster and metal, and water-based paint that can be used on wood is becoming more widely available. They are made using pigments derived from natural plants, minerals and resins, such as linseed oil, and waxes also derived from plants, which act as binders and media for the pigments. Natural paints are more subtly coloured than conventional ones and generally smell nicer as they are often made with essential oils.

There has been much research into the effects of conventional paints on health and some studies have found that petrochemical solvents, often in paints, such as turpentine (white spirit), emit toxic gases including toluene and xylene, which are known carcinogens. This has led to an increased demand from consumers for natural paints instead of the more commonly used petrochemical-based varieties.

The disposal of paint pots also poses a big problem – particularly those that are not completely empty – because the toxins can leach out into the water table. Leftover paint should ideally be passed on to someone who can use it, such as local schools or community groups. Conventional paint should be taken to a recycling centre – never poured down drains – however, it will almost certainly end up on landfill.

In 1989 the World Health Organization's International Agency for Research on Cancer found that professional painters and decorators faced a 40 per cent increased chance of developing cancer.

Natural paints and stains are water based and are made using plant-based dyes, solvents and fillers, which are biodegradable. This means that they can usually be composted safely as long as they have been dried out properly first.

As well as improving the aesthetic quality of your home, natural paints and finishes also help to create a healthier living space for you and your family. On a practical level, they allow the walls to "breathe", which in turn reduces the likelihood of the long-term structural damage that can result from moisture being trapped behind sealed, non-breathing, non-porous surfaces.

Some natural paint manufacturers have developed products to help combat the air polluting effects of formaldehyde and other pollutants in the home, such as solvents and VOCs given off by synthetic furnishings. Wall insulating paints are also available that help regulate the inside temperature throughout the year. For more information on manufacturers, see Resources on pages 244–5.

If you are planning to redecorate or have recently moved house, be aware of the hazards of dealing with paint. Lead is often found in old paint so take great care not to inhale the dust or fumes when rubbing or stripping down old surfaces. When you are doing this sort of work, wear a mouth and nose cover made out of an old T-shirt or sheet and keep windows open to make sure there is sufficient ventilation. The least harmful way of stripping paint is to sand it off, rather than applying harmful paint-stripping chemicals.

* **Look out for low-odour paints.**

* **Use paints made from natural resins, essential oils, chalk, India rubber and linseed oil.**

* **Don't throw unwanted paint down the drain – let it dry first and contact your local authority regarding responsible disposal.**

* **Whenever possible, opt for natural, unpainted finishes.**

* **Look for limewash, mineral- or plant-based paints for walls and ceilings.**

* **Check whether the pots are recyclable.**

* **Try to use paint "kits" so you can make only as much paint as you need.**

* **Buy solvent-free products.**

* **More environmentally friendly paints are those thinned with milk casein or natural glue.**

* **Be aware that water-based paints, such as lime distempers and whitewash may, not be very durable or washable.**

Wallpaper

Until recently wallpaper had been out of fashion, but a number of designers have modernized it and it is once again a good way to cover your walls. But how acceptable is it on an environmental level? Many wallpapers are vinyl based and wallpaper paste is a solvent that often contains fungicides. Vinyl and plastic wallpaper actually stops the wall from breathing, which can lead to structural problems.

More manufacturers are developing environmentally-friendly wallpaper made using chlorine-free paper sourced from managed forests. Look out for wallpaper made using water-based inks that have less impact on the environment. For stockists, see Resources on pages 244–6.

Conventional paint strippers all contain a solvent known as dichlormethane (DCM), which is thought to be carcinogenic. Water-based paint strippers that are biodegradable and do not give off toxic fumes are available, but they vary in their effectiveness.

Flooring

Indoor pollution can be caused by the very materials you introduce into your home to furnish it, so do not forget this when you are choosing the floor covering. In order to avoid the volatile organic compounds (VOCs) (see pages 41–3) given off by artificial fibres and synthetic materials, make sure you are aware of exactly what your new carpet is made from. An immediate indicator of how harmful it might be is the smell of a new carpet or floor covering. Although the odour does eventually fade, the carpet could continue to emit harmful gases into your home environment.

Most carpets and floor coverings are made from petrochemical-based synthetics manufactured using non-renewable resources. This makes them non-biodegradable and difficult to recycle, so they end up on landfill sites or in incinerators once they have been disposed of. Vinyl flooring, whether on a roll or in tiles, should always be avoided as it uses polyvinyl chloride (PVC), the manufacture of which is extremely hazardous to the environment.

A growing number of companies are starting to cater for people who want a greener home, and many do-it-yourself giants are developing eco-friendly ranges. In the meantime, materials to look out for are: natural linoleum, wood (as long as it is from a sustainable source or salvaged), cork and local slate. Wooden floors might seem like the most natural option and they certainly look good, but to be sure of green credentials, check where

> Cut down on noise pollution by adding a layer of acoustic insulation under floorboards or carpets. Try using coconut fibre matting or mats made from recycled rubber tyres.

the timber is from and how it has been forested (see Wooden Flooring, page 52).

INSULATION

Before you decide which flooring you want for your home, first make sure the floor is properly insulated against draughts and sound. This is a relatively straight forward, albeit time-consuming, job, but it is well worth the effort. Lift the floorboards and fit wooden slats or netting to support the insulation material then fill the space with the insulation material – you could use anything from old pieces of carpet to compressed wood fibre – making sure you leave some gaps to allow for ventilation. You can then fit your new flooring over the top of this insulating layer. (See also Insulating Floors, page 27.)

CARPET CONCERNS

None of us like to think about the amount of dust and dirt trapped in our carpets, but we all know it is there, no matter how conscientious we are with the vacuum cleaner. Recent research has shown that dust mites in carpets can cause and exacerbate allergic reactions, particularly among children, so choosing environmentally friendly flooring can be beneficial both to the planet and to your family.

Buying a wool carpet might seem like a good eco-option, but not if it has been treated and dyed with chemicals, so check the processes it has been through. There are often VOCs (see page 41) present in the binders used in the fabrication of materials such as carpet padding, as well as in the adhesives used to apply carpet padding and tiles. Natural and organic wool that has not been treated with chemicals is one option – just make sure it has not been backed with a synthetic material. Look out for woollen felt backing, which as well as being natural provides a comfortable surface to walk on and has the added benefit of offering good sound insulation.

If you cannot bear to live without it, there are a number of green alternatives to having carpet throughout your home and it does not have to be cold, scratchy or minimalist. Environmentally friendly flooring comes in many different forms, so you could choose a different material for each room. Flooring made with materials such as cork, coir and sisal can look very good and will give your home a clean, modern style.

COIR

Most commonly used to make doormats, coir is a 100 per cent natural and renewable fibre made from the husks of coconuts that would otherwise be thrown away. The colour varies with the annual cycle – coir harvested in the wet season is lighter than the summer crop. Coir fibres are softened, spun into yarn and then woven to make coarse matting, which is ideal for kitchens and bathrooms.

Flooring made from coir is very long lasting, as well as being eco-friendly – coir was traditionally used to make rope and twine because it is such a durable material. The fibres are non-oily and therefore prevent bacteriological activity, which helps to eliminate the chances of an allergic reaction, such as eczema or asthma, which can be caused by synthetic carpets.

* Coir and jute are very durable and ideal for areas in the home that get a lot of wear and tear, such as stairs and hallways.

* Sisal is more delicate and would be better used in areas that have less traffic, like the living room or bedroom.

* Linoleum is ideal for use in the kitchen because drips and spills can be mopped up easily.

* Reclaimed ceramic tiles, locally produced or salvaged stone, cork or bamboo are all good choices for the bathroom.

SISAL

Sisal is traditionally grown in Mexico. Its 1 m (1 yard) long leaves are soaked until they disintegrate into tough fibres. The fibres are then spun into yarn and woven to make carpets or matting. It is the most commonly used natural fibre and makes carpets and mats of various textures and colours. However, there is concern about the intensive cultivation methods, which can lead to soil erosion, and the effect of sisal dust on factory workers.

JUTE

Grown in India and then exported. The jute fibres are extracted from the stem of the plant and soaked in water. It is then used to make a number of products, including hessian (burlap) cloths and sacking, as well as wall coverings and backing for carpets and rugs. Jute is less hard-wearing than sisal.

CORK TILES

A sustainable, natural material that comes from the bark of the cork oak tree. Once it is 25 years old, the tree can be harvested once every nine years without being damaged. Cork trees can live for up to 150 years and, as well as producing cork, they also support a diversity of wildlife. As a natural product, cork is biodegradable, sustainable and non-polluting.

The cork industry is currently under threat because of an increase in popularity of the plastic wine "cork". This is due to the large number of wines that are "corked", or contaminated, by a faulty cork. Corked wine costs the wine industry thousands every year and there are increasing calls for producers to use plastic corks instead

Look for flooring adhesive made from natural materials when you are laying cork, linoleum or carpet.

so as to prevent this loss. The wine industry is the single biggest user of cork, with most other products, such as tiles, being made from wine cork leftovers.

Floor tiles made of cork are useful in areas such as the bathroom and kitchen. Cork is made up of millions of air pockets so it makes a very good insulation material, for both noise and warmth. The best option if you decide to buy cork tiles is to look out for unvarnished tiles. You can then seal them yourself with an innocuous sealant such as a water-based varnish or beeswax polish, which will also make them easy to clean. For a more colourful effect, try staining cork tiles with a plant-based stain. There is also the added bonus that you can replace odd tiles if they get spoiled or damaged, rather than having to re-lay the entire floor, so it is always worth buying a couple of extra tiles just in case. There are some interesting "designer" cork tiles around at the moment, which really bring the material bang up to date with unusual designs and colours. While these are tempting, a lot of them are finished with a PVC laminate – one of the most toxic, non-biodegradable materials around.

SEAGRASS

Grown in seawater paddy fields, seagrass is used to create flooring that is water and stain resistant. The seagrass is twisted and then woven to make coarse, rustic-looking flooring. Make sure that the company you are buying it from does not use chemicals such as dyes or bleach to alter the look of the fibres. Also, check that it does not use synthetic backings on the seagrass, which defeats the object of buying natural flooring, as these are non-biodegradable. There are concerns that harvesting seagrass can disrupt the delicate eco-system it is part of, and you should also take into account the amount of energy used in transporting materials from different countries.

LINOLEUM

Linoleum is another good natural flooring option. It is made from softwood powder, linseed oil, pine tree resins, cork, chalk and jute backing. The cork used in linoleum is sustainably harvested from the cork tree. Linoleum will cost more than vinyl flooring but is by far the better choice. When laying a linoleum floor, try to use a plant-based adhesive rather than a solvent-based one. If you are using linoleum as a flooring material, make sure that you have a damp-proof surface as moisture can damage the backing of the linoleum.

RUBBER

This comes from the white, milky latex extracted from the rubber tree, which is indigenous to South America. Although it is a natural substance, the rubber we use today is vulcanized in a production process that is very energy consuming. It is combined with sulphur under heat and pressure to make it resilient and elastic, and to get rid of smells and stickiness. As it is tough and waterproof, rubber is often used to make flooring for bathrooms and kitchens.

RECLAIMED TILES

Unfired clay is a very eco-friendly material; in fact it is quite literally the earth beneath our feet, and is eminently biodegradable. The problem with tiles is that they need to be fired – a process that uses a huge amount of energy and causes a great deal of pollution, although some types of kiln are more energy efficient than others. The best option is to look for salvaged or reclaimed terracotta tiles. Also, bear in mind that if you are using tiles on your floor, the glazes often contain toxic chemicals and compounds, including zinc and lead. Generally, the brighter the tile colour, the more toxic the glaze.

STONE

For centuries people have used stone such as granite, slate, flint, limestone and sandstone for building. The high cost of materials such as granite is caused by the rarity and quality of the stone and the fact that its transportation is very labour intensive. Transportation costs can also be high due to the weight of the stone. This means that using these materials for flooring is not very green unless it is salvaged stone from old buildings and is also available locally.

Stone is hard, strong and water resistant. A raw material like slate can be made into thick slabs for floors. Stone is a non-polluting, natural material that is ideal for use in kitchens and bathrooms. The disadvantages of using stone are really the expense and possible problems with radon, which materials like granite can emit, so make sure it is tested by an expert first. Natural stone can give an earthy, natural but contemporary feel to a room.

Wood

This is one of the best environmental choices when selecting materials to use in your home. Wood is waste efficient, recyclable, biodegradable and non-toxic, but this is valid only if the wood is harvested from a renewable source. Trees stabilize climate and global temperature, so deforestation causes a number of problems, one of which is the reduction in the number of trees that soak up excess carbon dioxide. Even with sustainable forestry there is the potential problem that although it provides us with a renewable resource, it does not support the same diverse wildlife as natural woodland.

Although trees are a renewable resource there is still concern that we are using too many and that this is affecting the delicate ecological balance. Look for certified wood that has been grown under a sustainability management scheme such as the Forest Stewardship Council (FSC). This indicates that it conforms to specific criteria regarding the protection of the environment, including water resources and soil structure, as well as social issues such as the welfare of forestry workers and the rights of indigenous peoples. The FSC was set up in 1993 as a non-profit organization with a membership of timber traders, community forest groups, forest workers' unions and retail companies across the world. It is recognized as international certifier of sustainable forestry by environmental groups such as Greenpeace and Friends of the Earth.

When you are buying new timber, find out exactly what type of wood it is. If possible, buy sustainable timber local to where you live, to try to reduce the amount of imported wood, and at all costs avoid all endangered tropical hardwood species. Also avoid wood alternatives like composite boards, such as fibreboard (MDF) and plywood, as they contain adhesives and formaldehyde.

The following are threatened tropical hardwood species and should be avoided:

- Teak
- Mahogany
- Rosewood
- Kapur
- Ebony
- Ramin

Trees are felled when they reach maturity, which varies depending on the species: oak matures at 100 years while ash takes 50.

TIMBER IS DIVIDED INTO TWO GROUPS

These are softwood and hardwood (which does not always reflect the hardness of the wood).

Hardwoods such as oak come from broad-leaved trees in temperate regions and softwoods such as pine come from coniferous trees. Hardwoods grow more slowly than softwoods and are more able to resist fungal and insect attacks.

Softwood is more susceptible than hardwood to water and insect attacks, so a lot of softwood timber is treated with toxic fungicides and insecticides such as lindane and pentachlorophenol (PCP). There are safer treatments, however, such as borax, linseed oil, potash and beeswax.

WOODEN FLOORING

Many older houses have wooden floorboards hidden beneath the carpet, which can make very attractive flooring if sanded down and polished. This kind of floor needs less cleaning than a carpet because dust is simply swept up without the need for a vacuum and other dirt can be wiped away with a damp cloth. A wooden floor also has excellent insulation properties, which makes it cool in the summer and warm during the winter months.

If you do choose to have floorboards, look for natural, vegetable-based wood stains and polishes, and apply a water-based varnish to create a smooth, attractive and easily cleaned surface.

Rugs make wooden floors more comfortable. They also have the added advantage that they can be shaken and aired outdoors, unlike carpets, which are there for good. To stop them slipping you can stick them down using strong tape or special grips designed specifically for this purpose. Don't buy rugs with non-slip backing because the backing material will probably be foam or plastic. Wooden floorboards are the cheapest and greenest choice of flooring for many older buildings.

If you do not have floorboards, fitting a new wooden floor on top of the existing one is an option. Most do-it-yourself stores sell wooden blocks that can easily be fitted onto different types of flooring. This has the added advantage of insulating cold concrete floors. Always make sure that the wood comes from a renewable source – look out for the FSC stamp. Even better, look for salvaged wood from old buildings. Try to buy untreated and unvarnished wood whenever possible and then treat it yourself using natural products. This allows the pores of the timber to stay open and enables the wood to breathe, which can help to stabilize the level of humidity in the house.

VARNISHES

Traditional varnishes are based on natural resins from tropical trees such as shellac and manila, which are good for sealing. Shellac is a pure resin that is used as a varnish and it can seal up to 80 per cent of the fumes emitted by chemically treated materials such as composite boards. Although many varnishes and stains are made using solvents, there are some natural stains, varnishes and waxes that use plant-derived resins and oils, such as larch or copal, with scented turpentine oil and pigments. Turpentine (white spirit) is distilled from a volatile essential oil called oleoresin, which comes from the bark of certain species of pine tree. Plant-based solvents in natural varnishes and stains allow the wood to breathe because they react with the oils and resins in untreated wood. They are less durable than chemical treatments, but smell and look better.

The only treatment that is really necessary for interior wooden furniture and fittings is a finish of beeswax or linseed oil. Pure beeswax is a good option for finishing wood surfaces – it gives a beautiful shine, helps to combat static and gives the room a rich, wholesome smell. Liquid beeswax is a natural treatment that can be used as a finish on wood, clay, stone and cork.

Wood panelling is an excellent way to utilize wood in your home. Although we tend to associate it with the 1970s and with Swedish saunas, a bit of creative thinking can bring it up to date. Panelling is most appropriate for those areas of your home that need extra protection, such as the hallway, because it is a very durable material and will protect the walls from wear and tear. It is also a good thermal insulator, keeping cool in the summer and warm during the winter.

Plastics

Plastic comes in a variety of different forms and it is impossible to avoid in today's world. We pack our sandwiches in it, sit on it and even wear it. It is also widely used in the construction of our homes for windows, doors and floors. Technological advances mean that it can be used to create highly original furnishings and equipment, which look great, but plastic really is an environmental nightmare.

Plastic has become known as a disposable material when we should really treat it as a valuable material due to the environmental damage caused by its manufacture. It is a by-product of the energy-intensive petroleum industry, so it is part of a much bigger problem. There are more than 50 different types of plastic, which fall into two main categories: thermosets and thermoplastics, both produced from petroleum and natural gas.

PLASTICS IN THE HOME

- ◆ **Phenol and formaldehyde are often used in adhesives and binders.**
- ◆ **Polyurethane is used in foam insulation.**
- ◆ **Polyesters are used in synthetic fabrics and carpets.**
- ◆ **Melamine is used for covering work surfaces and furniture.**
- ◆ **Silicones are found in sealants.**

Soft plastics or thermoplastics are among the most harmful because they can offgas (leak out) into the atmosphere and even into foods. They account for around 80 per cent of all plastics produced and include polyvinyl chloride (PVC), polychlorinated biphenyls (PCBs), polypropylene, nylon, acrylics and polythene. Thermoplastics emit harmful vapours known as VOCs, which are potential carcinogens (see below and box opposite). Thermosets are hard plastics that cannot be softened again, unlike thermoplastics. They include polyesters, urea formaldehyde and silicones, and can be found in composite boards, paints, carpets, adhesives and certain fabrics.

The production of plastic products, along with metal manufacturing, is right up there at the top of the most energy-consuming processes. The oil that plastic is made from is itself a limited resource, and other valuable resources are used in what is an incredibly energy-intensive and polluting process. Another major problem with plastic is that only a small percentage of plastics can be recycled and, as it is not biodegradable, waste plastic will never decay. Some countries use incineration to dispose of plastic, but this is an extremely hazardous process: toxic chemicals such as dioxins are emitted, and even after this process around 90 per cent of the plastic burned remains as toxic waste.

All plastics are potential fire hazards because they burn twice as fast, and hotter, than traditional materials, as well as giving off toxic fumes that can kill quickly. Polyurethane foam, once widely used in furniture upholstery, is a very dangerous fire hazard and its use in furniture has now been banned in a number of countries.

Avoid using clingfilm
(plastic wrap) as chemicals in it can be
absorbed by fatty foods – use cellophane or
greaseproof (waxed) paper instead. The same goes
for plastic containers: look for stainless steel ones that
you can reuse, or pack food in paper bags or empty
bread bags. Pollution from plastics can also come
from the PVC floor tiles, toxic adhesives and
laminates that are common in
many houses today.

VOLATILE ORGANIC COMPOUNDS

When talking about plastics it is impossible not to mention volatile organic compounds (VOCs) – pollutants given off by plastics in the home, which have been linked to a number of physical symptoms. VOCs include a wide range of plastic compounds, such as the organochlorines polyvinyl chloride (PVC) and the highly toxic polychlorinated biphenyls (PCB), which are found in many household cleaning products, paints and adhesives. These have been linked with headaches and nausea, and PCBs are carcinogenic (see box on page 54).

ENDOCRINE DISRUPTERS

A number of noxious chemicals, including DDT, lindane, dioxins and PCBs, have become known as "endocrine disrupters". This is because they contain hormone-disrupting compounds (HDCs), which mimic the female hormone oestrogen and can cause such disturbing and long-reaching effects as low sperm count and male infertility. Cancers and tumours thought to be a result of the effects of HDCs have been found in fish and mammals in the North Sea and America's Great Lakes.

The main culprits are: phthalates, which are widely used in plastics, vinyl flooring, paint and ink; alkylphenolic compounds, which are used in detergents, paints and shampoos; bisphenol A, used in food cans and bottle tops; organochlorines, which are widely used in pesticides, plastics and synthetic materials; and dioxins.

Dioxins are known to be carcinogenic and have been shown to affect foetal development and the immune system. Organochlorines accumulate in fatty tissue and can be passed down the food chain. These gender benders or hormone-mimicking chemicals are found everywhere in the average home – from pesticides in non-organic food to food packaging, children's toys, detergents and cosmetics.

Metals

We use a vast range of metals in our lives today, including steel, zinc, aluminium, copper, cast iron and brass. They appear in our homes in various different guises: copper pipes, aluminium gutters, steel windows and brass wiring. Metals also appear in a number of household items and appliances such as washing machines, toasters, coffee makers and aluminium foil.

All of us should be trying to reduce the amount of metal we use because they are very expensive materials, manufactured in an energy-intensive way. The mineral ores from which they come are a non-renewable resource, and some metals, in particular zinc, lead, tin and tungsten, are becoming extremely rare. In addition, the manufacturing process for some metals uses huge amounts of energy and creates even more pollution with emissions of carbon dioxide and acid gases. Metals are also extremely toxic to humans – dust, fumes and particles can accumulate in the body and lead to toxic levels. Aluminium has been linked with Alzheimer's disease and lead can cause poisoning.

Around half the iron used for steelmaking comes from scrap and around one-third of the aluminium produced is recycled, but it should be much more. Recycling aluminium is much more energy efficient, as secondary aluminium requires only 5 per cent of the energy it takes to process iron ore.

STEEL

Steel production is one of the most energy-intensive industries, but it does create clean waste heat, which can be recovered and used. The production process causes emissions of carbon monoxide and hydrogen sulphide, as well as dioxins. Stainless steel is produced in much the same way as steel but is heated to higher temperatures. It is made mainly from recycled steel and has the benefit of being able to be continually recycled.

ALUMINIUM

Aluminium production uses huge amounts of electricity, which is extremely expensive and polluting, producing twice as much carbon dioxide as steel. Some countries have developed hydro-electricity schemes for aluminium production. These sound quite promising but in fact often end up disrupting wildlife and people on a grand scale as villages and valleys are flooded to create reservoirs. Aluminium is made from bauxite, which makes up part of the earth's crust. While it is now in great supply, eventually it will run out. The plus points are that aluminium can be recycled using far less energy than the original production cost.

LEAD

Lead is a very poisonous metal, which can attack our immune systems and can be fatal. It used to be widely used in paint but has now been phased out. Lead production involves burning off impurities from the ore, smelting and refining. Emissions produced during this process include lead oxides, zinc, mercury and copper.

COPPER

Copper is produced in a similar way to lead and gives off large quantities of sulphur dioxide and nitrous oxides, which cause acid rain. Being a very conductive material, it is widely used in the home for electrical cables and water piping.

- ◆ **Recycle all your food and drink cans.**

- ◆ **Don't use aluminium or zinc pots or pans.**

- ◆ **Choose greaseproof (waxed) paper over foil for the kitchen.**

- ◆ **Don't collect rainwater from lead gutters or roofs.**

Fabric

Most of us enjoy using fabric in our homes. Decorative cushion covers and throws can be very attractive additions to living spaces, but are you aware of how your gorgeous embroidered throw has been produced? And what about the processes involved in creating the vivid colours on your favourite rug or towel? All of these issues need to be looked at carefully and this includes gaining an understanding of what is meant by "natural" fabrics.

Textiles are an integral part of our lives – in our homes and on our backs. By reusing and recycling fabric whenever possible we can reduce the impact of the chemicals used to grow raw materials such as cotton and also cut down on the pollution caused by the dyeing process.

COTTON

Many people are under the impression that cotton is an environmentally friendly fabric because it is a natural product, but this is simply not true. It is, nonetheless, the most widely used plant fibre for clothes and for furnishings. However, cotton is one of the most intensively produced crops in the world and the cotton industry uses vast amounts of fertilizers, pesticides and growth regulators. Cotton is made from the Gossypium plant, which is also used for making more coarse fabrics such as rayon, as well as in papermaking. It is the intensive farming processes used in cotton cultivation that make it such a very environmentally unfriendly fabric. Insecticides are sprayed on the crops throughout the growing season – cotton production alone accounts for 25 per cent of the global pesticide market. These chemicals can cause skin irritations and allergic reactions when they come into contact with our skin. The number of cotton farmers suffering acute pesticide poisoning each year is between 25 and 77 million worldwide, according to a report published earlier this year by the Environmental Justice Foundation (EJF) and the Pesticide Action Network (PAN).

The demand for cheap cotton has also lead to ethical issues such as child labour and poor working conditions and pay. Research by the EJF reveals that in Egypt during the cotton harvest an estimated 1 million children from the age of 7 work 77 hours a week.

There are also problems incurred by the high demand for irrigation during cotton production, which can cause or exacerbate local water shortages. It takes 6 litres (1.6 gallons) of water to produce one cotton bud and irrigation for cotton production has drained the Aral Sea, leaving behind a dusty sea-bed larger than Germany. Most cotton available today has been chemically bleached and if dyes have been used, they are more than likely chemically derived.

As a solution to these problems a number of companies have chosen to start producing basic organic cotton. Buying organic is really the only way of being sure that harmful pesticides and insecticides have not been used in the production process. Organic farming also guarantees that workers are not exposed to harmful chemicals and that their working conditions are monitored. Some organic farmers are even growing coloured cotton, which eliminates the need to use toxic dyes. Demand is definitely growing for organic cotton products and the most recent report from the Soil Association revealed that the organic cotton market in the UK grew by 30 per cent in 2007. The report also revealed that its market value was expected to be worth £107 million in 2008.

❖ **Avoid fabrics that are labelled "non-iron" as they may have been treated with formaldehyde and could cause allergic reactions.**
❖ **Use organic cotton, linen or hemp bed linen.**
❖ **Buy items you will want to keep/ wear for a long time.**
❖ **Look for vegetable-dyed fabrics.**

AVOID VOCS

ORGANOCHLORINES: These are compounds often found in synthetic chemicals such as those used to make household cleaners and air fresheners. They include polychlorinated biphenyls (PCBs) and polyvinyl chloride (PVC), and chloroform and chloramines, which are both toxic gases. Organochlorines have been linked with skin irritation, depression and headaches.

PHENOLS: These carbolic acids are to be found in plastics and disinfectants, and phenolic synthetic resins containing formaldehyde can be found in paints, plastics and varnishes. Phenols are suspected of causing damage to the respiratory system.

FORMALDEHYDE: This is widely used as a binder and preservative in hundreds of household items, including wood sheets, bed linen and cosmetics. It is also used in furniture upholstery. Formaldehyde releases toxic vapours at room temperature, which pollute the atmosphere. It has been associated with a number of physical symptoms, including nausea and nosebleeds, and it is a suspected carcinogen.

HEMP

A very good alternative to cotton and linen, hemp is a totally natural fibre. It grows prolifically, takes only four months for a crop to mature and it can do this without the use of any fertilizers. Hemp also grows in such a way that it naturally squeezes out any unwanted weeds, thereby eliminating the need for the use of herbicides. This means that it is pretty much organic without even trying. For a crop to be certified as organic, a great many other factors have to be taken into account, but by its growth habit even non-organic hemp produces a very environmentally friendly fabric that deserves to be used much more widely.

After the crop has been harvested, hemp leaves rot down and return a high proportion of nutrients back to the soil, making it an ideal rotation crop for a sustainable organic farming system. But despite its apparent desirability, hemp has had quite a chequered history in terms of production due to its close association with the plant *Cannabis sativa* – or marijuana. Cannabis contains a much higher level of the narcotic ingredient tetrahydrocannabinol (THC) than hemp, which cannot be used as a narcotic but which closely resembles one. Because of its unfortunate family connections, hemp was an illegal crop in most of the world for nearly 60 years, but it is now starting to be grown again under special government licence in some countries, including the UK and the USA.

HEMP HAS BEEN USED TO MAKE:

* Sails for ships.
* The first pairs of Levi jeans.
* Writing ink.
* Rope.
* Paper – the American Declaration of Independence was thought to have been printed on hemp paper.
* Dollar bills.

**Avoid buying fabrics
that need to be dry cleaned.**

**Keep your dry cleaning to a
minimum because the chemicals
used are toxic.**

**Buy duvets and pillows filled
with natural down or feathers
rather than polyester.**

WOOL

Conventional wool production uses far fewer chemicals in the manufacturing process than conventional cotton. Wool is incredibly versatile and has the added advantage of being naturally flame resistant and receptive to dyes. This means that natural plant-based dyes can be used to good effect on woollen fabrics. Wool also repels dirt, so it requires less energy-consuming washing. Its role as a by-product also means that it is well suited to an organic farming system. The simple manufacturing process required for wool products means that it can be done on a small scale with minimum impact on the environment.

When buying wool products, be sure to check that they are naturally dyed, 100 per cent new wool. As most conventionally produced wool is moth-proofed with chemicals it might be possible that people who think they are allergic to wool are actually allergic to the chemicals used to treat it instead. Look out for wool that is certified as organic, which guarantees that the sheep are from farms where no organophosphate dips have been used on their coats. Once the sheep have been shorn, the wool is washed using soap flakes without the use of chemicals or bleach and it is not treated to make it flame retardant.

Felt, which is made using wool, has become popular again over the last couple of years. It is created by

SILK

Silk is made by the silkworm – a caterpillar that feeds on the leaves of the mulberry tree. The worm spins a cocoon made of fine, long filaments and then meets its death when the cocoons are heated in water to separate the strands. Silk is the finest natural textile fibre and it can be dyed easily. To be sure the silk has been produced in an environmentally friendly way, buy it only from ethical and environmentally responsible suppliers who can vouch for the production process.

steaming and pressing wool to achieve a durable structured fabric that can be used on walls as well as furnishings. Flax is another green fabric option – it is derived from the same plant as linseed oil, *Linum usitatissimum*, and can be used for textiles, insulation and paper.

WHAT WE WEAR

Most of us enjoy shopping for new clothes to extend our wardrobes, but the two concepts of being fashionable and being environmentally conscious are irretrievably opposed. The kind of conspicuous consumption associated with keeping up to date with fashion can be a hard habit to break. Indeed, the well-known buzz of so-called "retail therapy" is familiar to many of us, but only by taking responsibility for our actions can we improve the ecological situation.

As well as the amount of waste produced by mass-manufactured clothing, there are other issues to take into account, such as the welfare of the workers. Sweatshops where workers are exploited to push up profits still exist. Only by buying clothing made from organic fabric can you be certain that standards regarding working conditions have been adhered to throughout the production process.

* **Look out for innovative fabrics such as eco-fleece and Tencel – eco-fleece is made from post-consumer recycled plastic bottles.**

* **Look out for hemp clothing.**

* **Buy fewer, higher-quality items, which will last you a long time, rather than lots of cheap, poor-quality pieces.**

* **Join a sewing or knitting club and start making your own clothes, or at least customize pieces you would otherwise throw away.**

* **The average dustbin (trash can) contains 10 per cent unwanted household textiles, clothes and shoes, which may end up being buried along with other refuse in landfill sites. Take unwanted fabric to a textile bank for recycling.**

* **Buy vintage and second-hand clothing, shoes and jewellery.**

RECYCLING

Most of us could probably benefit from a major rethink about the amount of things we consume and the waste we create. Although this section is called "recycling", it also looks at how we can reduce the amount of waste we produce in the first place, as well as how we can reuse existing items to cut down on the amount of waste going into landfill sites and creating more pollution. Reusing and reducing the number of unwanted items is more important and fundamentally greener than simply deciding to use your local recycling bins. Nonetheless, recycling unwanted items is very important and something that most of us can introduce into our lives fairly easily.

Modern labour-saving devices designed to revolutionize housework are, on the whole, "disposable" and therefore not environmentally friendly. After all, what exactly does disposable mean? Manufacturers create disposable items so that people buy more, but what right do they have to say whether it is acceptable to keep buying sponge cleaners and throwing them away a week later? The manufacture of these items contributes to the pollution of the environment and the resources being wasted. We can happily live without them by making a few simple decisions about how to change our lifestyles.

Join Freecycle – an international online group which enables people to swap unwanted items that would otherwise end up on a landfill site. Visit www.freecycle.com to find your nearest group.

THINK GREEN

Before you even start to think about recycling your household garbage, why not give some thought to ways of reducing the amount of waste you create in the first place? There are hundreds of ways we can cut down on the amount of rubbish we produce each week, such as reducing unnecessary consumption and reusing and repairing items that might otherwise end up being thrown away. Most of us have heard the saying "buy cheap, buy twice" and it does make sense to buy fewer, better-quality items, which will last for longer and which can be repaired if they break down – this applies to everything from towels to televisions, from can openers to dishwashers. Even better, give your next purchase some real thought rather than carelessly laying out your hard-earned cash: do you really need another salad bowl, pair of flip-flops or toy for the cat? With a little effort we can all opt out of the culture of conspicuous consumption.

An essential point to remember is that it is far more important to live in an environmentally responsible way – to introduce changes to our everyday habits and actions – than simply to practise "green consumerism" as a salve to our environmental consciences. However, careful decision making about where to spend your money can still play a part in a greener society. Use your purchasing power to encourage large manufacturers to be more environmentally responsible and to promote recycling. When you are making big purchases, ask manufacturers and suppliers what their respective environmental policies are, and whether they use any reusable packaging or have on-site recycling facilities for staff and customers.

TRANSPORTATION AND PACKAGING

When you are doing your grocery shopping take time to discover where your food products are from – why buy an apple that has had to be transported for thousands of miles when you can purchase one that was grown on a tree much nearer to home? The transportation of imported goods, with its high fuel use, adds to pollution and energy waste, as well as congestion. A lot of food packaging is made from non-renewable raw materials and all manufacturing processes cause some level of pollution. The production of plastic, which is made using oil, is a major contributor to environmental pollution. There is also concern that a certain amount of toxins can be absorbed by food in cans and plastic containers (see Plastics, pages 54–6). Buy in bulk to cut back on packaging waste. In some US supermarkets up to 250 items can be bought in bulk, including flour, rice and pasta. Food packaging now makes up around a third of the typical UK household's waste and waste food packaging that isn't recycled ends up going to landfill or being incinerated.

Always take your own reusable bags to the supermarket when you are shopping. In the UK around 17.5 billion plastic bags are given out by supermarkets annually (2006 figures) and only one in 200 of these are recycled – the rest end up in landfill sites or as litter. Try to use organic cotton hankies instead of tissue paper and cloths

instead of paper towels in the kitchen. They might seem slightly less convenient but once you get into the habit of using them, you will wonder why you ever spent money on reams of paper towels that were used up very quickly.

LANDFILL SITES

The next time you throw something away, try to picture what will happen to it once it leaves your house – this makes it much harder to dispose of things that can be reused or recycled. Almost everything we throw out ends up on a landfill site, which basically means that it will be dumped in the ground. All of the organic matter rots down and produces methane gas, which contributes to global warming. Organic domestic kitchen waste should ideally be used as compost for your organic garden and vegetable patch – or even flower boxes if you are not lucky enough to have a garden. You could also find out whether there is a local composting scheme in your area. (This is explored in greater depth in Composting: see pages 180–7.)

The rest of the rubbish in landfill sites just sits there, creating patches of polluted land unfit for use. There is also the added danger that poisonous chemicals from toxic waste such as batteries can leach into the water supply. As we begin to run out of places to dump our rubbish, the authorities are being forced to look at alternatives. One of these is incineration. This is not a very acceptable option to environmentalists because burning plastics and other products can release harmful chemicals into the atmosphere, as well as creating toxic ash, which itself must be disposed of.

Batteries

✪ Think twice about disposing of batteries. They are a serious source of toxic waste and should not be thrown in domestic waste receptacles. If they end up on landfill sites they can enter the water system.

✪ Batteries contain a wide variety of toxic substances and it takes around 50 times as much energy to manufacture them as they actually hold.

✪ Find out if your local authority has a facility for toxic-waste disposal, or even better, invest in a battery recharger rather than throwing out batteries.

✪ Batteries contain strong corrosive acids that can cause harm or burn the eyes and skin.

✪ Heavy metals from batteries, such as mercury, lead, cadmium and nickel, can contaminate the environment.

✪ Encourage your family to use appliances and toys that do not rely on batteries.

REDUCE, REUSE, RECYCLE

✿ When you are buying new items, be aware of the amount of packaging that they are wrapped in.

✿ Avoid pre-packed foods and try to shop in places where you can buy loose items sold in paper packaging or reusable containers.

✿ Junk mail can be recycled, but you should block companies sending it to you in the first place.

✿ Swap old clothes with friends.

✿ Cut down on the amount of newspapers you buy – make sure you get only one per household and read someone else's at work.

✿ When buying paper products and stationery, make sure that they are recycled.

✿ Use old newspapers for composting – when you are chopping vegetables have a newspaper handy to collect the scraps, then just fold it up and throw it straight on the compost heap.

✿ Keep a big container handy for recycling used paper.

✿ Use both sides of sheets of paper.

✿ Encourage children to get involved in recycling at home by turning it into a game.

✿ Use old mugs and plates for picnics and parties rather than buying plastic ones.

✿ Reuse old envelopes.

✿ Think carefully about everything you purchase – do you really need it?

✿ Buy fewer, better-quality items that will last longer and you are less likely to get bored of.

Many unwanted household items can be donated to second-hand stores, but remember that it is not good enough simply to give your old clothes and books to charity if you do not buy second-hand goods yourself – it is crucial that there is a market for recycled goods or the whole system will grind to a halt. People tend to think only new things are good enough, but can find the most original items at car boot (garage) sales and second-hand stores. When you are shopping, look out for recycled items – there are increasing numbers of plastic, paper and glass products available and even some clothing.

Create a recycling system at home using boxes that can easily be carried and emptied. Allocate containers for different materials: one for paper, another for cans and so on. Stackable bins are a good idea because they take up less space

Nappies (diapers)

So-called disposable nappies (diapers) can make up 4 per cent of total domestic waste. A lot of parents feel that their lives have been revolutionized by the introduction of the disposable nappy – no more washing and drying. But the pollutants caused by the manufacture of nappies, combined with the amount of waste they produce, are unacceptable and over the last few years there has been a move by environmentally-conscious mums and dads back to more environmentally -friendly nappies. These include both the old-fashioned terry towelling nappies, as well as modern pre-folded styles.

Prefolded nappies are shaped like disposable nappies with convenient velcro fastenings so there is no need to use pins. Some companies make paper liners, which can be flushed down the toilet this gets rid of the worst before the nappy is soaked and washed. As most of us have access to a washing machine, there is no need for endless hand washing. If you have a young baby there are plenty of other items that need washing, such as bedding and clothes, so adding a few nappies will not make much difference to your wash load. Cotton nappies do not have to be boiled; a machine wash at 60°C (140°F) is good enough. If you do not have access to a washing machine, there are now a number of nappy-washing services available where you can pay to have them collected, laundered and then delivered back to your door. These services are also kinder on the environment than home washing. Another benefit of reusable nappies is the money you save. It is estimated that the number of nappies a child gets through before he is potty trained is between 4–6,000, which works out at as much as £700 (about $1,000). Washable nappies cost about £100 (about $145) for the initial outlay, but after that the only costs are those incurred by washing and detergent.

Sanitary protection

Conventional sanitary protection creates a large amount of waste and can also cause serious health problems. A by-product of the chlorine-bleaching process is dioxin, a poisonous chemical linked to reproductive problems, cancer and birth defects.

ITEMS THAT CAN BE RECYCLED

✿ **Clothing and shoes**

✿ **Paper**

✿ **Aluminium cans**

✿ **Plastic carrier bags**

✿ **Cardboard**

✿ **Plastic bottles**

✿ **Glass**

✿ **Household appliances**

✿ **Aluminium foil**

✿ **Steel cans**

✿ **Kitchen waste**

The pesticides used on non-organic cotton can also be harmful, so the safest and greenest option is to buy reusable products. This might seem like a step too far for many people, but it really is just a case of adapting. Reusable sanitary towels come with a holder and just require washing after use. Once you have made the initial outlay of buying a pack with enough towels to see you through a cycle, you will save yourself a lot of money as well as help the environment. Another form of reusable protection is natural sponges, which can be rinsed out and reused. An even better option is to use a Mooncup – a reusable menstrual cup around 5 cm (2 in) long and made from soft silicone rubber. It is worn internally like a tampon but collects menstrual fluid rather than absorbing it.

Many women do not know the best way to dispose of their sanitary towels and tampons. The answer is to throw them away – don't flush. Sanitary protection pollutes our beaches and can disrupt sewage systems if it is flushed away. There is really no ideal way to dispose of it, but it is preferable that it is sent to landfill sites rather than flushed down the toilet into our water system. Cut down on the amount of waste in the first place by avoiding products with lots of packaging such as applicators and unnecessary wrapping. There are companies that manufacture unbleached, biodegradable protection, so look out for their products in your local healthfood store.

Plastic

In society today, plastic is a big problem and its production has been associated with diseases such as cancer and liver dysfunction. Plastics are made from petrochemicals in polluting factories. They do not decompose and when burned and emit toxic fumes into the atmosphere that makes their disposal a major problem. Most people already have a lot of plastic in their homes, but it is good to get out of the habit of buying and using plastic products such as food containers whenever possible. Use a metal sandwich box rather than clingfilm (plastic wrap) or a plastic container for transporting food, and use greaseproof (waxed) paper for wrapping and storing food at home. Another great way to cut down on plastic is to have your milk delivered to your doorstep in glass bottles rather than buying it in plastic containers. Glass milk bottles are reused up to 40 times and then recycled to make more bottles. This is a far better option than plastic bottles because recycling plastic is much more energy-intensive than glass recycling.

Glass

Although glass is created from natural materials that are readily available, such as sand and limestone, the manufacturing process for glass products is very intensive and energy consuming. Try to reuse glass wherever possible – wash out jars and containers and refill them with loose foods such as breakfast cereals or rice. Look out for stores that practise a bottle refill system, such as local delicatessens and healthfood retailers. When recycling glass, make sure that bottles and jars are rinsed thoroughly clean before you take them to the bottle bank. Remove all the lids, corks and labels, and make sure you put the right colour glassware in the right bin.

By recycling glass you are saving energy that would go into the production of new glass products. It takes around 20 per cent less energy to make a bottle using recycled materials rather than raw ones.

Also, it's important to buy recycled glass products when possible. Glass is 100 per cent recyclable and because it doesn't degrade during the recycling process, it can be used over and over again

Paper

Paper is made from cellulose fibre, which comes from a number of sources, including rags, cotton, hemp, grass and straw. Most of it, however, is made from waste paper and wood pulp. By recycling paper we are helping to reduce the number of trees that are cut down each year. The UK Department for the Environment, Food and Rural Affairs (DEFRA) estimates that recycling 1 tonne of paper saves 15 average sized trees. However, the main benefits nclude a reduction in the loss of wildlife habitats as old forests are replaced with managed plantations to meet increased demand for paper.Less energy is used to produce recycled rather than virgin paper – between 28-70 per cent less, according to the charity Waste Watch and, as a result, less polluting emissions are released into the environment.

Paper that ends up on landfill sites biodegrades to produce methane gas – a potent greenhouse gas and contributor to global warming. By reducing the amount you will also be helping to cut down on methane emissions.

Cans

When you recycle food and drink cans, make sure they are clean, then crush them. It is really important to recycle aluminium cans because it is such an energy-intensive and polluting material to produce. It is, however, easy to recycle and can be reprocessed over and over again. Because of this, aluminium drink cans are a valuable raw material and the aluminium industry pays collectors cash for empty cans. Recycling 1 kg (2.2 lb) of aluminium saves 8 kg (17.6 lb) of bauxite, 4 kg (8.8 lb) of chemicals and 14 kWh of electricity.

Textiles

When we think about recycling it is most commonly with regard to paper and glass, not textiles. Textile banks are almost as common as bottle banks these days, however. They act as a collection point for unwanted textiles, which are then sorted into different categories. Items in good condition are sent to charity stores and sold to the public, or exported to developing countries. Textiles that are not reusable are sold to merchants for recycling. Woollen garments are colour sorted and sold to specialist firms where the fibres are shredded to make something called "shoddy", which can then be respun and used to create fabric. Rags are sold to what is known as the "filling and flock" industry. They are then shredded and used as fillers for car insulation, roofing felt, loudspeaker cones and furniture padding, among other things.

Textiles are not recyclable once they have been contaminated by household waste and tonnes of discarded textiles end up on landfill sites every year. This is a massive waste of a potentially useful resource. Don't throw out that old T-shirt with holes in it simply because you don't think the charity shore would want it. Either rip it up and use it for cloths at home or keep it until you have a chance to get to a textile bank – they are usually situated near supermarkets and in public car parks.

We could also take a leaf out of our grandmothers' books by being a lot more resourceful. The attitude then was "make do and mend" and there is still plenty of scope to be creative by reusing things you might have thrown away. Instead of getting rid of an item of clothing just because you are bored with it, try to adapt or customize it into something new.

- ♻ **Donate unwanted textiles to charity stores or textile banks.**
- ♻ **Scour second-hand stores for curtains and bedding – you can often find large lengths of really interesting retro fabrics, which are back in vogue.**
- ♻ **Be creative – get out the sewing machine and make some cushion covers, for example, from second-hand fabric rather than buying new items.**
- ♻ **Learn how to knit so you can make throws and blankets with leftover balls of wool.**

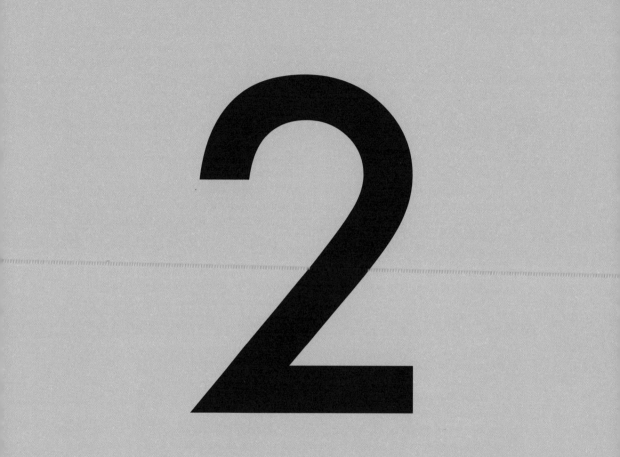

THE GREEN HOUSE

The interior of your home is very important and has a big impact on your frame of mind and general wellbeing. Once inside the average household there are a lot of challenges if you are serious about living in an environmentally friendly way. We are so accustomed to items like wall-to-wall carpeting and mass-manufactured furniture that we do not always stop to consider what their impact might be on the environment and our health.

To create a green, natural home we have to look at everything – from the furniture we buy to the energy rating of our cooker. A painter and decorator who uses organic paints told me that the biggest problem we face is being unwilling to compromise. Rather than luxuriating in plush carpet we should consider wooden or cork floors, and instead of painting the walls a deep, vivid blue, select a lighter shade of paint, which has been made with non-synthetic, plant-based ingredients.

As well as wasting large amounts of energy, the average household is also responsible for creating huge amounts of waste. From paper to plastic – we throw out tonnes of rubbish and hardly spare a thought for where it goes. This chapter looks at what action to take when your refrigerator reaches its final day, for example, and what you should really be doing with those unwanted toner cartridges.

If all this sounds slightly intimidating, remember, you can always start small: place a recycling bin for newspapers and magazines in the living room. This will get the ball rolling and has the added bonus of tidying up the room. There are plenty of other ideas in this chapter, on ways both small and large scale, to change your home. Ideally, it should be fun and you will achieve a sense of satisfaction that at last you are part of the solution rather than the problem.

The worlds of design and technology have caught up with the environmental movement as a result of increasing demand for well-designed, cutting-edge products that don't cost the earth. And now there is a huge range of products for green living, including everything from organic cotton bed linen to organic skin and body care.

Heating and hot water are the greatest energy users in the home but we can still make big savings around the house by taking another look at the appliances we have and how we use them. If your washing machine, or any other appliance, needs replacing, why not look out for one carrying the Energy Star (in the US) or the Energy Saving Recommended logo (in the UK) – both identify products that have met strict criteria set by an independent panel. Even if you make just a couple of changes, such as recycling your paper or starting a compost heap, you will be helping, rather than adding to the situation.

THE KITCHEN

At the heart of every home is the kitchen. We all have an image of a perfect kitchen, whether it be a minimalist vision in stainless steel or the romantic dream of a cat snuggled next to the Aga, a pot of soup bubbling on the hob (cooktop) and a cosy chair pulled up to the range. No matter what kind of kitchen you have in reality, there is one thing that it will have in common with most others – it is the location of many of the home's most energy-guzzling appliances and some of our least environmentally friendly habits. So it is a great place to start if you are keen to go green.

It does not take much to make a difference – you could make big changes by replacing your appliances with greener versions or doing away with them altogether, but changing the way in which you use your kitchen is just as important, especially when it comes to water and energy.

Appliances

Most people's kitchens in the developed world are crammed with appliances. Fridges, freezers, washing machines, dishwashers, tumble dryers, ovens and microwave ovens are common, even in small kitchens for just one or two people. Obviously, they have become essentials for many of us and the thought of losing them fills us with dread and horror – so don't worry, we are not about to suggest a return to the good old hand-washing days of yesteryear! But the way in which we use our appliances and the type of product we buy can still have a massive impact on the environment as does what we do with them when they are no longer working. The starting point has to be a careful consideration of your needs. Sure, kitchen appliances can wear out fast, but find out first if they can be repaired. Do you really need a huge fridge with ice and water dispensers plus LED display? Can you justify having a large chest freezer in your garage just so you've got room to keep the Christmas turkey? If repair is not viable, the next best option could be to buy a secondhand appliance – there are now plenty of websites offering used appliances, for example.

If you are in the market for a new appliance, however, then it is vital that you become familiar with the energy rating labelling in your country as appliances account for about 20 per cent of your household's energy consumption with refrigerators, clothes washers and clothes dryers at the top of the list. In the UK, we use £800 million worth of electricity by using washing machines, tumble dryers and dishwashers, thereby producing 5 million tonnes of CO_2 each year.

In the EU, by law all refrigeration appliances, electric tumble dryers, washing machines, washer dryers, dishwashers, electric ovens must carry an EU energy rating label which displays how energy efficient they are. The label rates products from A (the most efficient) through to G. If everyone in the UK used an A-rated fridge, energy wastage would be cut by over two-thirds, saving over £1 billion, about $1.4 billion, on bills.

The UK also has the Energy Saving Recommended scheme that ensures only products that meet strict criteria on energy efficiency carry its logo. For example, for fridges it endorses A+ that are more energy efficient than A-rated products and washing machines must be AAA – A for energy, A for wash quality and A for spin. The criteria is set by an independent panel and reviewed annually.

Meanwhile, in the US, the Federal Government requires most appliances display an Energy Guide Label, which will tell you the annual energy consumption and operating cost for each appliance so you can compare them. The American Council for an Energy-Efficient Economy lists the energy performance of top-rated energy-saving appliances on its website. You can also look for the Energy Star logo, which is given to certain appliances, including fridges, freezers and washing machines if they meet strict Government energy efficiency guidelines.

In the future you may also be able to purchase Dynamic Demand controlled appliances such as fridges and freezers that will be able to reduce the amount of electricity they use during peak periods. Small electronic controllers could be installed to track peak times on the electricity grid, helping to reduce demand and, it is hoped, eventually save an estimated 2 million tonnes of CO_2 emissions a year when fully integrated across the network – the equivalent of taking over 665,000 cars off the road.

FRIDGES AND FREEZERS

Other than reviving the use of the larder or "cool room" in your home or no longer using foods that need refrigeration, there is little choice but to have a fridge and, for many of us, a freezer as well.

If you are buying a new fridge or freezer, investigate the kind of refrigerant it uses, as well as its energy efficiency. In the past, chlorofluorocarbons (CFCs) were commonly used as cooling agents. By 1986 a quarter of all global CFC production was for refrigeration, but once the hole in the ozone was discovered and CFCs blamed, fridge makers were forced to find a new gas.

They turned to hydrochlorofluorocarbons (HCFCs) and hydrofluorocarbons (HFCs) for the coolant and in the foam insulation, but these have now been found to contribute to global warming. HCFCs are being phased out, but HFC fridges are still being produced, accounting for 3 per cent of the UK market in 2004, and they continue to exacerbate the greenhouse effect.

But there is a "green" alternative developed by Greenpeace called Greenfreeze, which uses a natural gas, hydrocarbon, for the refrigerant. Hydrocarbons have no effect on the ozone layer, less impact on global warming than CFCs and HCFCs, are cheaper and also non-toxic. The energy efficiency of these hydrocarbon fridges has also proved to be as good as, or better than, those cooled with CFCs or HFCs – they can use up to 70 per cent less energy. Today, there are over 150 million Greenfreeze refrigerators in the world, produced by all the major European, Chinese, Japanese and Indian manufacturers, and now is available in most major markets, with the exception of the US.

Disposing of your old appliance is also a key environmental issue. It is estimated that up to 3 million domestic refrigeration (fridges, fridge-freezers and freezers) units are disposed of in the UK each year. Approximately 95 per cent of the materials in your refrigerator or freezer can be recycled, including the metal cabinet, plastic liner, glass shelves, the refrigerant and oil in your compressor, and the polyurethane foam insulation. However, the ozone depleting substances in many old fridges, such as HCFCs used as a blowing agent in insulating foam, require specialist disposal techniques.

In Europe, the Waste Electrical and Electronic Equipment Directive means that those who make and sell electrical equipment, including kitchen appliances, must make it easier for their products to be recycled, which in the UK includes both actively assisting in delivering a UK-wide collection infrastructure and encouraging the participation of consumers in recycling electronic equipment.

In the US, you should contact your local solid waste disposal service provider and ask their policy on refrigerator or freezer disposal, but many stores and private companies also provide recycling services. Look out too for a Bounty Program, often sponsored by local or regional utilities, where you can be paid a "bounty" to allow the recycler to recover and recycle their old, inefficient unit and sometimes receive rebates and discounts towards the purchase of new Energy Star qualified models.

If you are not in the market for a new fridge or freezer, there are still ways in which you can improve the energy efficiency of your current model.

For example:
❋ Minimize the number of times you open the door: for each minute that a fridge door is open, it will take your fridge at least three minutes to regain its temperature.

❋ Defrost your fridge or freezer regularly (especially in summer): on average a fridge/freezer should be defrosted every three months and a fridge every month.

❋ Make sure your fridge or freezer is not in a sunny spot in your kitchen and is well away from other hot spots such as the cooker, boiler, tumble dryer or washing machine – putting it in a cool garage or cellar helps save energy.

❋ Check the condition of the seals on your fridge and freezer by trapping a piece of paper in the door when closing it; if the paper can be pulled out easily, the seal should be replaced.

❋ Keep the coils at the back-dust free as accumulation of dust on condenser coils can increase energy consumption by up to 30 per cent.

❋ Insulate around the sides of your fridge or freezer, using aluminium foil (recycled if possible).

❋ Always cool food before putting it in the fridge.

❋ Do not fill your fridge more than three-quarters full to allow for circulation of cold air. Many items commonly put in the fridge may not need to be there at all, such as bread or root vegetables.

❋ Keep a thermometer in your fridge or freezer to check that the temperature is kept constant – 3–5°C (37–41°F) for fridges and lower than -18°C (0°F) for freezers. If your appliance is not maintaining constant temperatures, then it needs to be serviced.

COOKERS AND MICROWAVE OVENS

Choosing the right heating method for the job is the key when cooking food. If you want to reheat a meal for one, then opt for the microwave oven, and when toasting just a single slice of bread, don't use the grill (broiler), go for the toaster instead – both use less energy.

Although microwave ovens are more energy efficient than conventional ones – they use 75 per cent less energy than conventional ovens and don't produce surplus heat – don't be fooled into thinking that by surviving on a diet of pre-prepared and heavily packaged microwave meals you are helping the environment. The environmental costs involved in processing this kind of "convenience" food, packaging it and shipping it to your local supermarket, which you may well have driven to, far outweigh the benefits of one cooking method over another.

When choosing a cooker or a microwave oven, ask the supplier for as much information as possible regarding energy efficiency and environmental policies. Go for a gas cooker rather than an electric one if you have a choice – gas is more energy efficient – and look out for cookers with options such as electric grills that allow you to switch on just half of the element for smaller jobs, or double ovens, so that you can use the smaller one for everything except the family roast. Glass doors allow you to check if your food is ready without wasting heat by opening the door and fan-assisted ovens use less energy to cook your food.

In terms of hobs (cooktops), gas is considered more energy efficient than electric with the exception of induction hobs (cooktops). These use an induction element – a powerful, high-frequency electromagnet. When a pan made from a magnetic material is placed in the magnetic field, the field transfers energy into that metal, which causes the pan to heat up. The heat may be instantly raised or lowered by adjusting the strength of the magnetic field so a rapidly boiling pan can be reduced to a simmer in about two seconds. Once the pan is removed heating zone switches off. Plus, all induction hobs (cooktops) include a power-boost button that will boil a pan of water in around 90 seconds. This type of hob (cooktop) does not work with non-ferromagnetic cookware, such as glass, aluminum and most stainless steel, nor with ferromagnetic material covered with a conductive layer, such as a copper-bottomed pan.

Induction hobs (cooktops) are more expensive than traditional ones, but consume half as much electricity as electric hobs (cooktops) and are more efficient in heat transfer. Manufacturers estimate that power savings of 40–70 per cent are achievable in comparison with conventional hobs (cooktops).

Consider also using a pressure cooker, which can cook three or four times quicker than a conventional cooker, saving energy.

ENERGY-SAVING COOKING TIPS

✪ Use the right size pan for the job and make sure it has a tight-fitting lid – a pan with a lid on will use three times less energy than one without.

✪ Use only as much heat as necessary – if the gas flame is licking the sides of the pan then you are wasting energy.

✪ Defrost food by leaving it in the fridge the night before you use it instead of using the microwave to defrost or cook food from frozen, which will take longer.

✪ Multitask – use a layered steamer to cook several items over the same heat source or steam vegetables in a colander on top of a saucepan of rice or pasta. It's healthier too.

✪ Avoid using a self-cleaning oven function too often – standard self-cleaning ovens use extra heat to burn off cooking debris. They use up a lot of energy, but they also include extra insulation, which makes them more energy efficient. If you use the self-cleaning cycle more than once a month, you will consume more energy than you save.

✪ Avoid putting too much water in a pan, as it will take longer to heat.

✪ Make sure that the flame on your gas stove is a bluish colour. If the flame turns yellow, the gas may not be burning correctly and the stove should be serviced.

✪ Only use your oven only when you are cooking large dishes. For smaller dishes use a toaster, toaster oven, grill (broiler) or a microwave oven.

✪ If you live in a sunny climate then you could try solar cooking using just the heat of the sun. A variety of solar cookers are available in three main categories: box cookers, panel cookers and parabolic cookers.

✪ Turn your oven off ten minutes before the end of the actual cooking time and allow the residual heat to complete the cooking process.

WASHING MACHINES AND TUMBLE DRYERS

Okay, so we could all hand-wash more than our delicates, but be honest, who wants to, let alone has the time? The washing machine has freed up millions from the drudgery of hand-washing and few would want to sacrifice their beloved washing machine.

But washing machines use phenomenal amounts of energy and water just to keep you in clean shirts all week – they can account for around 13 per cent of household electricity consumption and 12 per cent of domestic water usage. So it is best to opt for the most energy-efficient model possible, no matter if there is an initial cost premium. For example, an Energy-Star qualified washing machine cleans clothes using 40 per cent less energy than standard washers and most full-sized Energy Star washers use 68–95 litres (18–25 gallons) of water per load, compared to the 151 litres (40 gallons), used by a standard machine. In addition, most Energy Star qualified washers extract more water from clothes during the spin cycle, so reducing the need to use a tumble dryer to dry clothes.

All washing machines sold in the UK must carry the official EU energy label and a small number of the best machines may also carry the European Eco-label – a voluntary label that can only be applied to washing machines (but not twin-tubs or washer-dryers) that meet certain minimum requirements.

Design options to look out for include eco-buttons, which define wash temperatures and loading levels, higher spin speeds that will reduce the moisture content of clothes and consequently decrease the energy used if tumble drying, and automated detergent dosage.

Other tips include buying a machine with the right capacity for your needs – if the machine is too large, you will be wasting energy on your small loads. And look for a machine with a hot-fill facility that uses hot water from the household water supply, preferably gas-heated, and with a short distance between the hot-water tank and the machine so that heat is not lost en route.

How you use your machine, new or old, is important if you are keen to save energy. Try these tips:

✿ Do a full load whenever possible.

✿ Pre-soak dirty clothes in bicarbonate of soda – this cuts down on the need for detergents and allows for a cooler wash.

✿ Up to 90 per cent of the cost of washing clothes comes from heating the water, so select the lowest possible temperature for your washing needs – 30°C (86°F) will do the job for the majority of your wash and on average reduce your energy consumption by 41 per cent – and always use cold water in the rinse cycle.

✿ Make sure your washing machine has the highest possible energy efficiency rating for its spin cycle as this will reduce the need for tumble drying.

✿ Wash clothes less often – a single washing-machine cycle uses up to 100 litres (26 gallons) of water and the average family uses its washing machine five times a week, amounting to 26,000 litres (6,868 gallons) of water a year.

✿ Use a magnetic ball (available from certain mail-order companies) to prevent calcification in washing machines, improving the operating life of your machine and reducing the amount of detergent needed.

✿ Check out eco-friendly washing powders and fabric conditioners (see Resources page 245).

When disposing of an old machine, make every effort to recycle it. If it is still working, try to find a new owner by donating it to a charity that collects unwanted white goods, such as the YMCA; otherwise sell it to your local scrap dealer. Steel can be recycled from a washing machine, offering energy savings of up to 76 per cent when recycled.

If you do not have a machine, support any green initiatives your local Launderette (Laundromat) may try to introduce. In the future these could include using computerized machines that weigh the laundry and calculate the correct amount of detergent and water required; using waste heat from the tumble dryers to heat the washing water and the building; and using the final rinse water from one wash in the first rinse of the next wash.

Drying clothes on a clothing line in the garden or backyard is the greenest option, but if this is not possible, consider investing in a wooden clothes dryer (using wood from a sustainable source) to spread clothes out in a warm room and allow them to dry naturally. If you must use a tumble dryer – and remember that on average a tumble dryer will use more energy than it took to wash the clothes in the first place – make sure you buy the most energy-efficient machine available. Keep the dryer clean and free of fluff, and make sure clothes are as dry as possible before putting them in.

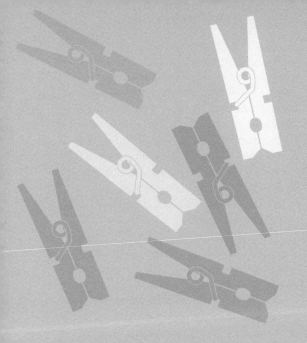

DISHWASHERS

As with the tumble dryer, once you have one you probably cannot imagine how you managed without it, but you should reassess how much you actually need to use it. However, if you do use one regularly, you can take heart from the fact that on the whole it is more environmentally friendly to use a dishwasher than wash dishes by hand. Research has found that dishwashers use only half the energy, one-sixth of the water and less soap than hand-washing.

The most energy-efficient dishwashers in the UK will carry the Energy Saving Recommended logo developed by the Energy Saving Trust in conjunction with industry and government. An energy-saving dishwasher uses 40 per cent less energy than an inefficient appliance. In the US Energy Star appliances use 41 per cent less than the federal minimum standard.

If you use a dishwasher, it is worth remembering the following: always use a full load – half-load settings use more than half the water; don't use the pre-wash or rinse dishes before putting them in the machine. Also avoid the drying programme by always opening the door at the end of the wash cycle and allowing the air to dry the dishes. Remember also to be sure that your dishwasher detergent is as green as possible or you might like to try soapnuts instead. As well as being used for washing clothes (see pages 101–2), these natural products can get lightly soiled dishes and glasses sparkling clean – just place three shells in the bottom of the cutlery holder and some vinegar in the rinse aid dispenser.

Other tumble dryer tips:

✿ Look out for the following: a moisture sensor option that automatically shuts off the machine when the clothes are dry and heat-pump dryers that use waste heat to warm the air going in, so they are more efficient.

✿ Choose a high-spin speed or extended spin option when washing clothes to reduce the amount of remaining moisture, thus starting the drying process before you put your clothes in the dryer.

OTHERS

There are many other appliances in the kitchen that contribute to our electricity bills such as juicers, food processors, sandwich makers and yogurt makers. The golden rule with all of them is to use them as little as possible – do you really need them or are there manual alternatives?

Products exist that help you do the same job by hand, such as a mouli for puréeing vegetables instead of a blender. And remember that while most appliances appear to offer the quick and easy option, they might not be quite so convenient when you consider the time spent setting them up and then washing them out afterwards.

If your heart is set on having a particular kitchen helper, then try to avoid plastic if you can. Buy a stainless steel kettle rather than a plastic one, for example, and an old-fashioned, but incredibly chic, stainless steel and glass blender.

Utensils and accessories

While these may not have such an obvious environmental impact as washing machines and fridges, given the amount of washing-up brushes and kitchen cloths that we will get through in a lifetime it is still important to seek out green alternatives, where possible.

The main way to make a difference is to avoid all plastic in your kitchen. Much of it can easily be replaced with wood – you can buy wooden washing-up brushes with natural fibre bristles made from sustainable resources, preferably with replaceable heads, for example. Metal, especially stainless steel, can also be more green than plastic; look for metal sieves, potato mashers, and so on. Getting rid of plastic washing-up bowls and using the metal sink is also advisable from a hygiene as well as a green viewpoint. Washing knives used to cut raw meat, for example, can leave a washing-up bowl harbouring particularly nasty germs.

In your quest to avoid plastic you may be tempted by natural alternatives such as bamboo mats, but do not assume that they are necessarily eco-friendly. While bamboo can be grown sustainably, it is not always done so, and there are concerns about the impact of bamboo harvesting on pandas in China, for example. There is also the pollution to consider as a result of the mats having been shipped halfway across the globe and the question of toxic treatments, such as DDT or lindane, being used on the bamboo.

When it comes to choosing a set of pots and pans, look for those made from stainless steel or cast iron and try to buy the most expensive set you can afford since they are likely to last a lot longer and thus reduce waste. Aluminium is a big no-no for both environmental and health reasons (see box opposite). Non-stick coatings on pans can release toxic fumes, if they are overheated, and although glass is great for casseroles and baking, it does not conduct heat that well so is inefficient as a cooking pan.

WRAPPING AND BAGGING

- Wrapping your food in either clingfilm (plastic wrap) or foil is a habit worth breaking. Not only is the production of both the low-density polyethylene used in clingfilm (plastic wrap) and the aluminium, used in foil wasteful in terms of energy, raw materials and pollution, but they could also pose quite serious health threats.

- Soft plastics contain plasticizers, which are known to be hormone disrupters (see page 56). These can leach into warm and fatty foods in particular and so wrapping these in clingfilm (plastic wrap) is inadvisable. Nor should you opt for foil instead. The aluminium can also leach into food – particularly acidic food – and it has been linked with a variety of health problems, such as Alzheimer's disease.

- The safest alternative for wrapping your food is greaseproof (waxed) paper or cellophane, which is made from wood pulp. Try to do away with wrapping altogether and store your food in glass or china bowls instead. If you cannot give up on foil, then make an effort to recycle it, using it again for covering foods or try taping it down under an ironing board cover to reflect extra heat onto your garments.

- Look out also for the plethora of recycled and biodegradeable wrapping and bagging options now available. From recycled aluminium foil to biodegradeable and compostable bags, there are plenty of other, more eco-friendly options.

- In Europe, you will be able to indentify products which comply with European standards for materials that degrade in aqueous environments, compost, home compost and soil conditions, and are flushable and disposable in waste water. These include the OK Compost, OK Home Compost, OK Biodegradable Water and OK Biodegradable Soil marks and the Compostable/Kompostierbar logo. In the US the Biodegradeable Products Institute certifies products, including compostable plastics, and awards its logo to those that meet the American Society for Testing and Materials international standards.

- These products are meant to be composted in a commercial compost facility, where high composting temperatures can be reached. Their ability to degrade on your home compost heap or in a landfill may be reduced. Landfills are not just large-scale compost heaps. Rubbish is not chopped, kept moist or turned regularly and few of the necessary micro-organisms are present to biodegrade the contents of a landfill.

The non-plastic message applies equally to plates and cutlery – even if you are keen on picnics or have a family of small children. Stainless steel bowls will not break when tossed over the edge of the highchair and can be taken on picnics every year. Teach children to use silver or stainless steel cutlery from an early age and wrap the cutlery in a tea towel for taking on outings with you. If you would rather avoid glasses when out and about, then the greenest option is waxed paper cups – at least they can be recycled. If, for some reason, plastic cutlery and cups are essential, do not trash them – take them home, wash them and use them again, even if it is only as jam spoons or for storing screws.

Kitchen paper and other paper products are popular kitchen accessories, but here it is essential that you buy recycled. Choose unbleached paper, if available; the manufacture of white paper requires large amounts of chlorine bleach, which pollutes the waterways downstream of paper mills. It also leads to the production of cancer and disease-causing dioxins, some of which have been found at low levels in bleached paper products for the kitchen, especially milk cartons and coffee filters.

Kitchen design

Fashion has come to the kitchen. As one celebrity chef after another appears "at home" in their own kitchen so we become ever more aspirational with regard to the design of our own kitchens. But the style of your kitchen should be about more than good looks. It should facilitate green habits, such as composting, recycling and energy saving. Examples include: ensuring your fridge isn't sitting next to your oven or beneath a south-facing window; building storage for compostable items next to your food preparation area, making it as easy as possible to just slide the peelings into the right container and creating space for several recycling bins to assist with the separation of materials.

CABINETS

In most kitchens, cabinets and work surfaces (countertops) make up the major elements. When it comes to your kitchen cabinets the healthiest material to use is untreated wood that you are certain originates from a sustainable source, preferably with FSC certification (see page 50).

Untreated wood is expensive and higher maintenance, but it is also probably the best ecological choice. You might consider using recycled wood recovered from an old house or barn, but be sure that if the wood is already painted then the paint used was lead-free. If you decide to paint your wood cabinets, it is best to use one of the many non-toxic, low-emission paints now available.

Some of the cheapest and most popular materials for kitchen cabinets are particleboards or chipboards covered in plastic laminate, but they offer mixed blessings in terms of the environment. While they often make good use of small bits of timber that are produced in sustainable forestry, the glue used to bind them together can contain the health-threatening chemical formaldehyde – a suspected carcinogen,

which can offgas (leak into the air) around you. Up to 10 per cent of the weight of some boards is made up of this glue. Look instead for formaldehyde-free board or low-formaldehyde chipboard.

Formaldehyde-free fibreboard is made out of materials such as straw, wheat board and Medite II – a nonformaldehyde, medium-density fibreboard. If these quite costly alternatives aren't feasible, look for plywood made with phenol-formaldehyde rather than urea-formaldehyde as the phenol variety is considered much less hazardous. If you do end up with regular particleboard cabinets, then you are advised to place them outside your home for three months before installing them in order to allow them to offgas.

SURFACES

Kitchen surfaces can make all the difference when it comes to how your kitchen looks – be it the clean, minimalist look of stainless steel or the robust, but beautiful good looks of granite. As with kitchen units, however, the most eco-friendly choice will probably be wood – provided it has been harvested from a sustainably managed forest.

Wood is not necessarily the most practical choice, though. With a tendency to stain and absorb water, it must be protected in some way – look out for environmentally-friendly resin and oil finishes.

The hard-wearing nature of granite or slate may be more attractive to you, but the energy used in quarrying, cutting and transporting these and other stone surfaces makes them a high-cost option in terms of the environment. Also be sure to get granite checked by the supplier for levels of the radioactive gas radon, which it contains naturally and continues to emit.

Stainless steel is becoming increasingly popular as a kitchen surface but its production is a pretty polluting process. It is, however, incredibly durable and non-polluting in the home, plus it has a high recycled content in the form of scrap steel and can be reused relatively easily.

For a more rustic look, ceramic tiles are popular but these are often glazed with toxic chemicals and the energy required to fire them is enormous. Look for reclaimed tiles and at least you will be doing your bit in terms of recycling. Recycled glass tiles are another option.

Plastics, such as melamine or Formica, are a common material used for kitchen surfaces, but they are to be avoided if at all possible, since their manufacture is detrimental to the environment and impact on our health uncertain (see pages 54–6). You can, however, buy recycled plastic worktops.

Concrete has become a popular option for a simple and durable look and the good news is that it is recyclable as a slab or crushed, but large amounts of energy are needed for its transport and manufacture. Concrete is often also used in terrazo – an aggregate using glass or stone chips, which are often recycled.

Other materials increasingly being used to manufacture greener kitchen surfaces include: post-consumer recycled waste paper and bamboo fibre with an organic resin made from cashew nut oil. These are well worth investigating and have become increasingly popular in the US.

FLOORS

Above all, kitchen floors need to be hard-wearing and waterproof. For the best in durability and eco-credentials, opt for linoleum, which is made of natural materials (see page 48). Do not be tempted to go for the cheaper option of vinyl linoleum. Since this is made using PVC, the manufacture of which is polluting and wasteful in terms of energy, and it does not biodegrade.

Other green flooring options in the kitchen are cork and terracotta tiles. Make sure you seal cork tiles using a "green" product. If you opt for terracotta,

look for reclaimed tiles and again make sure they are sealed against water.

WALLS

The kind of paint you use in the kitchen is important, since steam and condensation are likely to be problems., but before you reach for conventional paints designed for kitchens – which usually contain fungicides among their long list of toxic chemical ingredients – seek out organic alternatives (see pages 42–3). Tiles and stainless steel can also be used on walls, especially for splashbacks behind the sink.

Using your kitchen

You can have the greenest kitchen in the world, but it will not make a jot of difference if you do not act in a green way once you are using it. In fact, the way in which you use your kitchen on an everyday basis could probably have more of an impact on the environment than all the cabinets, appliances, pots and pans put together.

SAVING WATER

**If you do nothing else make an effort to
save water:**

- Fix dripping taps (faucets) immediately. Around
4 litres (7 pints) of water can disappear down
your drains this way every hour or so, and
90 litres (23 gallons) of water if the drips start
to form a stream.

- Fill the kettle with the correct amount of water
needed for your cup of tea, thereby saving
water and energy. If you find it difficult to
measure the exact amount of water you need,
then you might find it worthwhile to invest in
a new kind of kettle that allows any quantity
of water – from a single cupful to full capacity
– to be released into the separate chamber for
boiling. It is estimated that one of these kettles
uses 31 per cent less energy than a regular
kettle. No matter which kettle you use, you
should also de-scale it regularly to ensure that
it is operating at peak efficiency.

- Don't leave taps (faucets) running when you are
washing and rinsing dishes – running the tap
(faucet) can use 10–14 litres (2½ –3½ gallons) of
water a minute (enough for a small bath in just
five minutes) and washing a mug under a running
tap (faucet) uses about 1 litre (1¾ pints) of water,
while six mugs is the same as a bowl of washing-
up.

- Save the water leftover from washing the dishes –
it can be used for watering the plants or flushing
the toilet.

DRINKING WATER

Most of our drinking
water comes from rainfall,
but on its way into our pipes it
can pick up whatever pollution exists
in the air and on the land. At the same
time, it is dubious whether expensive bottled
water is any better for us than water from the tap
(faucet), due to the toxins absorbed from the plastic. In the
past there have been worrying stories regarding well-known
brands of bottled water, which have been contaminated as a result of
poor sanitation due to heavy flooding. Because of the manufacturing and
transportation involved in the production of bottled water, not to mention
the amount of water bottles that are thrown away each year, it is a far less
environmentally friendly option. If you are determined to buy bottled water,
choose large bottles made out of glass that can be recycled.

Filtered tap (faucet) water is a much better option. There are various types of filter
available, from jugs with disposable filters to special systems that can be fitted
under the sink. If you use the plastic jug version, make sure you change the
filter regularly to prevent contamination by the release of bacteria and heavy
metals back into the water. There are different types of fitted water filters:
activated carbon, reverse osmosis and distillation. A distilling filter
is the most effective solution, but is expensive to install. Seek
professional advice as to what system would best suit
your needs and budget.

Whenever possible, buy products that have some recycled content, such as kitchen paper, bin bags and glassware, and don't forget to do your own recycling. You can tear up old T-shirts to use as dusters; use old toothbrushes for tricky cleaning tasks such as the grater and the juicer; empty jars of pasta sauce are ideal for storing dry goods such as rice or beans and use washing-up liquid or drinks bottles with the ends cut off as protective cloches around young seedlings in the garden. Recycle plastic shopping bags by using them to line your wastepaper basket or take them back to the stores with you.

Instead of buying new, consider car boot (garage) sales, secondhand stores or markets for unwanted kitchen items – you will save money as well. For the ultimate in recycling, consider setting up a composting system – either a traditional compost heap or bin in the garden, or a wormery. You will save on bin bags as you will have less than half the amount of refuse that you did before and you will also see your garden bloom with the help of all your leftover vegetable peelings.

For cans, glass and plastic bottles, newspapers and magazines, aluminium foil and cardboard set up a recycling system in your kitchen or look out for a local recycling service, which gives you a recycled plastic box in which to store recyclables, which are then picked up weekly. For more on recycling, see pages 123–6.

FOOD MATTERS

What you choose to fill your cupboards, fridge and freezer with has a direct impact on the environment. Make sure you buy food as near its natural state as possible, which has the least amount of packaging and is preferably organic (see Green Food and Drink, pages 222–43).

Ideally, you will be able to supplement your store-bought items with home-grown goods – such as tomatoes from hanging baskets and lettuces from your window box. Even the most time-pressed among us can manage to grow a few herbs in our kitchens and the pleasures of freshly-cut herbs might be all you need to inspire you to greater things in your cooking.

CLEAN GREEN

The pressure on modern homeowners to keep their kitchens spotless is intense. We are bombarded by advertisements promising sparkling taps (faucets), sinks and surfaces with a liberal sprinkling of whatever spray, liquid or cream that is being promoted. These days, many people have grown up thinking that a different product is required for each item to be cleaned, and thus the average home contains numerous plastic bottles full of noxious, polluting cleaning agents. Statistics show just how dramatic a rise there has been in our consumption of cleaning products. Over the past two decades, expenditure on household cleaning materials (other than soap) in the UK has increased by 60 per cent in real terms.

The irony is, however, that many people's kitchens are no cleaner than they used to be. Most bacteria are killed by the application of hot, soapy water – something that is increasingly ignored now there are wonderproducts on the market that promise shining results without the elbow grease. And the advent of antibacterial products such as scourers, chopping boards, washing-up liquids and handwash is not a long-term answer. There are real concerns that the bugs they are designed to kill may be developing resistance to the disinfectant used (see box on Superbugs, below).

Plus, there is a considerable body of evidence that chemicals in cleaning products have an impact on human health. In 2003, a report by the Royal Commission on Environmental Pollution in Britain concluded that the number of manmade chemicals in the environment (including cleaning products, toiletries and other sources) posed an "unacceptable" health risk. Meanwhile, another report carried out by WWF and Greenpeace on newborn babies and their mothers found that every sample of blood tested positive for an array of manmade chemicals, including some used in household cleaning products such as musks and antibacterial agents.

SUPERBUGS

♦ Using soaps, toothpastes and other products that contain disinfectants may do more harm than good. Recent research has found bacteria that is supposed to be killed by the disinfectant triclosan – commonly used in soap, toothpaste, chopping boards and so on – could become immune to the chemical in the same way that some bugs are becoming immune to antibiotics.

♦ Triclosan affects a broad range of bacteria and fungal infections, so broad in fact that scientists had thought bugs would be unable to develop immunity. But this is no longer thought likely.

♦ Good hygiene practices using hot water and soap will not lead to superbugs and your kitchen will still be clean.

DETERGENTS

So you have your green washing machine and you are already making sure you do full loads at no more than 30°C (86°F), but you could ruin all your hard work if you do not pay attention to the detergent you use. Conventional washing powders contain several chemicals, such as pigments, fluorescent whitening agents and silicone defoamers, but many of these are not even listed on the packaging. A study by *Ethical Consumer* magazine in the UK found that a typical laundry detergent has 12–16 ingredients, only five or six of which are commonly listed. The problem with most of these chemicals is their impact on the environment, both when they are manufactured and after use when they are dispatched into the sewerage system and potentially our waterways.

For example:
◆ Phosphates and phosphonates, used as "builders" to keep dirt from being redeposited on clothes, can cause algae blooms, which distort the natural balance in rivers and lakes; not all sewage plants can remove phosphates from the water, so they can get through to our waterways.
◆ Bleaches in most mainstream powders can pollute waterways and undermine the bacterial action that helps to break down sewage in sewage plants.
◆ Surfactants, such as alkylphenol ethoxylates (APEs) and linear alkyl benzene sulphonate (LAS), which reduce the surface tension of water in order to dislodge ingrained dirt, are slow to biodegrade and can damage plants and animals.
◆ Optical brighteners and perfumes may be harmful to fish.

A LINK WITH ASTHMA?

◆ **A British study has found that frequent use of household cleaning products and other chemicals in the home could be linked to cases of asthma among children. In the 10 per cent of families who used the chemicals most frequently, the children were twice as likely to suffer from wheezing problems as those where they were used least. The exact chemicals involved have not been identified, but the researchers say they have established a clear link between use of chemicals in the home and wheezing in young children – which can go on to develop into asthma.**

◆ **A more recent Spanish study has found that using household cleaning sprays and air fresheners as little as once a week raises the risk of asthma. The risk of developing asthma increased with frequency of cleaning and the number of different sprays used. Spray air fresheners, furniture cleaners and glass cleaners carried the highest risk.**

◆ **Other studies throughout Europe and the USA have demonstrated an increased risk of asthma for people working as cleaners.**

CLOTHES WASHING TIPS

- For mainstream brands, a washing powder is better than a liquid, and a concentrated powder better than a standard powder.

- Look for soap-based detergents, or the ones with a high soap content, as soap is completely biodegradable.

- Vegetable-based surfactants are better than petrochemical-based ones.

- Use a product without phosphates, phosphonates or carboxylates.

- If you cannot do without bleach, then buy a separate product made of sodium percarbonate – you will be using it only when you have to, and it needs no stabilizers (which in other bleaches have been linked to toxic-heavy metal pollution in waterways).

- Don't use the manufacturer's recommended amount of detergent – half as much will usually get your clothes clean.

- Add a little bicarbonate of soda to hard water to help minimize the redeposit of dirt on clothes.

- Look for eco-friendly alternatives to lots of detergent, such as balls, discs, rings or soapnuts.

- Remove stains prior to a wash by soaking clothes in a bicarbonate of soda solution or making your own stain remover with a quarter of a cup of borax dissolved in two cups of water – this is good for removing blood, chocolate, mud, coffee, mildew and urine stains. Lemon juice and vinegar can also be applied to fruit and vegetable stains.

Even when these products do biodegrade they can create other compounds which may be harmful. For example, in laboratory research the product of surfactants (APEs) breaking down has been shown to inhibit the growth of male sex cells. Indeed, surfactants are considered by the Environmental Detergent Manufacturer's Association to be the most toxic constituents of laundry products.

As a general rule, you should seek to use a phosphate-free washing powder, with as few other chemical additions as possible. Ideally, the ingredients should be plant based and biodegradability should be rapid. Concentrated varieties are usually a better green bet since they do not contain the non-active "filler" ingredients used to bulk up ordinary powders and they reduce the packaging and energy used in transport.

Liquid clothes detergents generally contain two to four times as much surfactant as powders, and usually come in plastic bottles. Liquids are therefore less environmentally sound than powders.

There is an increasingly large selection of eco-friendly laundry products available, so finding an alternative should not be hard. These products are generally based on plant and natural mineral ingredients. They avoid phosphates, petroleum-based additives and chemicals such as optical brighteners, artificial enzymes and chlorine-based bleaches.

You could also try a device that promises to help you cut down on the amount of detergent you use. A doughnut-shaped ring made of hard-wearing recycled and recyclable polyethylene, called an Aquavator, can reduce the need for detergent by 49 per cent, according to the Fabric Care Research Association. It works by rubbing against clothes, helping to remove dirt and stains, and creating a jet of water through the hole in the middle, which helps lather up a detergent.

Consider opting out of detergents altogether by using a washing ball or discs which, when agitated in the machine, produce ionized oxygen which reduces the surface tension of the water, allowing it to penetrate fabrics and release dirt. You may save on detergents and feasibly dispense with the rinse cycle on your machine (if you are close enough to stop it) since there is nothing to rinse! Heavy stains will need to be treated prior to washing (see box, opposite), and it may take some getting used to the lack of scent in your clean clothes, but you could always put a few drops of lavender essential oil in the wash. Washing balls are reuseable for over 1,000 washes. Even in hard water, they soften clothes meaning fabric conditioner isn't as necessary. They are also antibacterial.

Another product to try is soapnut. Soapnut is the fruit of the Ritha – a tree found primarily in India and Nepal. The shell contains saponin, which is known for its ability to cleanse and wash, and they can be used in washing machines and dishwashers. Put six to eight half shells into a cotton bag (or knotted sock) and place in your washing machine. This amount will be effective for four to six consecutive washes. The nuts will look darker and soft when they are no longer of use, so remove them and put on your compost heap.

Other products you may currently use in your wash include fabric softeners, stain removers and bleach. If you must use them, and you really should try to avoid them, look for eco-friendly brands, with as few petrochemicals as possible.

With bleach, you should particularly avoid the chlorine variety, since it is highly reactive and can combine with other elements in the environment to create toxic substances. Opt for chlorine-free powdered bleaches, if absolutely necessary.

Other commonly used detergents in the kitchen are washing-up liquids (dishwashing detergent). The average house uses around 8 g (¼ oz) of washing-up liquid (detergent) a day while dishwashers use around 30 g (1 oz) of detergent, so the detergent you use for your dishwasher will have a big environmental impact. There are eco-friendly dishwasher detergents and washing-up liquids. Look for those that are available to buy in bulk or as refills (in the case of washing-up liquid), avoiding the packaging waste. One company estimates it saved over 500,000 1-litre bottles, which is more than 26,000 kg (57,319 lb) of plastic, from being trashed with its refill scheme in the UK. Another option is to buy concentrated washing-up liquid and use it sparingly or dilute it yourself. Again, the important issue here is the kind of surfactant used – make sure it is vegetable based – and avoid any product with synthetic perfume and colourings.

Cleaners

Open the cleaning cupboard in most kitchens and you will find a veritable arsenal of products for use around the home. Not only do these products pollute the home environment, but when you throw away the last remnants, they continue to pollute the wider environment. In addition, greater quantities of bleach and detergent are discharged to sewers from domestic households than from factories manufacturing them. Don't forget, too, the cumulative effect of all that plastic packaging on our landfill sites.

Unfortunately, manufacturers are not required to list specific ingredients on labels so you do not necessarily know what you are getting. Many products not only threaten the environment but may also trigger allergies and diseases in those people using them and living in the chemical fog they generate. For example, Volatile Organic Compounds (VOCs) found in oven cleaners and surface cleaners have been linked to respiratory problems such as asthma and solvents, such as perchlorethylene found in some carpet cleaners, which is a known animal carcinogen. Triclosan, an antibacterial agent often found in surface cleaners, has been discovered to be bio-accumulative (it builds up in our bodies) and has even been found in human breast milk.

No one needs more than one or two cleaners at most, and you could probably get away with non-toxic, homemade versions. But if you do wish to buy a particular cleaning product, go for the one without synthetic chemicals, that is rapidly biodegradable, phosphate-free, chlorine-free, vegetable oil-based, unscented, dye-free and concentrated. Liquid soap, for example, is a safe option, especially if it is perfume- and colour-free, so make sure you have plenty of the best-quality, natural soap you can afford – it will meet most of your cleaning needs.

Sodium carbonate crystals, or washing soda, once featured in most kitchens. More eco-friendly than detergents, it can be used to clean floors, tiles and work surfaces – just dissolve the crystals in warm water. If you add some crystals to your washing-up water, you can also reduce the amount of washing-up liquid you need to use. Washing/soda crystals are also useful for cleaning fridges, freezers and plastic containers. Try soaking clothing in dissolved crystals before washing to remove stubborn stains.

MOPPING AND POLISHING

Cloths and mops come in a variety of materials, some of which do not appeal to the environmentally aware. The greenest products are those that can be reused rather than thrown away, so avoid foam mops and sponge scourers, and go for cotton dishcloths and string mops that can be washed and used again.

Alternatively you could try an E-cloth, which wipes away dirt, including grease, using just water. These micro-fibre cloths are sold for a variety of uses, including cleaning kitchens and bathrooms, stainless steel, glass, mirrors, plastics, chrome, television and computer screens, car dashboards and wood. The cloth can also be boil-washed up to 300 times to ensure germs are not being harboured (although do this rarely to avoid wasting energy on a hot wash).

When you are buying household cleaners, try to purchase them in the largest possible containers, avoiding PVC packaging, and refill small pump-action spray bottles for use around the home to save on packaging.

Homemade cleaning products

It is not that long ago that homeowners had to be more resourceful when it came to keeping a spotless kitchen and home, using many items that were already in their pantry. Such traditional methods are still as effective today for those of us wishing to avoid the worst of the chemical industry.

The following are a few of the basics that would be useful to have on hand, with some of their uses.

SALT

When added to bicarbonate of soda, salt can help cut through grease; a sprinkling on the inside of a bin (trash can) reduces unpleasant smells; it removes burn marks from the edges of dishes and stains from china and earthenware; it whitens discoloured wooden draining or bread boards if used with cold water as a daily scrub; it removes fish or onion smells, if rubbed on damp hands; and it cleans stained cutlery, if applied with a soft cloth.

WHITE VINEGAR

A solution of half-vinegar and half-water cleans windows, tiles and mirrors, and if wiped off

immediately, it can remove dust and fingermarks on polished wood. Mixed with olive oil, it can polish off cup rings and other stains on wood; in a stronger solution it makes a good toilet cleaner and limescale remover for sinks, kettles and irons. It will keep bread fresh, if wiped on with a cloth inside a freshly washed breadbin; and 300 ml (½ pint) vinegar mixed with 300 ml (½ pint) boiled linseed oil, which has been allowed to cool, makes a natural polish for leather upholstery.

FRESH LEMON JUICE

This can be used instead of bleach to disinfect surfaces and the toilet; used neat it will remove grime at the base of taps (faucets), it cleans bath edges and showers plus grouting. Warm water and lemon juice will polish silver as long as a piece of aluminium foil is present when soaking, in order for a chemical reaction between the aluminium and the foil. A cut lemon can remove fresh fruit juice stains and smells left on chopping boards by fish or garlic, and you can return cotton socks to their whitest by boiling them in a saucepan with a few slices of lemon.

BICARBONATE OF SODA

This can be added to washing powder to soften water; diluted, it leaves sinks, cutlery, tiles and floors clean and very shiny; it can be added to washing-up liquid and dishwasher powder to improve performance and cut back on the amount required; a hot strong mixture dissolves grease on grill (broiler) pans; it is good for cleaning fridges, freezers and plastic food containers; it will remove stains on garments left to soak in a solution; weak mixtures can be used on cork tiles, wooden floors and paintwork; it helps clear blocked drains, if followed by boiling water; it cleans brooms and brushes; and it deodorizes trainers (sneakers), if left in them overnight.

BORAX

This is a naturally occurring mineral which has no toxic fumes and is safe for the environment, but which can irritate skin and eyes and should not be ingested. Mould and mildew can be tackled with a mix of borax and water – simply spray on and wipe off, and sprinkle borax on a damp cloth for wiping down baths, tiles and sinks.

HERBS

The leaves and flowering stems of rosemary, eucalyptus, juniper, lavender, sage and thyme can all be simmered in water for 30 minutes to make disinfectants, which will last up to a week if stored in the fridge. Clean metal or pewter items by soaking for five minutes in an infusion of horsetail – combine 25 g (1 oz) of herb with 300 ml (½ pint) boiling water, infuse for two to three hours, then bring to the boil and simmer for 15 minutes before straining. Rhubarb and sorrel will clean pans (though not aluminium ones) if placed in water and boiled in them. Make furniture polish from herbs and beeswax (see box, right) or rub ground sweet cicely seeds on woodwork as a polish.

HERBAL FURNITURE POLISH

❋ Grate 100 g (3½ oz) beeswax into a bowl containing 300 ml (½ pint) turpentine (white spirit). Stand it in another bowl of warm water on the stove until the beeswax dissolves (be careful as turpentine catches fire incredibly easily). Or leave the mixture for a few days and the beeswax will dissolve of its own accord.

❋ Add a few drops of essential oil – try lavender, thyme, pine or rosemary. Pour the polish into a can or jar to set. Use a soft cloth to rub it onto furniture and buff with a clean cloth once dry.

❋ You can add a herbal infusion – try mock orange, lemon balm or sweet marjoram – and around 15 g (½ oz) olive-oil based soap (melted in the infusion once it has boiled) to the beeswax and turpentine mixture, when cool.

Pet care

Most of us are crazy about our pets, but do we love them enough to care about what chemicals we put in and on their bodies? Sadly, commercial pet foods, pest controls and pet medicines all contain some pretty unfriendly ingredients, so it may be time to integrate your pets into your green living plan.

PET FOOD

With regard to food, the same rules that apply to humans also works for pets – organic food is the best bet for the environment and their health; this should also be as fresh as possible, and appropriate for the particular species' needs. Organic certification does apply to pet foods, so look out for the relevant symbols or numbers on packaging (see page 243 for more on certification); the choice is growing ever wider.

The added bonus is that organic pet food does not contain the artificial colourings, flavourings and preservatives that are so prevalent in conventional pet foods and which have been implicated in a number of animal diseases. There are over 100 permitted chemicals approved for inclusion in pet foods by the European Commission.

It is best not to feed your pet on a diet of prepared food only; supplement it regularly with fresh food. Most animals will do well if they are fed on organic fresh vegetables, while some birds thrive on organic fresh fruits, and organic hay is a must for rabbits and horses.

As with human food products, choose pet-food packaging that can be recycled or reused. This means leaving those brightly coloured, individually packed foil sachets on the supermarket shelf and instead buying food in paper bags or cardboard instead. Pet foods in cans are estimated to contain 60–85 per cent water, which means that you will probably need to buy twice the amount to satisfy your pet, generating twice the of waste. And when feeding your pet, avoid using plastic feeding bowls and opt for ceramic, clay, stoneware or enamel bowls instead. Not only is plastic bad for the environment but the chemicals and dyes used can leach into the pet food and harm the animal.

PEST CONTROL

Fleas are probably the number one pet pest and the cause of more chemical use on pets, via sprays, collars and injections, than any other problem. Each year, over 50 million flea collars are bought and eventually dumped, leaching often highly toxic insecticides into the environment. Common pesticides include the organophosphate diazinon or carbamate carbaryl – both of which are nerve poisons and also suspected endocrine disrupters, potentially causing cancer, reproductive disorders and various other ailments. In addition, many flea collars are made from PVC, which has its own environmental cost (see pages 54–6).

There are greener alternatives, such as herbal flea repellents, but regular flea combing, the use of flea traps, washing your pet when you first see the fleas and disinfecting the house through washing and vacuuming should be your first and more environmentally friendly line of attack.

For dogs, regular bathing in diluted tea tree oil or eucalyptus oil – 20 drops to 600 ml (1 pint) of water – should help you keep on top of the fleas. You could also try adding Brewer's yeast or garlic to your pet's food, or cider vinegar to its water, in order to deter the fleas from biting in the first place. Other deterrents include spraying your pet with citronella, eucalyptus or citrus peel essential oils well diluted with water and putting penny royal on a fabric collar.

If you must use chemicals to sterilize your house to prevent reinfestation, use a pump-type spray to apply the pesticide where it is needed rather than an aerosol "bomb" that coats all surfaces. Follow directions and be careful not to mix pesticides.

CAT AND DOG WASTE

Cleaning up after your pet is a key environmental necessity. Faeces on pavements could be washed into water courses during heavy showers and will damage aquatic life, while certain parasites have been known to survive sewage treatment and again threaten marine life. Ensure your pet defecates away from drains and clean up after them – ideally using biodegradeable poop bags and putting them in a designated bin for animal faeces now provided in most urban areas.

In the case of cat litter, avoid the clay-based variety which doesn't rot and is often dusted with silica, a known carcinogen which can cause respiratory disease. Instead choose a litter made from recycled material such as sawmill scrap or waste from wheat or corn. This has the added bonus of being lighter and less smelly than clay.

PET HEALTH

Pets cost their owners dear in vets' bills and the environment dear in terms of the manufacture and disposal of animal medicines, so it would be great if you were familiar with green pet first aid.

Obviously prevention is better than cure, so a good organic diet and plenty of exercise is the first step, but there are also many supplements that you could consider adding to your pet's diet. These can prove particularly effective when treating conditions like arthritis or in building up the immune system prior to winter, for example. There are books that provide advice on specific herbal and dietary supplements and also an increasing number of pet remedies in the areas of aromatherapy, flower remedies, herbalism and homeopathy.

A few handy items for a pet first-aid kit include: aloe vera gel and spray for cuts and burns; arnica tablets and cream for shock, bruises, swelling and most kinds of injury (although the cream should not be applied to broken skin); tea tree oil and grapefruit seed extract for disinfecting wounds and comfrey tincture or ointment for healing wounds and helping broken bones mend.

Should the problem with your pet prove too serious to solve always consult a vet, but try to find one who is qualified in natural medicine and nutrition, such as a homeopathic vet.

First-aid kit

Knives, hot saucepans, boiling water and naked flames – most people's kitchens are an accident waiting to happen, so it would be as well to have a first-aid kit handy. But don't be tempted to reach for the same old chemical products; this is your chance to try out natural medicines, such as herbal remedies, aromatherapy, homeopathy and flower remedies that are safer for you, your family and the environment.

But just because they are "natural" does not mean they are necessarily green. With up to 80 per cent of medicinal herbs gathered in the wild and many herbs now appearing on lists of threatened species worldwide, it is important to find out where your remedy actually comes from.

Always pick the organic variety, if available; plants used in herbalism, aromatherapy, flower remedies and homeopathy may all have been bombarded with an array of toxic chemicals, unless they were grown organically. And conventional growers may ignore natural environmental conditions, cashing in by planting huge areas with a popular plant, with little care for the impact on local flora and fauna – something that organic growers are unlikely to do. Try to use the least-processed form of remedy possible. Fresh herbs and homemade herbal teas or tinctures will have had less added to them and take less energy to produce than tablets, for example. And keep an eye on the packaging of the product – homeopathic tablets should be stored in glass, but can now be found sold in foil and plastic blister packs or plastic and glass dispensers. Suppliers with clear environmental objectives will make an attempt to use recycled materials and/or package their products in something that can itself be recycled.

So, armed with this knowledge, you are now ready to go out there and stock up on the remedies required, or even better to start growing your own in the garden or window box!

**Below are some key plant-based remedies for
treating minor ailments.**

MIGRAINE AND HEADACHES

The herb feverfew is widely used to treat migraines and headaches – eat the leaves or make a tea with them. It is best taken regularly as it has a cumulative effect. Lavender and valerian may help reduce tension if this is a cause of headaches. Essential oil of peppermint rubbed on temples can suppress nerve pain, while willow bark supplies the same chemical as aspirin to help relieve pain and inflammation – try taking the tincture.

MINOR BURNS

Aloe vera is the remedy to have on hand for minor burns (and sunburn). If you have a plant, then cut a leaf off and slice it down the middle; apply the inside surface to the cut. Aloe vera can also be bought in gel form, so if you do not have your own plant, pop a tube of gel in your kit and purchase a tube of calendula ointment or cream – it is soothing and especially good as the burn heals.

STOMACH UPSETS

Camomile tea can soothe an upset stomach; to relieve nausea, try freshly grated ginger or powdered cinnamon steeped in boiling water – this will also help with diarrhoea. Peppermint has antispasmodic qualities so it will help stop vomiting when your stomach is empty – again, try drinking it as a tea.

CUTS AND BRUISES

Arnica – which is so useful that it should be in everyone's first-aid kit – is great for treating bruising and shock. Use it in ointment form (on unbroken skin only) and consider also investing in calendula and comfrey ointment to speed healing. A fresh comfrey leaf poultice will also greatly help any bruise or strain, so head for the garden.

For cuts, reach for another first-aid favourite: tea tree oil. It is antibacterial, antifungal and antiviral, so will see off any bugs that might have got in through the cut. Use either the diluted essential oil directly on the cut or buy a tube of tea tree oil cream for such an occasion. Use St John's wort oil to help ease the pain and diluted echinacea tincture to disinfect the wound, if infection seems likely.

INSECT BITES AND STINGS

Peppermint and lavender oils are the remedies to have handy, should you get too close to some insects, and tea tree oil can also be soothing – all of them may be applied directly to the bite or sting. For wasp stings, try applying onion slices or vinegar on the spot and once you have removed a bee sting you can dab the inflamed area with bicarbonate of soda dissolved in icy cold water. Chickweed from the garden will soothe a sting, if rubbed between the hands first to release the juices.

COUGHS AND COLDS

Echinacea is a must in all first-aid kits. At the first sign of a cold, start taking the echinacea, preferably in tincture form, and follow it with elderberry tincture to tackle any flu bugs. If this fails and the cold takes hold, use eucalyptus, peppermint or bergamot essential oils in steaming water as inhalants for a blocked nose and a cough; liquorice tea is one to consider for a cough and marshmallow root tea can work wonders with a sore throat. Try to build resistance to colds by drinking rosehip tea, which is high in vitamin C.

DIGESTIVE PROBLEMS

Drinking a cup of peppermint tea after meals can help you avoid indigestion, and chewing aniseed, caraway, dill and fennel seeds after a meal is a common digestive remedy in India. For constipation, try chewing liquorice root, eating flax seeds or taking syrup of figs.

ALLERGIES

Hayfever is one of the more common allergies and millions of people pump chemical sprays up their noses each summer. An alternative and more natural approach is to take bee pollen throughout winter to build up resistance to pollen and to drink nettle tea and to bathe the eyes in diluted eyebright tincture to soothe inflammation.

HANGOVERS

Good old peppermint tea crops up again here – have a cup when you wake up to ease your aching head and dodgy tummy. Milk thistle is the herb beloved of all serious party goers as it supports liver function – have the tincture on hand for when you need it.

It is very important that you check with your doctor before using any natural remedies if you are already taking any prescribed medication, if you have an existing medical condition and/or you are pregnant.

Consult only qualified herbalists, aromatherapists, homeopaths or other natural practitioners for advice on natural, alternative medicines and for remedies tailored to your individual needs.

THE LIVING SPACE

The living space is usually host to a number of different activities such as watching television, listening to music, relaxing and eating. It may not seem so at first glance but there are plenty of things that you can do to "green" your living room. Simple practices, such as switching off appliances like DVD players and televisions rather than leaving them on standby will save energy, reduce carbon emissions and save you money. It is also worth taking another look at your furniture and fittings. Furnishing the living room with natural materials, such as wood flooring and fabrics, will help reduce pollutants in the atmosphere (which can be released by manmade materials) and will create a warm, comfortable atmosphere at the same time.

Furniture

The most important issue when considering furniture is the material it is made from. Good eco options include any furnishings made of wood from a sustainable source (and ideally carrying the FSC logo). As well as the materials used in modern furniture, there is also the issue of the glues and finishes which have been involved during the manufacturing process. Some furnishings contain VOCs, which are then released into the environment where they pollute the atmosphere (see page 54).

In an ideal world furniture would be upholstered using natural, organic materials, however, these pieces are often hard to find and over most peoples' budgets. A good compromise is to buy secondhand furniture or look for items on recycling sites such as Freecycle.

Good, solid, well-made furniture will last much longer than modern, mass-manufactured pieces. The most environmentally friendly items of furniture are simple pieces made without energy-intensive processes.

com. This has two benefits: you prevent something from potentially ending up on landfill and you save the energy and materials that would have been used to manufacture a new piece of furniture. Car boot (garage) sales and auctions are also good hunting grounds for interesting old items such as lampshades and stands.

If you are buying new pieces of furniture look for items made from timber with natural finishes, or even better, unfinished pieces you can treat yourself using natural stains and varnishes. Choosing furniture with natural fillings such as cotton, linen or hemp, and upholstery made from natural fabrics, will help to maintain a good level of humidity in the room because they are more porous and absorbent than synthetic materials. This will also help to combat static caused by electrical equipment such as televisions and stereos.

If you have a generous budget there are some really interesting examples of furniture design using green and recycled materials like recycled drink cans, but as with anything "designer", they will cost more than standard furniture. Another idea is to visit wood salvaging centres where you can sometimes find beautiful pieces of wood which are offcuts from sawmills and that you could use to make unusual shelving with a bit of sanding and waxing. An offcut of walnut or cherry wood from a sawmill needs only planing, sanding and waxing; it can then be made into an unusual table or even a breakfast bar. It is far more satisfying to have furniture in the room that you have created yourself rather than something bought from a store.

- Have a large basket in the living room in which to dump old magazines and newspapers before they are sorted out for recycling.

- If you have a solid-fuel fire, buy a log-making machine. This squashes wet newspapers into "bricks", which will burn for up to an hour.

- Look for secondhand items of furniture and have them re-upholstered using natural materials.

- Source wooden furniture made with traditional joints such as dovetails rather than metal hinges.

- Visit design students' graduation shows for original items – lots of students are exploring environmentally-friendly design for furniture.

- Check out local auctions, car boot (garage) sales, house clearances and thrift shops for interesting pieces. Look for furniture made from recycled items, too.

Home entertainment

Televisions use around 10 per cent of their usual energy and DVDs use around 20 per cent when they are on standby so it is worth making sure that everyone in your household makes the effort to switch them off properly when they are not watching.

If your television or DVD doesn't have an off switch (and many don't), then your only option is to switch it off at the wall. This is also true for digital set top boxes, which may then take some time re-setting themselves once they've been switched back on. Televisions, stereos and PCs in the living room contribute to atmospheric pollution and use a lot of energy. The plastic used in the production of the components and casing of electrical

- **Visit record fairs and secondhand stores for unwanted vinyl and CDs.**
- **Use your local library to borrow CDs and videos rather than always buying them.**
- **Use your local video rental store. Swap CDs, records and videos with friends.**

Always switch electrical equipment off rather than leaving it on standby as it still takes around a quarter of the energy used when it is fully operational. Arrange the room so that you are sitting a good distance away from the TV screen and do not let children sit close to it.

equipment can contribute to pollution in the room. All electrical equipment generates electromagnetic fields (see pages 128–9), radiation and static, so try to eliminate the amount of equipment you have in any one room. Natural fibres rather than synthetic carpet will help reduce static. It is also important to make sure the room is well ventilated as this will reduce the amount of static and pollution.

There is also the problem of what to do with defunct electrical equipment so that it does not end up on a landfill site. (See pages 123–6 for information on recycling electrical equipment.) Try to have electrical equipment serviced regularly to maintain it in good working condition and always check if it can be repaired before getting rid of it.

Conservatories

If your living room faces south (in the northern hemisphere) and leads into the garden, you might like to consider building a conservatory or sunroom, which is a great way to use passive solar energy. A conservatory is a cheap way to insulate your house because it acts as a protective zone between the house and the outside. It traps the sun's heat and can be warm and comfortable even on winter days – so you can make the most of the sun's non-polluting free energy.

The conservatory should be as large as you can make it and the floor must be well insulated. Make sure, too, that it has adequate blinds to shield against the sun on really hot summer days. By adding a conservatory onto a house you are essentially creating another room, which can be used in the winter and summer.

Walls

Both clay and lime plaster have good insulating and breathing qualities, which makes them ideal for walls. Natural plasters can look good as a room finish, rather than painting or wallpapering over the top. You will cut back on buying unnecessary items, which saves money, and also achieve an original and individual look. Unpainted plaster can really bring out the best in a room furnished with natural materials; use different colours and textures of plaster to create a decorative finish. It is also possible to add pigments to the plaster to alter the tone and create effects like marbling.

If you decide to paint your living room, use paints made with natural solvents and pigments to avoid offgassing of VOCs (see pages 41–3) by petroleum-based paints. Other ideas for green wall coverings include natural materials such as bamboo, jute, sisal and seagrass. They help to absorb more noise than uncovered walls and also act as extra insulation.

Natural wall coverings come in rolls like wallpaper and are fixed to the wall using wallpaper paste. Look out for paste made from natural materials and free of fungicides, preservatives and synthetic resins, too.

For more on walls, see Materials, pages 40–63.

Lighting

When you are lighting the living room try to do so according to the different activities that take place there. For example, there is no need for a bright overhead light when everyone is watching television. If someone enjoys reading or doing other close work, such as needlework in the living room, place a directional light where they usually sit. Energy-efficient bulbs come in lots of different sizes and can be used in lamps as well as the main light fitting in the room.

For more on lighting, see pages 127 and 165.

Make the most of your windows and the natural daylight received in the living area. If you have enough room, build a window seat where people can read or enjoy the view. Make sure your windows are well insulated for the winter months and use shutters and heavy curtains to block out draughts.

GREEN DO-IT-YOURSELF

✔ Use plant-based products.
✔ Keep windows open even when using natural paints or varnish.
✔ Don't throw waste paint down the drain.
✔ Wear gloves and a mask when dealing with solvents.

Flooring

The flooring you choose for your living room should be comfortable and practical. Wooden flooring is a good idea – just scatter rugs where people might want to sit on the floor to add colour and comfort. Sheepskin rugs are great because sheepskin is self-cleaning and can be refreshed just by hanging it out in the fresh air. Otherwise, look out for pure new wool or felt rugs. Even better, learn how to make your own rag rugs; they're very environmentally friendly. You might also try making your own beanbags using some thick, hard-wearing fabric like hemp filled with a mixture of dried beans and wood chips so it is not too heavy – you could even add some dried herbs to make it smell good.

Instead of synthetic carpets choose a floor covering made from sisal – a plant indigenous to Mexico. The tough fibres from sisal are woven into mats or carpets that look simple and beautiful. They give the room a fresh, natural smell. If your living room gets a lot of wear and tear, and is the scene for gatherings and parties, think about laying an FSC-certified wooden floor as it is a more hard-wearing surface.

For more on flooring, see pages 44–52.

Freshen up floors and keep them free of germs by adding six drops of a combination of essential oils, such as tea tree, lavender and pine, to 300 ml (½ pint) water. Put the mixture into a water spray container and spritz it onto the floor after vacuuming.

Fragrance in the living room

Smell is a very evocative sense and pleasant smells can help to create an inviting environment. However, don't be tempted to use air fresheners to improve the quality of the air in your living room. A recent study reported in *Time* magazine found that many air fresheners contain phthalates which have been linked with health scares such as cancer and developmental problems in infants.

In addition to the health concerns there is also the energy employed in the manufacture of these products, which are often used once and thrown away. Additionally, many air fresheners these days are "plug-ins", which use energy on a constant basis. Research indicates that a single plug-in is responsible for generating around 13.35 kg (29 lb) of CO_2 a year.

Another good way to scent a room is to use bunches of flowers and herbs – they also add colour and life to any interior. Avoid buying cut flowers unless you are certain of their origin. Flowers bought in supermarkets have often been air-freighted, causing carbon emissions by flying and the energy used to refrigerate them during transit.

There is also the issue of pesticides used in commercial flower production, which have an impact on the environment as well as the workers' welfare. Try to use flowers that have been grown organically, ideally in your own garden – these will not cost you anything and will be free from chemical pesticide treatments. Fresh herbs in a flower display make it more interesting and add to the fragrance – try rosemary or mint. Or place herb-filled cushions on the sofa so that the fragrance is released when someone sits down.

Plants are great for maintaining a good degree of humidity in the living room. Another method is to use bowls of water – these could have flower petals, herbs or candles floating in them for decoration.

Use aromatherapy candles made with soya or vegetable wax to create soft ambient light and burn your favourite incense to create a relaxing atmosphere.

Homemade potpourri can look amazing and smell wonderful.

To make a relaxing potpourri for the living room, take a handful each of:

dried lemon verbena
dried rose petals
dried lavender flowers
dried calendula petals
dried camomile flowers
angelica root
orris root

Combine the dried leaves and flowers in a bowl. Sprinkle on some essential oils of your choice, mixing between each drop, and then place the mixture in a sealed container. Store in a dry, dark place for six weeks and then display in your favourite ceramic or wooden bowls.

Warming up

The idea of having a solid-fuel fire in the living room is very attractive. Socializing with friends and family around an open fire is very enjoyable. A "real" fire looks extremely inviting and can act as a centrepiece for the living room. The problem is that open fires are not energy efficient and therefore do not really have much of a place in the natural home.

Domestic fuel use for an open fire adds to atmospheric pollution. It can release gases such as benzopyrene into the indoor air and on a wider level adds to dioxide emissions that cause global warming.

Open fires are very inefficient and most of the heat goes up the chimney with only around 10 per cent making it into the room. You can, however, improve the efficiency of a solid-fuel fire so that it is better for you and for the environment. Invest in a well-designed fireplace with a flue, smoke shelf and air dampener

under the floor duct, which brings in air from outside. Incorporate a heat-storage system to make the most of the heat it generates. Remember that heat loss is greater from a fire on an external wall. If you have the choice, build the fireplace in the centre of the house as a heat store, or in the middle of the living room. Use solid masonry for the fireplace and chimney as it stores heat more efficiently than bricks.

High-performance stoves have lower emissions and create more heat; they can be refitted into existing chimneys and may be a good option to a solid-fuel open fire. The best choice is a woodburning stove, which can be charged up once or twice during the day using fast-burning sticks and will give off heat gently between firings. Avoid burning damp or unseasoned green wood, and try sourcing sustainably managed seasoned wood from a local supplier, which will also keep emissions from transport down.

- Keep warm by putting on extra layers.

- Have handy a soft, pure wool blanket to wrap up in when it is cold.

- Use natural materials like wood, fabric and cork in the living room, which help maintain an even temperature.

If you have a solid-fuel fire:
- Don't overinsulate the room against draughts.
- Keep the chimney clean.
- Use only smokeless fuel.
- Buy a log-making machine for your old newspapers.
- Don't use firelighters made from paraffin.
- If you have a solid-fuel fire, you could add a couple of drops of essential oil to the fuel before you place it on the fire. Do this when it's not burning too fiercely, otherwise most of the aroma will go up the chimney.

Stone such as granite, slate, flint and limestone has been used in building for centuries and is still used for fireplaces and flooring. There are environmental problems associated with stone: Quarrying disfigures the landscape and there are high transportation costs involved in moving such a heavy material. It is natural, however, and has a place in the eco-friendly house as long as it is of local origin, salvaged or reclaimed.

THE HOME OFFICE

Developments in technology, such as email and broadband, have made working at home a much more realistic option for lots of people. Many households have a home office, or at least a workstation that is used for admin, checking emails and the children's homework.

Working at home has many environmental benefits such as reducing the emissions caused by the daily commute. Home workers are also more in control of their environment and can save energy by switching off PCs rather than leaving them on standby as they are in so many offices. Environmental factors such as heating and lighting are also much more controllable when you are working from home.

For this reason it is also preferable to position your computer in a room where other activities are taking place. This means that resources such as lighting and heating can be shared by household members, rather than having to light and heat a separate room in the house. Working at home can be an enjoyable experience if you are prepared to reassess your working conditions and make a few changes. If it is possible, move your office space to an area that is bright and airy – try to position your desk near to a window to make the most of the available natural light, preferably one that looks out onto something stimulating such as a garden. Research has shown that people working in areas well lit by natural light have increased productivity, which is another bonus.

Changing your habits

One of the key energy-saving tips when it comes to working at home is to make sure you switch off appliances rather than leave them on standby. Computers on sleep mode use between 20–60W of power (the average is around 80W when they are in use) and so the general rule with a PC is if you are not going to use it for 15 minutes or more, switch it off.

Another major culprit for energy-wastage are battery chargers for mobile (cell) phones and laptops which still use energy unless they are switched off at the wall.

Look out for computers and monitors that carry the Energy Star mark, which was developed by the American Environmental Protection Agency and has been highly successful internationally. If your machine has this mark, it means that it has the ability to "sleep" when you are not using it, thereby cutting energy usage by up to 65 per cent. So-called screensavers are, unfortunately, not energy-saving devices at all.

Recycling

If you are working from home you have to consider how to dispose of used office equipment such as printer ink cartridges, paper, pens and floppy disks, as well as the computer hardware. A growing number of companies have take-back policies, and some of them make it even easier for you to recycle by providing envelopes for returning used toner cartridges. Sending your old printer cartridges and mobile (cell) phones to charities such as Oxfam also helps them to raise money because they can sell them on to companies that recycle them.

According to Oxfam International, around 60 million inkjet cartridges are used each year in the UK alone, but only 10 per cent are recycled, and each cartridge can take up to 1,000 years to biodegrade. Empty inkjet cartridges can be donated to Oxfam to raise money for their charity programmes around the world.

This take-back policy extends to some responsible manufacturers of PCs and photocopiers, so if you are thinking of investing in new equipment, make a few phone calls first to find out which companies deserve your support. Many companies, such as Hewlett-Packard, take back cartridges for free, and provide mailers or labels for you to ship them back. If you are considering getting rid of an old computer, find out if there are any IT recycling schemes in your area before you throw it out. Another option is to advertise it in your local paper or to offer it to a school or community centre. Upgrading a PC can also extend its lifespan.

RECYCLING PAPER

The major source of waste from the home office, and indeed the average domestic home, is paper. Household paper products such as newspapers, magazines, telephone directories, pamphlets, coloured paper and cardboard can all be recycled. It takes around 28 per cent less energy to produce recycled paper than virgin paper, and by recycling you will help reduce the waste-disposal problems.

Although recycling paper does not save trees because sawmill waste and tree tops – by-products from the building and furnituremaking industries – are generally used for papermaking, it can certainly play a role in

reducing energy and waste. Paper is made from cellulose fibre obtained from wood pulp, textiles, cotton, grass and straw. The amount of paper we use is increasing, partly because it is a very attractive material to use – it is biodegradable, comes from a renewable source and is recyclable. The problem is that we often take it for granted and do not take care to recycle the paper products consumed by us on a daily basis. But there is nothing particularly new about recycling paper, since papermakers have traditionally bought their raw materials from waste-paper merchants. What is new is that individuals and companies have now started to take responsibility for the disposal of the waste paper they create.

Set up your own recycling system for your home office. Use wooden boxes or baskets to separate the different types of paper for recycling and have them near to your desk to make it as easy as possible. A stacking system of containers or boxes for different grades of paper is a good idea because it takes up less floor space. Almost all paper that is used in the home can be recycled but it is important to keep different types separate as this will affect the quality of the recycled paper.

Contact your local authority to find out where your nearest recycling points are situated and whether it operates a kerbside collection scheme in your area. It is also worth looking in the telephone directory for community-based schemes that collect paper and other waste for recycling for a monthly fee – probably not much more than the cost of petrol (gasoline) to and from the recycling bin if you add it up.

Other options are to take your waste paper to a paper bank – usually situated in car parks near to supermarkets or public amenities. The three main types of waste paper are white, newspapers and magazines, and it should be indicated which bank is appropriate for each type. Once the paper is in the bin (trash can), the next stage is for it to be collected by the local authority or paper merchant and sorted into different grades. It can then be delivered to the paper mill, where it is reprocessed into different kinds of paper. This process cannot, however, go on forever, as paper can only be recycled about four to six times before the fibres lose their papermaking qualities.

Recycling your own waste paper on its own is not enough; it is important that you also buy recycled paper. Many suppliers offer a range of recycled stationery, including envelopes, fax paper, mailing labels, files and document wallets, flip charts, storage boxes and sticky marker tabs.

IT equipment

Recycling old office equipment, like PCs and printers, is vital if we are to tackle the growing waste problem. It's estimated that 1 million tonnes of waste electronic and electrical equipment, including computers, is discarded by householders and commercial groups in the UK every year. In the US, according to 2005 figures by the Environmental Protection Agency, e-waste totals 2.6 million tons with only 12.6 per cent recycled – and that includes 133,000 PCs discarded every single day.

- **Be aware of your use of paper – don't use more paper than you need.**
- **Try to use both sides of the page, even when printing.**
- **Buy recycled paper for your printer and photocopier.**
- **Recycle the waste paper from your home office.**
- **Look out for notepads made from recycled paper and even old maps.**

The production of computers uses natural resources and involves the use of toxic chemicals. PCs are made up of modular parts, each of which has various components, quite often produced by different manufacturers. This makes it an incredibly wasteful and unenvironmentally-friendly industry, which produces tonnes of toxic waste. In a recent report on the PC manufacturing industry, *Ethical Consumer* magazine stated that "industrial illness is three times the average for other industries". Unwanted computers make up a huge amount of waste – in the UK alone, IT equipment accounts for around 39 per cent of the electrical equipment discarded by householders and commercial groups. A great deal of electronic equipment ends up on landfill sites, contributing to environmental pollution. The overall range of substances found in electrical equipment and the fact that many of them are toxic causes more problems.

SWITCH TO A GREEN ISP

A growing number of internet service providers now operate energy-saving business practices, such as encouraging staff to use public transport. Some use solar-power in their offices, while others offset their carbon emissions. For more information see Resources on page 246.

- **When choosing IT equipment, look for items that can be upgraded.**
- **Check if the company you are buying from operates a take-back system.**
- **When something stops working, try to repair it before thinking about disposing of it.**
- **Contact your local authority for information about reuse and recycling schemes for IT equipment near you.**

Ideally, you should be able to upgrade your computer easily by adding extra memory or a larger hard drive. If you are plan to invest in a new computer, find out about the scope for upgrading. If, however, your computer is still working but you are unable to upgrade satisfactorily, you can extend its life by donating it to a community group or a school. Alternatively, there are companies that buy and sell computers for refurbishment or spares.

Lighting your work space

The type of lighting you have in your working environment can make a lot of difference to your comfort. Harsh, overhead lights causing awkward shadows are not conducive to long periods of work. Standard tungsten filament lamps, also known as incandescent light bulbs, are very wasteful of energy because around 90 per cent of the energy produced is converted to heat rather than light. There are other problems associated with conventional lighting, too – when incandescent bulbs heat up they can cause pollutants to be released from their plastic fittings into the atmosphere.

It is a good idea to experiment with lighting your work area to make sure that you are using the right amount of lighting. Try out different levels of lighting to see what best suits your needs so as to avoid using more energy than you need. Task lights are often very useful as they concentrate light in the area you need it most.

The best kind of light on an environmental and personal level is natural daylight. Make the most of the light in your office space by positioning your desk near a window. Make sure you can pull blinds or curtains away from the window to allow the greatest amount of light in. If at all possible, think about installing a skylight, which is an effective and attractive source of natural light.

LOW-ENERGY LIGHTING

When you do need to have some artificial lighting there are a number of options. Low-energy light bulbs come in a range of shapes and sizes for different fittings. The most energy-efficient lights for the home office are LED desk lights. These give directional light with minimum emissions. Look out for desk lights made using environmentally-friendly and sustainable materials (see Resources on pages 247).

- **Turn off lights when they are not in use.**
- **Install a timer or remote-controlled lighting system.**
- **Use low-energy light bulbs for areas that need to be lit for long periods of time.**
- **Instead of having a stronger lamp further away, use less powerful task lighting.**
- **Keep bulbs clean to maximize their light output.**

Compact fluorescent light bulbs (CFLs) are efficient, economic and long lasting, and have low heat emission. These bulbs use a fraction of the energy used by standard bulbs and last for much longer, saving you money. They come with bayonet or screw fittings like standard incandescent bulbs and so will fit most lamps (see Lighting, pages 116–7). They are best used in areas where the lighting is left on for long periods of time so they are ideal in a home office space and they could be used for more general lighting in conjunction with task lighting on the desk.

Electromagnetic frequencies

In this highly technological age, a vast proportion of us spend the majority of our lives surrounded by electrical equipment without giving much thought to its effect on our wellbeing, let alone the consumption of non-renewable resources necessary to produce the electricity powering all these machines. There have been concerns that living in close proximity to power cables and lines can increase the risk of certain cancers in children and this has led to health fears about the levels of electricity in the home.

Sitting in front of a computer subjects the user to a constant barrage of strong electromagnetic fields (EMFs) and to low-frequency electromagnetic fields (ELFs), both of which have been linked with eye strain and headaches, as well as high blood pressure and stress. We are also exposed to EMFs from power cables, the radio and television, as well

as IT equipment, and although there is no proof that they are harmful, the amount of research is growing. You can reduce the ELFs and EMFs in your home by making sure that you switch off and unplug all unused electrical equipment.

Ionization

Ions are positive and negative electrically charged molecules and in a natural balance there should be slightly more positive ions in the atmosphere. All electrical devices alter the level of negative ions in the air and too many positive ions in an atmosphere are thought to have a detrimental effect on your health they have been linked with hay fever, migraines and increased stress levels. Certain weather conditions, such as thunderstorms, also cause negative ion depletion and are thought to evoke feelings of irritation and restlessness.

The best way to avoid this kind of atmospheric pollution is to limit the amount of electrical equipment you have in your office. Using natural materials and making sure that there is adequate ventilation can help to minimize the effects of a positive charge.

If you spend a lot of your time around electrical equipment it might be worth investing in an ionizer, which generates negative ions and is thought to improve the quality of the air. Although ionizers themselves are not very expensive, an even cheaper way to improve the atmosphere is to add plenty of indoor plants.

- Sit well back from the screen, but not to one side – this is where radiation is leaked.
- Use natural materials to maintain a good level of humidity in the room to counteract the dry air and negative ion depletion that is caused by electrical equipment.
- Keep computers and IT equipment away from sleeping areas.
- Reduce the physical strain of working in front of a monitor by using an anti-glare screen.

Static

Computer screens emit forms of high- and low-frequency radiation. This is why good ventilation in a home office is essential. Good ventilation also stops the build-up of static electricity, which is caused when weak charges of electricity cannot be earthed due to the presence of insulating materials such as rubber flooring and synthetic carpets.

You can avoid a build-up of static by using more natural materials such as wood and leather, which are conductive and allow the static to disperse. As metal is a good conductor of electricity it can become charged. It is therefore best to avoid having your bed near to your computer if it has a metal bed frame or springs.

Stop the strain

The increase in the number of computer-related health problems over the last few years should be a warning to make sure you take precautions against injuries like Repetitive Strain Injury (RSI).

It also makes sense to stop regularly for breaks – most experts recommend that you take a ten-minute break at least every 40–50 minutes. Another good idea is to adjust your depth of vision every 30 minutes or so by focusing your eyes on far-off objects. This should help with the "blurring" that is associated with VDU work, which is caused by the muscles in the eye becoming tired after focusing on short-range screens for a long time.

Make sure you keep your mouse clean, as a build-up of grease and dirt can slow the mouse down and make it harder to use, thereby increasing the risk of developing RSI. Try to use the keyboard commands rather than the mouse. Position the mouse at the same height as your keyboard to avoid shoulder strain and allow yourself enough desk space to use the mouse comfortably. A wrist rest positioned in front of the keyboard can also help to reduce the risk of RSI – use a light touch and keep your hands and fingers relaxed. To avoid sore eyes, have some eye drops at hand and remember to blink and look away from your monitor at regular intervals. As often as possible, move away from your screen and do a few stretching exercises or go for a ten-minute stroll.

- ✪ **Take frequent and regular breaks away from your computer.**
- ✪ **Place a book under your feet in order to raise your knees to the same level as your thighs.**
- ✪ **Make sure your chair supports the curve of your back – use cushions to fill the gap, if necessary.**
- ✪ **Place printers away from your desk.**
- ✪ **Look away from the monitor at regular intervals and focus on a distant object to avoid eye strain.**
- ✪ **Keep your desk as uncluttered as possible and make sure that it is large enough for everything it needs to hold.**
- ✪ **Buy a wrist rest to support your hands.**
- ✪ **Take up a yoga class to relieve stress.**

GOOD DESK PRACTICES

Your computer should be positioned so that it is at eye level to avoid eye strain by looking up or down. Try to keep your work space clear and free from unnecessary clutter. Have plenty of filing cabinets at hand so that you can put papers away immediately after use rather than have them lying around.

Office furniture

More companies are now designing ergonomic furniture for the home and office. Curved lines that reflect nature and allow for more comfortable working positions are becoming increasingly popular, but if you cannot afford to buy the latest desk and chair designs, there are still ways to improve your working environment.

Your desk should provide enough space for your monitor so you can sit about 50 cm (20 in) from the screen, with the top of the screen slightly below eye level. Curved desks are good because they stop you stretching for paperwork, which can put a strain on your back and upper body.

Avoid desks made with synthetic materials, such as composite boards. Instead, choose one from a company that uses Forest Stewardship Council (FSC) certified timber (see page 50). Any furniture made from chipboard, medium-density fibreboard (MDF), plyboard and particleboard is hazardous because it contains formaldehyde, which is present in the resin binder. Furniture made from composite board is often coated with laminates that may contain PVC to give a wood-effect finish. This is best avoided as it can offgas VOCs (see page 60) and is a major source of pollution during its manufacturing process.

Some companies are looking at alternative materials to composite board and are creating new materials for furniture construction made from natural non-wood fibres like hemp, flax and sugar cane, which are by-products of existing production processes. One of the most innovative materials is Tectan, which is manufactured by a German company using waste drink cartons. It is a good alternative to chipboard, but is not yet available to buy. Or have a desk made from reclaimed wood – you can find interesting pieces of salvaged wood that cost a fraction of what you would pay at a timber yard – and a joiner can make them into a desk for you.

A supportive chair is one of the most important items for working at home. Avoid those made from inflammable polyurethane foam, which poses a serious fire hazard. If you intend working from home for long periods, it is worth investing in a good-quality office chair, which is designed to support the small of your back so that you are not slouching. The height and backrest must be adjustable, and the chair should have castors for easy movement. Check out secondhand office furniture stores for old office chairs and filing cabinets.

Office products

Avoid using plastic office equipment, such as trays and files. Choose metal trays, which last longer and are less harmful to the environment, and wooden filing cabinets. Instead of buying boxes of disposable pens invest in a beautiful pen that you love to use and that will last for years. Look out for water-based correction fluid and marker pens rather than ones that contain toxic solvents. Use old CDs as coasters for your desk and dining table, and source unusual office accessories, such as stapleless staples, mouse mats and CD holders made from hemp and recycled plastic.

THE BATHROOM

For most of us our bathrooms are our sanctuaries. You can close the door on the noise and demands of your day-to-day life, fill the bath, light a few candles and suddenly you are in a serene world of your own. But just how relaxing would that long hot bath be if you knew that the bubbles around you contained a detergent so strong that it is used to degrease engines? And while you brush your teeth, consider that the toothpaste in your mouth may contain artificial colours, flavours, sweeteners and aluminium!

In fact, almost every bodycare product in your bathroom probably contains a long list of chemicals – many of which could be toxic to you and the environment. Add to this the amount of plastic packaging that comes out of your bathroom in the form of toothpaste tubes, toothbrush packs, shampoo bottles, pots of body lotion and so on, the water wasted and the power used to heat your bath and shower water, and the environmental impact of your bathroom becomes very clear. Your days of stress-free bathing may be over unless you start making some green bathroom choices.

Decor

Avoid using conventional paints for bathrooms, as these are likely to contain fungicides and other chemicals that can offgas into the room. Often, they are also impermeable and therefore likely to trap moisture, potentially causing damp. Instead, go for water-based microporous paint that will let your walls breathe, dispersing moisture and aiding drying. There is a variety of natural paints available that are suitable for use in bathrooms. You could also complement your painted areas with recycled or reclaimed glass tiles.

For floors, the choice is similar to that for kitchens since moisture levels and heat are the main factors in both rooms (see page 139). Natural linoleum, cork and terracotta tiles are the most suitable floor coverings for the bathroom.

THE BATHROOM SUITE

As with every other part of your house, try to avoid plastic when it comes to choosing a bath, basin or toilet. Alternatives include porcelain or enamel bathroom suites, which both hold the heat of the bath water better than plastic or fibreglass. Choose the best-quality fixtures you can afford as they should last longer.

Avoid power showers, as these are heavy users of energy, but be sure to have at least a shower attachment that fits to your bath taps (faucets), as normal showers are huge savers of water and energy (see page 135). Installing water-saving or low-flow showerheads can save you even more water, and opt for an electric shower which heats the water only as it is used, thereby saving energy.

Don't go for the biggest bath you can squeeze into your bathroom – think of the water and power that will be wasted (and the cost on your heating bills) in just getting it half-full. Remember that the less surface area of water exposed to air, the less heat that will be lost, so go for a short, but deep, bath tub if possible. In fact, you could dispense with a bath altogether – a shower will do the job and save you acres of space, too.

Your taps (faucets) should ideally be low-flow and sensor controlled, turning on only when your hands or toothbrush are beneath them. But if these are beyond your budget, choose mixer taps (faucets), which use a minimum amount of water to get the right temperature. Spray taps save water, too.

Toilets are particularly heavy users of water. For example, flushing accounts for around 30 per cent of total household water consumption within the UK and an old toilet can use as much as 9–12 litres (2⅓–3 gallons) of water every time it is flushed. A good way to save water is to install a dual-flush model – which has one flush using around 2–3 litres (½–¾ of a gallon) of water for liquid waste, and another, using 4–7 litres (1–2 gallons), for solids.

Another option is to fit a variable flush device to your existing toilet. These devices usually allow a half-flush or a full flush – the amount of water you save depends on the size of your cistern. They are suitable for most toilets and can be fitted yourself or will take a plumber ten minutes to fit.

For the determinedly green, there is no better option than the compost toilet. This uses no water and creates a valuable garden fertilizer out of your waste. Contrary to popular belief, compost toilets are not smelly if they are properly looked after and you can now buy compost toilet systems specifically designed for domestic properties.

Finally, say "no" to a bidet. They are really not necessary and will waste yet more water when a shower would do the job just as well.

Water-saving tips for the bathroom:

- Don't have a bath or shower just to wash your hair and remember you do not need to shampoo every day – in fact, it is better for your hair if you don't.

- Resist the temptation to install a large bath. Most modern tubs hold around 130 litres (34⅓ gallons), which is around 60 litres (16 gallons) of water with a submerged adult, but some larger baths hold more than 300 litres (79 gallons).

- Have a short shower rather than a long soak – a five-minute shower can use about a third as much water as a bath and in a typical household, bathing accounts for around 20 per cent of annual water use. But don't have a power shower! They can actually use more water than a bath in less than five minutes. Instead choose the lowest rated electric shower you can find. An 8-kilowatt shower uses far less water and energy than a 10-kilowatt model.

- If you do have a power shower you can sometimes cut back on water usage by switching off the booster pump. To do this you need to locate the pump and switch off the isolating switch to see if it is still possible to take a shower using gravity alone. As a guide, if you have at least 1 m (3–4 ft) vertically between your showerhead and the bottom of your cold water storage tank, you should be able to have a shower using gravity alone.

- Use a water-efficient showerhead. They reduce the water used by up to 30 per cent by either creating finer drops or introducing air. Typically, they work at a flow rate of 4–9 litres (1–2⅓ gallons) per minute. Most power showers use over 12 litres (3 gallons) of water per minute , but most people are satisfied with a shower flow rate of 10 litres (2½ gallons) per minute.

  In the US the upper limit set for showers is 9 litres (2⅓ gallons) per minute – there is currently no such limit in the UK. Consider installing a low-flow showerhead or an air shower.

- Try using a tap (faucet) insert that changes the water flow into a spray by only slightly opening the tap (faucet). This will save on water use but can be overriden if you need to fill the basin up quickly by turning the tap (faucet) full on.

- Get leaking taps (faucets) fixed as soon as possible, as up to 4 litres (1 gallon) of water can disappear down your sink every hour this way. A dripping hot tap (faucet) can waste 31 hot tanks of water each year.

- Find out if you have a leaking toilet cistern by putting vegetable dye in the water. If it appears in the toilet bowl without flushing, you know there is a leak, which needs to be fixed straightaway.

- Use a cistern displacement device – you can either buy one or make one yourself using an old water bottle filled up with water. Inserted in the cistern they will ensure it does not fully fill with water and save 1–3 litres (¼–¾ of a gallon) of water per flush. They are sometimes available free from your water supplier. You can also buy a kit that fits into a cistern which only allows the toilet to flush for as long as you hold the handle down.

- Flush your toilet less. One-third of an average family's water use is flushed down the toilet – the equivalent of two baths of water per day. If you are the only one in the house do you really need to flush it every time?

- Use a dual flush toilet – one study found an average reduction of 27 per cent in the volume of water used directly for flushing after installation of dual flush services.

- Investigate water-saving systems – there are various ways of collecting rainwater for use in your toilet and saving greywater from your bath for use in the garden. You will probably need advice from experts on the best system for your needs.

- Make use of the water in your bathroom air by growing humidity-loving plants in your bathroom, such as ferns.

- Turn the water off when it's not in use! Leave it running while you brush your teeth and you could be wasting 4 litres (1 gallon) of water.

BATHROOM ACCESSORIES

The look of your bathroom is defined by the accessories – a truly green bathroom will have no plastic in sight and the accessories (and those that are only absolutely necessary) will all be made from natural materials, such as wood.

So resist the urge to use a plastic shower curtain and have a glass screen instead. Don't buy a plastic non-slip bathmat unless you are really unsteady on your feet or have small children, and avoid cluttering up the place with a lot of unnecessary plastic soap holders, plastic storage boxes and plastic toothbrush holders. If you really do need all these bits and pieces, seek out those made of sustainable materials.

HEALTH TIP

**If your skin is dry and flaky, and your hair dull and lifeless, this could be due to the chlorine in your water. Chlorine is commonly added to water supplies. You can absorb it through your skin and, as the water is heated, it can give off vapours that you then breathe into your lungs. It has been estimated that during an average shower you absorb as much chlorine as you would by drinking eight glasses of chlorinated water.
You can remove the chlorine from the water in your shower by fitting a de-chlorinating shower filter. Alternatively, remove it from all water in your house by using a whole-house water purifier.**

Use a flannel (wash cloth) rather than a sponge. Real sponges are taken from the sea, disturbing precious natural habitats, whereas artificial sponges are another product of the plastics industry. Cotton flannels (wash cloths), preferably organic and unbleached, can be washed time and again, and used around the house for other cleaning tasks when they are past their best.

Unbleached, Fairtrade organic cotton towels are the most eco-friendly and if you have linoleum flooring, you may want to look out for organic cotton bathroom rugs as well. Or make your own bathroom mat by sewing together the best bits of old towels or by gluing leftover cork tiles onto a piece of hardboard.

For scrubbing under nails or giving your skin an all-over brush to help detoxify, choose wooden brushes with natural-fibre bristles. Check that the wood comes from a sustainable source – likewise for toilet brushes. You can also buy wooden duckboard-style slatted mats for stepping onto when you get out of the bath.

Avoid plastic in other areas of your bathroom, too. Don't buy disposable plastic razors – use metal ones with replaceable but durable blades, or an electric shaver. Look out for recycled plastic toothbrushes and razors – made from yogurt pots – and make the effort to recycle your toothbrushes. An old toothbrush makes a great cleaning aid for hard-to-reach areas around taps.

Finally, although not strictly an accessory and more of an essential, when it comes to toilet paper there is no excuse for buying anything other than recycled. The quality and softness are now the equal of most other papers. It can make a big difference too. The average British person uses over 100 rolls per year and, according to the World Wildlife Fund (WWF), around 270,000 trees are flushed down the drain or end up as rubbish all over the world every day. Look for products marked 100 per cent recycled and unbleached. Those carrying the FSC Recycled logo are guaranteed to contain only postconsumer waste material.

GREEN CLEANING TIPS

Here are some green solutions to a few of those tricky cleaning challenges in the bathroom:

* Limescale on taps (faucets): rub with half a lemon, rinse thoroughly and dry.
* Limescale on tap (faucet) nozzles: tie an old plastic bag filled with white vinegar around the ends of your taps until the scale is dissolved, then rinse.
* Blocked showerhead: remove the head and soak it in a bowl of warm, neat vinegar. A needle will help clear blocked holes.
* Hard-water deposits in toilet bowl: apply a paste of borax and white vinegar, leave for a few hours, then rinse.
* Hard-water deposits on shower doors: wipe with white vinegar, leave for 30 minutes, then rinse.
* Mildew on shower curtains: prevent mildew by soaking curtains in salted water before hanging, and scrub with a paste of bicarbonate of soda and water, then rinse.
* Mould around shower: wash down with borax and do not rinse – the borax residue will fight mould growth.
* Fungus on tile grouting: apply a paste of bicarbonate of soda and water, leave for an hour, then rinse with warm water.
* Bath stains: light stains can be treated by rubbing with cut lemon dipped in salt darker stains may be removed by applying a paste of borax and lemon juice – leave for an hour, then rinse.
* Drip marks in a bath: rub with warm vinegar, then rinse with warm water. Repeat daily until they disappear.

The next best choice is toilet roll with a high-recycled content or products carrying the FSC Mixed Sources label, which guarantees that the product is a mixture of fibre from an FSC-certified forest or a controlled source, or post-consumer reclaimed material. Ensure, also, that recycling claims don't just refer to the packaging and avoid the very brightest of white papers as this indicates that it has been heavily bleached.

Bodycare

Today bodycare means big business. There are products aimed at the moisturizing, cleansing, toning and all-out pampering of almost every part of your body, and now men are just as well catered for as women. But behind the alluring promise of beauty lies the ugly reality of thousands of chemicals polluting the environment, millions of plastic bottles sitting in landfills and the earth becoming ever more depleted of diminishing resources. So if you want to make a world of difference in one quick and easy step, make sure you buy only what is absolutely necessary and always check that it is as natural as possible. But beware: the term "natural" is used somewhat loosely in the bodycare world; in many countries very few ingredients need to be natural for this term to be applied to a product.

What you should be looking for are ingredients that are plant based, rather than petroleum based, since these are theoretically sustainable, non-polluting and better for our health (see pages 140–5). Certainly avoid products containing mineral oil, which is just another name for petroleum oil, but be aware also that the vegetable oil used may be palm oil and palm oil plantations are a major cause of rainforest destruction in countries such as Malaysia and Indonesia (see Green Buying Guidelines, pages 142–5)

It is also advisable to avoid as many manufactured chemicals as possible, which come in the form of fragrances, preservatives, detergents, chelating agents, thickening agents, colorants, antimicrobials, emulsifiers, and even UV absorbers to stop the chemical dyes in some products from fading in the sunlight (i.e. chemicals to protect chemicals!).

Bodycare products are notorious for their long list of bewildering ingredients, so it can be hard to distinguish which are the good or bad among them. Read as much as you can on the subject and, if in doubt, choose the product with the least number of ingredients of any kind.

Always choose certified organic bodycare products or products that at least contain organic ingredients. Again, beware of the hype here – the term "organic" can be freely used on bodycare product labels in many countries without it meaning anything at all. Your first step is to look for bodycare products that are certified organic – not just those containing organic ingredients. In the US, organic bodycare products will display the USDA certified organic symbol, while in the UK the Soil Association now certifies bodycare products and is working with a group of EU certification bodies to develop a common European organic beauty and cosmetic standard. To achieve certification the products

ENERGY-SAVING TIPS

✱ If you have a problem with condensation in your bathroom then you will need to consider ventilation. The most eco-friendly way of airing your bathroom is obviously to open the window, but if feeling a draught around your ankles while you stand in the shower does not appeal then you will almost certainly require an extractor fan.

✱ To save energy, it is best to use a wind-operated fan in your window that draws air out of the house using the difference in pressure alone. If you do not have a convenient window then you are likely to need, or already have, an electric extractor fan. Often these come on automatically when you switch on the bathroom light, but to save energy install a second light in the bathroom, say above the mirror, which can be switched on without the extractor fan going on as well. You can use this light when you are just brushing your teeth or putting on your make-up – use the main light (with the extractor) only when you are having a bath or shower.

✱ Finally, you will want to be sure that the bathroom door is well draught-proofed to prevent all your valuable, centrally heated, warm air being drawn out along with the condensation.

must use organic ingredients if they are available and the remaining ingredients must meet strict criteria to ensure that they are not damaging to our health or the environment.

Finally, try to avoid using as much packaging as possible. Aim to bulk buy, refill and recycle at every opportunity. You will then reduce waste and save yourself some money, too, while you are at it. And make sure that you let those manufacturers that consistently overpackage their products know that this is one of your reasons for no longer buying from them.

Health hazards

There has been an explosion in our use of chemicals in everyday products – between 1930 and 2000 global production of manmade chemicals increased from 1 to 400 million tonnes each year, but they are a major health issue. According to the World Wildlife Fund, hazardous manmade chemicals have contaminated every environment, including wildlife, such as birds, polar bears, frogs, alligators and panthers, and up to 300 manmade chemicals have been found in humans.

Three types of chemicals are of particular concern:

* Very persistent and very bioaccumulative chemicals which break down slowly or not at all, and accumulate in the bodies of wildlife and people

* Endocrine Disrupting Chemicals (EDCs), which interfere with the hormone systems of animals and people

* Chemicals that cause cancer, reproductive problems, or damage DNA.

Chemicals from all three of these groups are commonly found in beauty and bodycare products. For example, the following are used in a variety of products – phthalates, acrylamide, formaldehyde and ethylene oxide – and have all been found to act as carcinogens or reproductive toxins.

Once you use a variety of cosmetic and bodycare products there is then the unknown "cocktail effect" of chemicals to worry about. Further risks might come from the use of nanotechnology, which produces nanoparticles – dust-like fragments are one thousandth the width of a human hair. Nanoparticles are already used in many products, including sunscreens and cosmetics but some researchers are concerned about their impact on our health as they are known to be able to cross over into areas of the body that were previously never reached by larger particles.

A coalition of over 40 consumer, public health, environmental, labour and civil society organizations spanning six continents have jointly produced a paper calling for greater government oversight of this new technology and its products. The coalition cites evidence that shows current nanomaterials may pose significant health, safety and environmental hazards.

WHAT IS THE GOVERNMENT DOING?

Government regulations on this issue are weak. According to the Environmental Working Group (EWG), nearly 90 per cent of ingredients in personal care products in the US have not been assessed for safety by anyone.

In Europe, the laws have been tightened up first with the banning of certain chemicals that are known or strongly suspected of causing cancer, mutation or birth defects. More recently, new legislation – REACH (Registration, Evaluation, Authorization and restriction of Chemicals) – has been created which aims to ensure that persistent and bioaccumulative chemicals will have to be substituted if safer alternatives exist, plus companies will have to provide health and safety information for large volume chemicals that they produce or import into Europe. A European Chemicals Agency will be set up to enforce the legislation, but there are concerns that the Agency could be influenced by the chemicals industry and that the legislation may not be tight enough.

The situation is worse in the US, where chemicals can be used in personal care products with no testing, no monitoring of health effects and weak labeling requirements. The EWG has found nearly 400 products sold in the US contain chemicals that are not allowed to be in use by other countries, and over 400 products containing ingredients the US cosmetic industry's own safety panel has determined to be unsafe when used as directed. It is left to an industry-funded panel, not a government health agency, to review the safety of cosmetic ingredients in the US.

Some states in the US are, however, taking their own action on this issue. In California, for example, the California Safe Cosmetics bill is the nation's first state law on chemicals in cosmetics and it forces companies to notify the state when they use chemicals linked to cancer and birth defects.

WHAT CAN YOU DO?

The first step is to become more chemically aware. Various websites list the chemicals you need to look out for, the World Wildlife Fund even has a "Toxic quiz" to help you identify the risks in your home and the Women's Environmental Network also offers fact sheets and a "Toxic tour" on this issue.

However, many chemicals will never appear on the ingredients listing either because they are hidden within a generic word such as "parfum" or because they are not actually ingredients, rather they are a byproduct of manufacturing.

You can find safety information on specific products online by checking the Skin Deep database of nearly 25,000 bodycare products (www.cosmeticsdatabase. com). This database will also tell you if a company has signed the Compact for Safe Cosmetics, whereby they pledge not to use chemicals linked to cancer, birth defects and other health harms and replace them with safer alternatives within three years.

Look also for products that are certified organic – their ingredients have been assessed not to be harmful to human health, and their manufacture and use must cause minimum environmental impact. In the UK, the Soil Association standards have also been updated to ban ingredients resulting from nanotechnology until further research is available.

Green buying guidelines

SOAP

Buy your soap in bars rather than bottles and save leftover scraps – they can be put in a jar with boiling water to create a soapy liquid for use elsewhere or may be stuck onto the next bar. You really do not have to buy conventional chemical-laden soaps these days; natural, handmade, vegetable-oil soaps are widely available. Look out for those that use essential oils and herbs for fragrance and therapeutic value, or bran and seeds for a good scrub. Alternatively, you could give ground soapnut a try. Derived from a tree grown in India and used there for thousands of years, soapnut can be used for washing more than just your body – it can also be used for cleaning clothes and even the car!

BATHTIME

A plethora of products claim to offer relaxation or invigoration with the addition of essential oils, but most of them have too few oils of too low a standard to have any real therapeutic benefits. In addition, their main ingredients will undoubtedly be detergents, foaming agents and preservatives. Go for bath oils instead by either mixing your own (see page 148) or buying them from a reputable source, such as a healthfood store. (Remember that vegetables, nuts and essential oils can be certified as organic, so pick these if available.) The bonus of using essential oils is that many are natural preservatives – just remember to keep them stored away from sunlight, preferably in dark glass bottles. Bath salts are another green alternative – try Epsom salts for swollen ankles and volcanic mineral salts for muscular aches and pains.

POWDER

Don't use talcum powder after your bath – in recent years it has been linked with female reproductive cancers and it could be contaminated with asbestos fibre. Choose cornflour (cornstarch) products instead.

HAIRCARE

Shampoos, conditioners, dyes and other treatments are packed full of synthetic chemicals that place a heavy burden on our sewage system and our health. Don't be tempted by offers of gleaming, shiny locks; instead cut back on your hair products consumption. You do not need much shampoo to clean your hair and you really do not need to wash your hair every day. Try making your own products using organic herbs and essential oils (see page 149) or look for natural products from healthfood stores.

TOOTHPASTE

First of all, avoid pump-action toothpaste tubes – these contain even more plastic than regular tubes. Next, take a look at the ingredients. Do you really want to put petrochemicals, artificial sweeteners and flavours in your mouth? And just how important are those green stripes, because they are achieved only by the addition of artificial colours (some of which should be avoided if you are concerned about hyperactivity in your children).

Natural vegetable-based alternatives abound and there is even an organic standard for toothpaste in the UK – the first non-food product in the world to be accorded legal organic status. Some natural products contain fluoride and the detergent and foaming agent sodium lauryl sulphate, so check the ingredients panel if you want to avoid these.

FACIAL CARE

Cleanse, tone and moisturize – the three magic steps to fabulous skin are drummed into most women from an early age, but try to keep it simple. Use homemade products as much as possible (see pages 146–7); otherwise choose the least packaged, and least complex product you can find. Shop in healthfood stores or the increasing number of specialist natural bodycare stores for natural products that make minimal use of petrochemicals and other toxic chemicals.

Don't be fooled into thinking that the latest chemical ingredient is going to wipe your face free of wrinkles – nothing can do that, other than cosmetic surgery! Instead the chemical could agitate sensitive skin and will have wasted energy and possibly created pollution in its manufacture.

SHAVING

Aerosols are still prevalent in this area, but these should be avoided at all costs due to their use of propellants. The best option is to do away with shaving foam or gel altogether and just use good, old-fashioned soap and water. If you feel you need more, choose a plant-based product, preferably as a cream in a bowl, which you lather yourself with a brush (made of sustainable wood and natural bristles).

ANTIPERSPIRANTS AND DEODORANTS

Again these are still commonly sold in aerosol form – a real environmental baddie. There are also health concerns about the impact of using antiperspirants that prevent your body sweating on a regular basis, especially those with aluminium as an ingredient. A small-scale British study found concentrations of aluminium close to the underarm in breast tissue taken from 17 women who had had masectomies and another British study has found traces of parabens – preservatives that are commonly used in deodorants and other cosmetics – in tissue taken from women with breast cancer. Although this does not prove aluminium or parabens cause breast cancer – or that they originated from antiperspirants – it does suggest these chemicals can accumulate in our bodies and both are used in these products. Parabens have also been shown to be able to mimic the action of the female hormone oestrogen, which can drive the growth of human breast tumours.

There are natural alternatives, like mineral rock crystal deodorants. If you do buy a conventional product, look for plant-based ingredients and choose a roll-on to save packaging.

EYES

Contact lens solutions clutter up many people's bathrooms, with a huge cost in terms of waste packaging. If you wear lenses, choose the simplest possible lens-care system available and buy in bulk. Best of all, go back to glasses!

SANITARY PROTECTION

The main environmental issue is how it is disposed of. If you flush a tampon or sanitary towel down the toilet you will end up bobbing up and down next to it when you next take a dip in the sea! The other environmental concerns come from the materials used – cotton and plastic mostly – so do your best to avoid non-organic, bleached cotton products and choose the brand with the least amount of plastic packaging; in particular avoid individually wrapped towels. Options include rubber cups and natural sponges for non-disposable solutions. (See also page 70.)

For information on cosmetics, nail varnish and perfume see Bedrooms, pages 67–9.

Do-it-yourself bodycare

It is cheaper and less worrying to make your own products then you exactly know what is in them. You do not need many ingredients and if you have your own herb patch, or window box, you may have most of the ingredients already. Here are some homemade preparations to start off with.

Note: If you are pregnant, suffering from high blood pressure or a heart condition, or if you are taking regular medication, check first with your doctor or a qualified herbalist or aromatherapist before using essential oils or herbal extracts or supplements. Always do a patch test first to test for an allergic reaction and remember, a balanced organic diet, plenty of water, rest and relaxation is better for you than anything else.

NATURAL SKIN TREATMENTS

❖ Assess the type of skin you have and experiment with some of these herbs: lemon grass, witch hazel, elderflower and sage for oily skins; comfrey, rose and camomile for dry skin and coltsfoot, borage and fennel for sensitive skin.

❖ Make a cleanser by pouring a cup of boiling water over 4 tsp of your dried herb of choice. Leave it to stand for 10–15 minutes, then add 2 tsp of the herbal infusion to 1 tsp honey and 1 tsp almond oil (warmed first in order to dissolve the honey). This can be rubbed on the face and then rinsed off with warm water.

❖ A cleansing milk for dry skin can be made by gently heating half a cup of full-fat milk with 2 tbsp camomile flowers for 30 minutes. Cool for two hours, strain and keep in the fridge for up to a week.

❖ To cleanse dry skin, blend half a small pot of natural yogurt with ¼ tbsp lemon juice and 1 tbsp almond oil until smooth.

❖ Cotton wool soaked in cold milk can be used as a gentle, but effective make-up remover, as can sweet almond oil.

❖ Mix 300 ml (½ pint) milk with some puréed cucumber and use this as cleanser for oily skin. It will keep in the fridge for three days.

❖ Oily skin will also benefit from regular gentle exfoliation. Try a daily scrub with a handful of bran, oatmeal or cornmeal.

❖ Mix 1 tsp cider vinegar with a herbal infusion to make a great toner. Keep it in the fridge and dab it on with cotton wool or simply spitz it onto your face. Herbs to try include yarrow, sage, mint and fennel.

❧ Give tired skin a lift by steaming your face over a bowl of hot water infused with two handfuls of fresh herbs such as borage, calendula, comfrey and nettle. Cover your head in a towel to keep in the steam and stay put for five minutes. (Don't do this if you suffer from flushing or thread veins.)

❧ Natural yogurt may be blended with finely ground oatmeal and a herbal infusion to make a face mask. Mix the herbal infusion with 2 tbsp yogurt and then add enough oatmeal to make a paste. Oatmeal can also be used to soften the skin – soak a handful of oats overnight, then use the strained liquid as a face rinse in the morning.

❧ Another nourishing face mask can be made by beating the white of an egg, applying it to the skin and leaving it to dry before washing off with warm water. Add 1 tbsp honey or 1 tsp olive oil to the frothy mixture if you have dry skin and 1 tsp lemon juice if you suffer from oily skin.

❧ The yolk of one egg left overnight in a hole made inside half a lemon can be applied to the face and left for 15 minutes before rinsing. This will cleanse and tone your skin.

❧ For sensitive skin try mixing 2 tbsp bran with 1 tsp runny honey and 3 tbsp of a camomile infusion. After ten minutes rinse the mask off with more camomile infusion.

❧ Try applying a good-quality mayonnaise on your face at night to help combat fine lines and wrinkles. This is best done when you are sleeping alone!

❧ Another kitchen moisturizer can be made by blending a ripe avocado with 1 tsp honey, ½ tsp lemon juice and enough natural yogurt to make a stiff cream. Allow to cool and apply to the face for 30 minutes before rinsing.

BATHS

❖ Use three or four herbal tea bags or wrap some loose herbs in a muslin (cheesecloth) square and hang it beneath the running hot tap (faucet) to make a herbal bath infusion. Squeeze the tea bag or muslin square gently underwater to encourage the essences to be released.

Herbs to try include: camomile, lavender, valerian and hops for relaxation; lemon verbena, basil, bay and pine for stimulation; calendula, comfrey and yarrow for healing; and clove, cinnamon, thyme or ginger to boost circulation in winter.

❖ Powdered full fat milk can help soften the skin: put 3 tbsp in a muslin (cheesecloth) bag and add this to your bath while you are running the water. You can also add herbs to the bag – try using 125 g (4 oz) of fresh elderflower, camomile, rose petals, sage or lemon balm.

❖ Make your own bath oils by adding a few drops of essential oil to a quarter of a cup of carrier oil such as sweet almond or apricot oil. Try lavender for soothing, jasmine to relieve tiredness and sage to ease anxiety. You can also add a few drops of essential oil directly to the running water in your bath or mix it to a paste with milk powder first.

Some essential oils can be dangerous, so do not use them if you are pregnant or suffer from high blood pressure without consulting a qualified aromatherapist or a doctor. Always read the label and use only the recommended drops.

❖ Make your own herbal oil by infusing the herb of your choice in almond oil on a sunny window ledge for a couple of weeks. Use it in your bath and in the kitchen!

❖ If you shower rather than bath, you can still reap the benefits of naturally scented products. Either add a few drops of essential oil to a neutral shower gel, or make up an oil solution as for a bath and pour a small quantity onto a flannel (wash cloth) and rub it vigorously over your body.

❖ Exfoliating your skin will help you get the most benefit from your herbal or essential oil bath – try rubbing sea salt mixed with a little water over your body, or brushing the dry skin with a natural bristle brush. You can even use the rice bran or oatmeal that has been soaking under the hot tap (faucet) in your herbal bag – remove halfway through your bath and rub it onto your moist skin.

❖ For irritated skin and aching muscles, try adding a cupful of cider vinegar to the bath.

HAIRCARE

❖ Dilute a little cider vinegar in warm water and apply daily to the scalp to help combat dandruff. Another dandruff treatment is to rub lemon juice into hair roots and scalp.

❖ Identify the herbs that best suit your hair type – lavender, rose and rosemary for normal hair; burdock, elderflower, parsley and sage for dry hair; calendula, lemon balm, mint, sage and yarrow for greasy hair; comfrey, nettle and willow bark for dandruff; horsetail, rosemary, nettle and sage for lifeless hair.

❖ Give your hair a homemade herbal boost by adding a herbal infusion to the mildest, least chemical shampoo you can find. Make the infusion by steeping 6 tbsp fresh herbs or 3 tbsp dried herbs in half a cup of boiling water for ten minutes. Then, every time you wash your hair, add 1 tbsp of infusion to 4 tbsp of the base shampoo.

❖ Make your own shampoo by pouring 600 ml (1 pint) of boiling water over 25 g (1 oz) dried soapwort root. Let it steep for 12 hours, then bring the mixture to the boil and simmer for 15 minutes. Remove the pan from the heat, add 25 g (1 oz) of your chosen herb, cover and cool. Strain the mixture and keep in the fridge for up to four days.

❖ Use herbal infusions to make an after-wash rinse. Add 1 tbsp of the infusion to 1 tbsp lemon juice or cider vinegar before adding 600 ml (1 pint) warm water. Try camomile or yarrow if you are blonde; lavender, nettle or rosemary; mint or sage if you are brunette if you are dark; and calendula or witch hazel if you are auburn.

❖ If blonde, try a cold tea or diluted lemon juice rinse; if brunette, apply diluted malt vinegar.

❖ Make your own hot oil conditioner using almond or apricot oil into which you can add either 2 tsp of your herbal infusion or a few drops of an essential oil such as tea tree oil, which is especially good for treating dandruff. Heat the mixture gently, before carefully massaging it into your scalp and wrapping your head in a hot, damp towel. Wait for at least an hour before washing off to allow the treatment to work.

❖ Mayonnaise can also be applied to the hair, left for an hour and then washed off. Follow this with a cider vinegar rinse to recondition dry hair.

❖ Comb rosemary hair oil through your hair prior to washing if your dark hair needs some shine. Mix 2 tbsp of strong rosemary infusion with 6 tbsp almond oil and 30 drops of lavender oil.

TEETH

❖ Bicarbonate of soda (baking soda) makes a great toothpaste. Just mix 1 tsp with a few drops of peppermint essential oil and enough water to make a paste.

❖ Oil of cloves has been used for years to help ease toothache. Apply a few drops to sore gums.

❖ If you have any sage in the garden, try giving your teeth and gums a polish by rubbing a sage leaf over them. Sage tea is also good as a mouth-wash for ulcers and bleeding gums.

❖ Herbal infusions can be used as mouthwashes. Start with a mint and rosemary recipe – add 1 tsp fresh mint and the same quantity of fresh rosemary and aniseed to 600 ml (1 pint) boiling water. Steep for 20 minutes, then strain, cool and then use as an effective gargle.

❖ To remove stains on teeth try dipping your toothbrush in lemon juice and some sea salt. Brush as normal, but remember to rinse thoroughly. Or rub the wet side of half a lemon over your teeth (strawberries can also be used in this way).

❖ Try chewing on some fresh parsley to sweeten your breath.

❖ Keep your lips smooth with a homemade lip balm. Gently melt 1 tsp of beeswax in a bain-marie or a heatproof bowl over a pan of simmering water. Add 1 tsp each of apricot and calendula oil, stirring constantly. Remove the mixture from the heat and add a few drops of orange or lemon essential oil when it has partly cooled. Pour into a jar or small pot to set.

EYES

❖ Refresh tired eyes by placing a damp used tea bag over each eye for ten minutes, then rinse with cold water. You can use regular tea bags, or try camomile or rosehip bags.

❖ The herb eyebright can help soothe sore, strained eyes and give relief from hayfever symptoms. Try boiling 2 tbsp fresh herb or 2 tsp dried herb in two cups of water for 20 minutes. Cool and thoroughly filter the solution three times through a coffee filter paper before using in an eye bath.

Babies in the bathroom

From ducks in the bath to baby lotion in the cabinet, the arrival of a baby brings many new products into a bathroom, but which are the greenest?

TOYS

Plastic ducks, boats and cups litter most children's baths, but the best option is to avoid plastic altogether. Failing that, look out for toys that are PVC-free as the dangerous chemicals. It can leach into your baby if these toys are chewed regularly. The best option of all is to think creatively about what is already in your home – recycle plastic yogurt pots to make water scoops, for example.

BODYCARE

Baby skincare is big business, and most products sell themselves as being the gentlest available. But if you take a look at the ingredients often they contain a long list of chemicals which are bad for the environment and completely unnecessary for babies.

Baths are fun and can help babies to relax before they go to bed, but most babies who get daily baths only need the gentlest bath products. Therefore, detergents and other strong cleaning agents are unnecessary.

A splash-around in lukewarm water will suffice or, as your baby gets older, you can use a natural olive-oil based soap or one of the increasing number of natural products for babies – but be sure to check the ingredients lists and look out for organic versions. Be sure to steer clear of artificially perfumed and coloured products.

Equally, there is no need for special lotions and powders to care for your baby's skin, unless it is especially dry or if your child suffers from a particular problem such as eczema. In these cases seek out natural, plant-based products such as organic almond oil for dry skin. To heal nappy (diaper) rash, review how often you are changing them and let your baby go nappy-free for as long as possible.

Nor is there a need for chemically saturated wipes in order to cleanse a baby's bottom when you are changing a nappy (diaper). Some warm water on organic cotton wool will do the job just as well, or make your own wipes using organic or undyed cotton squares (which can be bought from some cloth nappy (diaper) companies). They can be dipped in a homemade solution of 50 ml (2 fl oz) distilled water mixed with 1 tbsp vinegar, 2 tbsp aloe vera gel, 1 tbsp calendula oil and a few drops of lavender and tea tree essential oil.

NAPPIES (DIAPERS)

Your choice of nappy (diaper) can make a big difference to the environment. Disposables can take between 200 and 500 years to decompose and in so doing, they emit noxious methane gas into the environment. They also contain all sorts of chemicals such as bleaches, perfumes, plastic and additives, which are not great for the environment either. Even biodegradable disposals contain absorbent gelling materials (AGMs) and need just as much fuel, energy and water to produce as ordinary disposables. In addition, 7 million trees are felled annually to meet the demand for the absorbent pulp in disposables and some of these trees are from mature forests in Scandinavia, Canada and the Baltic States, rather than sustainably managed plantations.

Consider also the possible health consequences of using disposable nappies (diapers). Concerns have been voiced about the chemicals used in disposables, which have been found to be a possible trigger for asthma. Plus, disposable nappies lined with plastic could be linked to declining fertility rates since they raise the temperature of a baby boy's scrotum, which in turn is critical to normal testicular development and sperm health.

There are plenty of alternatives to disposable nappies (diapers), including real washable versions, those with a disposable inner liner and a washable outer, and greener versions of disposables – using recycled pulp, for example. If you prefer to use real nappies (diapers), then try to use those made from organic cotton or hemp and organic wool waterproof overpants. Be sure also to wash and use them in the most eco-friendly way possible.

This should include:

❀ Wash soiled nappies (diapers) at 60°C (140°F) but washwet nappies and waterproof wraps at lower temperatures along with the rest of your laundry
❀ Avoid tumble drying and avoid soaking – store nappies (diapers) dry in a lidded bucket
❀ Avoid using unnecessary chemicals such as conditioners and sanitizers, and use an eco-detergent. Commercial fabric conditioner will reduce the absorbency of nappies
❀ Never iron nappies (diapers) or wraps
❀ Use washable liners.

If you can't face washing them yourself then there are laundry services available for real nappies (diapers), but choose one that uses eco-friendly laundry detergents.

It is also worth looking out for exchange services. One exists in the UK that gives parents an opportunity to source, sell, donate and buy used washable nappies (diapers) and accessories – for free.

If you really cannot bear the thought of giving up disposable nappies (diapers), then at least stop using plastic nappy (diaper) sacks. With all those nappies filling landfills the last thing we need is to have them all individually wrapped in their own plastic bags as well. Anyway, it is far better to keep soiled nappies (diapers) outside in a garbage receptacle rather than to leave them inside the house in artificially fragranced bags.

NAPPY (DIAPER) WASHING TIPS

The Women's Environmental Network gives the following nappy (diaper) washing tips:

If you wish to soak nappies (diapers) then try using the following
- ❖ White distilled vinegar (2–3 tbsp)
- ❖ Sodium bicarbonate (baking soda) (1 tbsp)
- ❖ Domestic borax (1 tbsp)
- ❖ Tea tree oil (5 drops)
- ❖ Sanitizing powder (1 tbsp)

Mix to dissolve, then add nappies (diapers) throughout the day. Change the solution regularly.

Please note that domestic borax and ordinary sanitizing powders should not be used on Velcro or waterproof fabrics. Some of these soaking and washing methods may not be suitable for certain nappies (diapers) – if in doubt consult the distributor.

- ❖ Adding half a small cup of vinegar in the last rinse cycle will keep nappies (diapers) soft.
- ❖ A few drops of lavender in the conditioner compartment of the washing machine will also keep the nappies (diapers) soft as well as smelling fresh.

THE BEDROOM

Your bedroom should be a place of tranquillity and
relaxation – your retreat from the outside world
(and perhaps from other members of your household).
In this section you will find practical advice and ideas on
how to create a far greener and, hopefully, more serene
sleeping space where you can rest easy.
As well as making green choices when it comes to
heating your bedroom you can also minimize its
environmental impact by choosing natural fabrics and
furniture. Organic bed linen is now easily available as are
natural materials for floors and walls.

Work out what your main activities are likely to be in the bedroom and light the room accordingly using energy-saving bulbs. You might want a quiet place to read, in which case placing a low table or seat near the window to make the most of natural daylight and the warmth of the sun would make sense.

As with the rest of the house, it is important to use as many natural materials as possible. It is also worth remembering that it is better to buy fewer, longer-lasting items that you love because even though they may cost more, they are less likely to fall out of favour or fashion. There should be adequate ventilation so the air stays fresh and unstuffy – avoid overheating. The best temperature is around 15°C (59°F); fitting a thermostat to the radiator will regulate this.

Avoid having electrical equipment such as televisions, stereo systems and radios in your sleeping space if possible because of the electromagnetic fields (EMFs) given off by such equipment (see page 158). Make the bedroom a telephone-free room so that you do not risk being woken with a phone call or feel obliged to take calls when you are resting and do not want to be disturbed. Keep whatever electrical equipment you do have in your bedroom as far away from the bed as possible.

❧ **Avoid synthetic fabrics.**
❧ **Look out for unbleached, undyed, organic fabrics.**
❧ **Choose organic cotton or hemp sheets and bed linen.**
❧ **Avoid pillows and duvets with synthetic fillings.**
❧ **Use a pure new wool underblanket for warmth.**
❧ **Look for duvet covers that use wooden buttons or cloth tie fastenings.**

Sweet dreams

A good night's sleep is crucial to our wellbeing, especially when you consider that we spend around one-third of our lives in bed. We all know that an interrupted night's sleep makes us, at best, bad-tempered and, at worst, unable to cope with the slightest problem or disruption that might occur during the day. To get a good night's sleep, you really need a good mattress and bed base. If you can afford to invest in only one good piece of furniture, make it your bed. Even if it feels like a massive initial outlay, it will be economical in the long term as a good mattress should last you between five and ten years, and the bed base much longer.

There are two main types of mattress – those with springs and those without. Within the sprung-mattress category there are two types: open-sprung and pocket-sprung. They are made by attaching layers of padding to the spring unit. The mattress should ideally be pocket-sprung – particularly if you share your bed – and made from natural fibres. Make sure that it is not too soft or hard as both can cause back problems in the future. Pocket-sprung mattresses are exactly that – each spring is sewn into a separate pocket of fabric. Poorer-quality mattresses tend to have fewer layers of padding, and some cheaper mattresses are made using synthetic foam, which can contain form-aldehyde and other toxic chemicals – not something you want to be lying on all night! The ideal covering fabric for a mattress is organic cotton but the majority of outer covers are still made using synthetic fabrics such as viscose or polycotton mixtures, and natural versions can be expensive.

Mattresses made with natural materials are less likely to cause allergic reactions (although natural fabrics do trigger allergies in some people). Natural fibres used as fillings in mattresses include coir, horsehair, hessian, cotton and pure new wool. There are three types of mattress finish: cheaper panel tops, quilted tops, and tufted mattresses, which are at the top end of the market. Latex is a foam made using natural rubber and can be a good for allergy sufferers. Organic mattresses, made from natural fibres like cotton and wool, provide comfort and reduce carbon emissions and pollution created in the manufacturing process. For retailers see Resources on pages 246–7.

BEAT THE BUGS NATURALLY

Treat mattresses and other bedding for bed bugs by regularly spraying with neem oil, a natural insecticide. Dilute some neem oil with water and use a spray dispenser to treat bedding including pillows and duvets. Readymade neem sprays are available to buy.

However, even an expensive mattress falls prey to dust mites, which are attracted by the skin particles we shed in our sleep, so it is recommended that you turn the mattress over once a week. Using an under-blanket may help to protect against dust mites and their faeces, which can cause skin irritations. Another good tip for guarding against dust mites is to vacuum your mattress regularly and neem oil is also a good preventative (see above).

As for the bed base, choose one made of wood with solid slats, which allows the air to circulate. There are a growing number of companies and cooperatives making use of reclaimed wood and sustainable timber so it is a good idea to browse the Internet for ones in your area – try to buy locally to cut down on pollution caused by transportation. Look out for bed frames made using traditional methods and FSC-certified wood, if possible.

Once you have chosen your natural mattress and bed base it makes sense to select bed linen made from natural, organic fabrics. Cotton, although natural, is not very environmentally friendly unless organically grown (see page 59). Around 16 per cent of all pesticides used worldwide are employed in conventional cotton production so it plays a large part in polluting our rivers and atmospheres. And no one wants fabric treated with potentially carcinogenic pesticides next to their skin! There is also evidence that fire retardants, moth repellents, easy-care and antipiling finishes which are routinely applied to bed linen may contribute to childhood asthma, eczema and even cot deaths.

Not only is there the environmental pollution to consider. A recent report by the Environmental Justice Foundation in conjunction with the Pesticide Action Network UK highlighted the dangers of pesticides used during cotton production for the workers. It claims that paralysis, coma and even death are some of the side effects suffered by farmers and children in the developing world, who are routinely exposed to pesticides, many of which are banned or restricted for use in the West.

Choose unbleached, undyed organic cotton, hemp or linen pillow slips, sheets and duvet covers. Hemp is a fantastically green fabric, which is now widely available. It is a great fabric for items that are frequently washed because it becomes softer with every wash.

Brushed organic cotton blankets are cosy, soft and warm, and organic cotton waffle bed linen looks good as well as being very comfortable. It is important to wash new bed linen, even if it is organic, before use to get rid of any smells and loose particles.

DUVETS AND PILLOWS

Duvets and pillows should be made with goose feathers or down, which are warm, but light fillings and can be covered with a cotton dust- and mite-proof case. They are produced without polluting the environment and have very good heat-insulating properties. The feathers should ideally have been gathered from the ground rather than plucked because the live plucking of the feathers will cause injury and distress to the birds.

Other natural fibre fillings include camel hair, which provides an even temperature and has excellent moisture regulating properties. Synthetic fillings may contain chemical residues which, as well as taking their toll on the environment, may cause allergic reactions. Organic bedding avoids all toxic fertilizers, pesticides, fungicides and herbicides that benefits consumer, farmer and the environment.

Electrical equipment

It is probably impossible for most people to avoid all electrical appliances in the bedroom – what about the alarm clock, bedside lamp and hairdryer? But all electrical equipment gives off EMFs and low-frequency electromagnetic fields (ELF), which are thought to have a negative impact on our health and wellbeing (see pages 128–9). It is therefore best to avoid non-essential electrical items, such as a television, in your bedroom.

There are some measures you can take to counteract the effects of electrical equipment in this area, one of which is to decorate the room using an ELF radiation-shielding wallpaint. They use non-toxic nickel pigment to provide a shield against electrical radiations in the home and claim to give up to 99 per cent shielding against ELF radiations. The paint colour is dark grey and is not intended to be a decorative finish but can

be overcoated with natural wall paint or wallpaper. It is especially useful for computer rooms.

There are some greener alternatives to items such as radios, which are often in the bedroom. The range of Freeplay wind-up radios designed by Trevor Baylis will give you hours of play time without costing you anything for the electricity. Originally, they were designed for communities in developing countries without an electricity supply. They do not require any batteries or mains supply and are powered by winding and solar energy – perfect for taking on picnics and camping trips. The latest version can store up to 15 hours of electricity, so you will hardly notice the difference between this model and a conventional radio.

Instead of using an electric alarm clock, look for a clock work alarm that simply requires winding. These have the added advantage of being much more attractive than the average black or white plastic electric alarm and you also avoid the risk of sleeping in, should there be a power cut or the electricity runs out during the night.

If you do use a battery-powered radio or alarm clock you could think about investing in a battery charger. They are fairly inexpensive and often come with a selection of reduced toxicity batteries, although there are chargers available that will work with most battery brands. Depending on the type of charger, batteries will last from ten to 50 charges.

* Buy a
battery recharger.
* Look for products that
do not require batteries.
* Keep electrical equipment
away from sleeping areas.
* Turn off unused electrical
equipment and also switch
it off at the mains.
* Choose a traditional
hot-water bottle instead
of an electric
blanket.

Fabrics in the bedroom

We are used to living among a variety of different fabrics dyed a myriad bright colours. In order to live a greener lifestyle, we need to wean ourselves off these synthetic, dyed fabrics and look to unbleached, organic fabrics in soft hues instead. Many natural fibres are treated with chemicals such as pesticides and fungicides, so natural does not necessarily mean green – organic is always the best option. Cotton, and to a lesser extent linen, crops are treated with vast quantities of pesticides.

In the bedroom we want to be surrounded by soft, comfortable materials like cotton and linen, particularly when they are next to our skin – like bed linen and nightwear. So choose unbleached organic cotton waffle towels, which are very soft and absorbent.

Wool is a very versatile fabric, which keeps us warm in winter and cool in summer (see page 62). To make sure that it is not mixed with other fibres, check that it carries the official wool mark – most certified organic wool comes from New Zealand, where organic standards are in place. Felt, which is made by matting together woollen fibres, is currently quite popular and fashionable. It may be used for rugs, wall hangings and furnishings. Other natural fabrics that can enhance our homes include silk, hemp, jute, sisal and animal skins – although there are other ethical issues involved in using leather and suede.

Avoid synthetic fabrics such as nylon and all non-iron and crease-resistant fabrics as these are likely to have been treated with formaldehyde. However, not all synthetic fabrics are a big no-no. Rayon is a synthetic fibre made from cellulose from trees and plants. It is similar in texture to cotton and is a good example of an environmentally-sustainable synthetic fibre.

MOTHPROOFING

It is common for both cotton and wool to be mothproofed using toxic chemicals, so try to buy untreated fabrics.

Moth balls often contain para-dichlorobenzene, which is highly toxic and carcinogenic. You can buy natural moth repellents based on essential oils – moths do not like lavender or cedarwood. Look out for them at your local natural products store.

Underfoot

Good flooring materials for bedrooms are natural and warm enough for bare feet. Wooden floorboards are great and you can use rugs to soften them. There is nothing nicer than stepping down onto a sheepskin rug in the morning. Take inspiration from the Japanese and use tatami mats, which are springy underfoot and absorb sound, to cover the bedroom floor. Natural sisal carpet is also a good option for the bedroom – but check that it does not have a synthetic backing.

Clothes

Fashion is anathema to environmentalism: it relies on a quick turnover of hundreds of different styles whereas "eco-chic" relies on fewer, long-lasting items made from natural fabrics. But you can be green and still have fun with clothes; you just have to be creative. A growing number of fashion designers and high street stores are developing and expanding organic, ethical and Fairtrade clothing ranges. In 2007 the estimated global market for sustainable clothing reached $1 billion.

Linen, hemp, cotton and wool are the most versatile natural fabrics and although expensive, linen is very durable and sometimes looks better the older it gets. Hemp is a very environmentally-friendly fabric and there are a number of clothing manufacturers who are starting to use it, particularly for items such as jeans as it is incredibly hard-wearing but actually softens each time it is washed. There are some innovative new clothing fabrics available today, such as Tencel, which is made from cellulose and fleece made from recycled, mostly post-consumer plastic bottles.

START SWISHING!

Swishing is essentially a clothes swap with a party atmosphere. Attendees arrive with at least one good quality item of clothing or an accessory and leave with a new outfit, having successfully recycled their unwanted clothes and without having spent any money. The official website even provides ready-made invitations available to download for your own party: visit www.swishing.org.

Green clothing does not have to mean smocks and sandals – look for exciting eco-fashion from innovative earth-conscious designers.

- ◇ **Keep dry cleaning to a minimum.**
- ◇ **Avoid crease-resistant items.**
- ◇ **Organize a "clothes-swap" party with friends.**
- ◇ **Look for clothes in second-hand stores.**
- ◇ **Purchase clothes that are easy to care for.**
- ◇ **Use aromatherapy bags to freshen clothes instead of fabric conditioner.**
- ◇ **Use wooden coat hangers.**
- ◇ **Avoid ironing when possible.**

Shoes

Leather shoes are essentially green because they biodegrade but a lot of chemicals are often used to treat the leather before being made into shoes. Some companies are exploring more environmentally-friendly design and have created footwear from old denim jeans. Other good ideas are wooden clogs and shoes made of felt with cork soles; they are biodegradable and very comfortable due to cork's natural insulation qualities.

Dyes

Fabric was traditionally dyed with natural colourings such as camomile, and techniques like weaving were used for decorative effect. Today we have a huge array of vivid, synthetic dyes at hand, which are incredibly harmful to the environment. We are used to bright colours and the way they lighten up our lives, but if we are going to live more organically, we need to get used to less vivid colours and fabrics in their natural, undyed state.

A good way to make individual furnishings or clothing is to buy lengths of unbleached fabric and dye or print it yourself using vegetable dyes. This is also a good way of livening up old T-shirts and trousers that you are bored with, although it will only work for pale items. Vegetable dyes can be quite hard to get hold of, but some specialist companies do make them and it is an area that will expand as the market grows. Some companies are experimenting with low-impact biodegradable dyes, which are more fade resistant than vegetable dyes. If you are feeling really adventurous, you could try making your own using natural materials such as onion, broom flowers and tea. There may be local crafts classes you can attend to learn the art of dyeing with natural plantstuffs, or see Resources page 247.

Blinds, shutters and screens

Different types of window covering are required in the bedroom throughout the year, depending on the season. In the summer months you will want to make the most of natural sunlight and during the winter, you will need to block out the cold for a cosy night. As well as using curtains you could think about alternatives such as wooden shutters, blinds (shades) or screens. Wooden venetian blinds are great for letting in plenty of light, but they can also act as a sunscreen on very bright days.

Reeds and grasses such as straw and bamboo are good materials for the natural home, and a lot of eco-friendly houses are being made with grass roofs. These materials are very versatile and can be used for blinds, wall coverings and floors. Bamboo is the world's fastest growing plant and can grow up to 1 m (1 yd) a day. It is grown without the use of pesticides and is incredibly versatile – it is so strong that it is used as scaffolding in parts of Asia! If you choose to have bamboo blinds, make sure the bamboo comes from a managed source – where the canes are cut leaving the young shoots to reach maturity, rather than being mechanically cut.

Even though it is a natural material, rattan should be avoided unless it is bought from an ethical trader because it is being overharvested and some species, along with certain species of bamboo, are in danger of disappearing. Other issues you need to consider are the production processes, because once harvested these materials are often treated with chemical finishes. Look for lighter-coloured bamboo, which is far less likely to have been treated than the darker varieties.

- ✪ Look for secondhand curtains made from retro fabrics.
- ✪ Change your window coverings according to the seasons.

- ✪ Look for salvaged shutters that can be adapted to suit your windows.
- ✪ Use bamboo blinds in the bedroom to cover up untidy areas such as shelves for clothing.

Softening up

The bedroom is no place for harsh lighting – use low-wattage bulbs for lamps and choose light shades made from paper, which give off a diffused light. Many people enjoy candlelight in the bedroom, as it is intimate and gentle. But many candles are made using petroleum and some still have lead in the wicks, although this has been banned in some countries, such as Australia. This means that burning conventional candles contributes to pollution on two different levels: during the manufacturing process and during the burning time.

The reason why some companies still put lead in the wicks of candles is to make them last longer. Metal wicks are most often used for scented and ceremonial candles – the metal in the wick makes the candle burn more slowly, but as the wick gets hot, lead is released into the atmosphere. There is an easy test to see if the wick contains lead: simply drag a piece of white paper over the wick. If a dark line shows up – similar to that drawn by a pencil – the wick contains lead. As with most metals, lead is a non-renewable resource so it should not be overused. The manufacturing process for lead is also very harmful to the environment, and it

is incredibly toxic. Lead has been known to affect the central nervous, cardiovascular and blood systems, and can lead to anaemia and kidney damage. So, do you really want to burn it in your bedroom?

Many companies today, however, make candles using natural ingredients such as soya wax, palm and coconut oil, unadulterated essential oils and unbleached papercore wicks. These are preferable for a number of reasons: they are made from a non-petroleum renewable resource, they contain no pesticides or herbicides, and they are biodegradable and safe.

Rather than using products made with synthetic fragrances, which can cause skin irritations as well as headaches and dizziness, look for candles produced using only essential oils. Some companies try to get away with using fragrance oils rather than 100 per cent essential oils – to be sure, look on the label to check the oil used is labelled "absolute" or "pure". Other things to watch out for are additives and dyes – buy candles in natural-looking shades rather than ones made using lots of vivid colours. Some companies are developing vegetable candles coloured with dyes such as beetroot, paprika and turmeric.

Incense

Along with candles comes incense – the perfect combination for creating an ambient atmosphere in your sleeping space, whether you are preparing for bed, reading or meditating. Natural incense is made using plant resins, essential oils and aromatic wood powders. Be suspicious of scents that are not attributable to any flower or plant you can think of – these are synthetic smells created using chemicals. Many ancient cultures have used forms of incense in prayer, ceremony, medicine and celebration, and it was often thought of as a way of contacting the gods. Today we use incense to help us relax or to stimulate us and to make our living spaces smell beautiful. Incense is also commonly used to aid meditation and creative visualization.

Stick incense is usually made using bamboo to aid the burning process, although some green companies are making bamboo- and chemical-free incense sticks now. Cone incense is made using sawdust compressed into the cone shape and saturated with essential or synthetic oils – the best ones are made using sawdust from a naturally aromatic wood such as sandalwood. Look out for incense made using only pure essential oils. It is possible to make your own incense.

NATURAL HOME FRAGRANCE

- Burn incense – available in cones, coils or sticks.

- Try non-burning fragrance sticks, which are absorbent sticks displayed in scented oils. They usually last for several months.

- Display bunches of freshly cut herbs or flowers, preferably from your own garden or grown locally.

- Make your own potpourri using dried lavender, rose petals or camomile flowers, mixed with a few drops of an essential oil.

- Light certified-organic soy candles. Available in a variety of scents, they are natural, clean-burning and biodegradable.

- Burn essential oils in a vaporizer, diffuser or ceramic oil burner.

- Add a few drops of an essential oil to a water spray container and use to spritz areas that need freshening up, such as the kitchen and bathroom.

Cosmetics

The bedroom should be your sanctuary from the rest of the house and as such, it is often the room chosen for the application of make-up, which can be a self-indulgent, therapeutic and enjoyable process. The international market for natural cosmetics is a major growth area. New research has revealed that global natural cosmetic sales are approaching £3 billion, about $4.3 billion, with the biggest growth taking place in North America and Europe. Growing concerns about the environment, combined with an increased awareness of health issues, mean that a lot of consumers are looking for natural, plant-based make-up products that are kind to the planet as well as our skin. Conventional make-up is full of artificial colourings, preservatives and fragrances, some of which ends up being absorbed through the skin. As awareness and demand grows for organic food and drink more people are also starting to question what they put on their skin and hair. Women in particular are realizing that because of the amount of cosmetics absorbed by our skin, wearing organic cosmetics is as important a practice as eating organic food.

The number of ingredients found in cosmetics can be quite staggering but often we do not look much further than the glossy packaging. The wearer of lipstick or lip balm will consume a certain amount of it while she is using it, which could amount to as much as three sticks of lipstick in a lifetime. This highlights the importance of paying attention to the cosmetics you buy, as well as the food you eat.

Cosmetic companies have vast budgets to spend on marketing their products and they are adept at selling us an image. Many of these manufacturers use minimalist packaging with words like "natural" and "organic" on the labels to tap into the growing market for natural products, which can be very misleading. It is always worth investigating further to find out whether they really are natural.

Most cosmetics, such as foundation, lipstick, eyeshadow and eyeliner, are made using natural or petroleum-based waxes, preservatives, colourings and thickeners. Look out for products made using natural waxes like beeswax or carnauba, rather than the commonly used petroleum-derived waxes such as ceresin. Synthetic fragrances can cause all sorts of symptoms, from dizziness to skin problems, so it is essential to read the labels of scented products carefully. Be aware that products marked "unscented" may use chemicals to mask unwanted smells and try to use products that are naturally fragranced with essential oils instead.

It pays to be cynical, however, especially in today's market where multinationals know there is money to be made in the natural cosmetics industry. Products claiming to be natural and organic, or made from essential oils may not be as pure as you would like. Always read the labels carefully and if there is something you do not recognize, contact the manufacturer. The only reason manufacturers will change their products is if they know there is a demand. In Europe and the USA a product can be described as natural even if it contains only 1 per cent natural ingredients.

ORGANIC COSMETICS

There are organic standards for cosmetics in place in Europe and the US. Look out for logos from the Soil Association, Organic Farmers and Growers and the Ecocert, as well as the USDA in the US.

NAIL VARNISH

Most nail products, such as varnish and polish remover, are chemical based. Nail polish removers contain solvents that dissolve the polish to remove it but they also dissolve the natural oils from your nails and the surrounding skin.

Many nail varnishes contain formaldehyde, phthalates and parabens as well as chemical fixatives. However, more natural varieties are now available, which are free from these ingredients and which avoid colour lakes – pigments which don't break down in the environment. Nail varnish remover without acetone, a known irritant which causes nails to become brittle, is also available. Don't be fooled by brands claiming to have added proteins and vitamins, as these cannot be absorbed by the nail and are therefore useless.

SMELLS GOOD

There is big business to be made from perfumes and scents, mainly because you are once again buying into a brand name and image. Most perfumes are made from petrochemicals, and labels claiming that products are made using natural fragrances can be misleading. Around 5,000 chemicals are used in the manufacture of fragrances and some reports suggest that around 95 per cent of these are made from petroleum.

When you start to consider that the fragrances that you wear can be absorbed through your skin, you will begin to understand that the fragrance industry is as bad for your health as it is for the environment. Synthetic fragrances can cause all sorts of symptoms, from dizziness to skin problems, so it is essential that you read the labels of perfumes and scented products very carefully.

❀ **Always check the labels carefully for synthetic fragrances, colours and preservatives.**

❀ **Avoid using very brightly coloured cosmetics – choose natural tones instead. Brighter colours are more likely to contain environmentally unfriendly pigments.**

❀ **Avoid overpackaged products.**

❀ **Always use refillable products whenever possible.**

❀ **Try going make-up-free for a day or two each week.**

❀ Make your
own fragrance by
adding a few drops of your
favourite essential oil to almond oil.

❀ Look for fragrance that is free
from petrochemicals and instead based
on essential oils. The majority of perfumes are
made almost entirely from petrochemicals.

❀ Avoid products with ethyl, methyl, propyl or
butyl parabens in the ingredients. Parabens have
been linked with cancer.

❀ Buy certified organic cosmetics – these
will be free from synthetic colours
and fragrances.

GREEN GROWING AND EATING

A green home isn't complete without a touch of nature in the form of some leafy plants. On a primeval level we need plants in order to exist, but most of us need plantlife in a spiritual sense, too. It connects us to nature, reminds us that we are part of a complex web of life and it is thus a fundamental part of green living.

By nurturing nature in our own homes we are also contributing to the planet's biodiversity, no matter how small this contribution may be. From a shiny-leaved houseplant in the living room to a herb-filled window box outside the kitchen, even the smallest of homes, in the most concrete-filled urban centres, can play its part in the greening of our environment.

Should you be lucky enough to have a backyard, a small garden or even several acres at your disposal then there really is a huge amount that you can do to help nature on its way. And should your green growing ambitions exceed the space available to you, then there is every chance that your area may have a community garden, allotments or disused land that could provide a larger arena for your green fingers to do their work.

But it is not only the environment that stands to benefit from your gardening efforts. Imagine the satisfaction you will feel serving your friends a plate of steaming, buttered asparagus, knowing that you grew it yourself. And think how much happier you will be eating food that you know has not been drenched in chemicals. The health benefits of all that fresh air and exercise are an added bonus, too.

Creating a garden is a wonderfully life-enhancing act in itself. Nature is not something that can be rushed or pushed ahead, it teaches us that there are natural rhythms and slows us down when every other part of our lives is speeding up.

It is a way of bringing creativity into our lives, accessing parts of our minds that may not have been used since we were children. And for children, there is nothing more exciting than seeing a tiny seed turn into a gigantic sunflower (and nothing more enticing than large amounts of mud and wriggling worms!).

Finally, your garden can be a sanctuary from the pressures of twenty-first-century life. Using natural materials, water features and atmospheric aids such as wind chimes, you can create a meditative space free from the telephone and television, where you can reacquaint yourself with thoughts and sensations that have long been forgotten in your day-to-day life.

Simply being outdoors working with the soil is a basic human pleasure, and so, too, is eating. And again, as with gardening, there are green options when it comes to food. It does not get much better than growing your own, but for those foods you cannot grow yourself, the best choice is to "go organic". You can then relax in the knowledge that you are supporting environmentally-friendly agricultural practices and that you are buying food you can trust. So get out your garden table and chairs, invite some friends over, light a few candles and cook an organic, outdoor supper that proves once and for all that green can be gorgeous.

THE GREEN GARDEN

The very act of growing plants would be considered by most of us as doing something green. Growing plants brings the experience of nature closer to our families and local communities, provides a home for a wealth of living organisms, and each and every one acts as a filter for the air we breathe, thereby contributing to a cleaner global environment.

But gardening can be an activity that is far from green. For many people, their gardens become an arena in which they wage war against nature through the liberal use of highly toxic pesticides. Each year, for example, American homeowners apply at least 90 million pounds of pesticides to their lawns and gardens.

Others think nothing of using products that have been created at the expense of precious natural resources, like peat from the fast-diminishing bogs and garden furniture made of wood plundered from tropical forests. And many gardens are grown with the help of excessive amounts of water drawn straight from the tap (faucet), despite the hundreds of gallons that fall from the sky each year and go uncollected in most areas.

The good news is that this environmentally wasteful approach to gardening is no longer in vogue. Gone are the days when a good garden was meant to be regimented in design, with uniform plants grown in weed-free, dark peaty soil surrounding a perfect sprinkler-watered lawn, without a daisy in sight. The new wave of gardening recognizes that a good garden is a complex ecosystem, with each element

REASONS TO GO GREEN IN THE GARDEN

❀ You can grow food that you trust – free from chemical sprays and other contaminants that have been implicated in health scares worldwide (see page 189).

❀ You can save the environment from the polluting effects of transporting fresh produce to you by growing your own.

❀ You are sparing the environment from the impact of pesticides, which kill many beneficial insects, birds, plants and animals, can pollute our water supplies and harm our children.

❀ You can teach your children where food comes from and the wonder of nature in a safe environment.

❀ Your garden will become a haven for wildlife, such as bees and butterflies, and be safer for your own pets.

❀ By growing rare or unusual seeds you can contribute to global biodiversity and introduce new flavours to your diet.

❀ Gardening is great exercise and fun.

❀ Going green gives you the chance to recycle in one of the most exciting ways, turning your food scraps and garden cuttings into compost, which, in turn, will support the growth of further food.

❀ You will save money by not having to pay for fertilizers, pesticides, compost and so on, and by growing your own food.

❀ Recycling will also prevent you spending a fortune at the garden centre.

❀ You will be saving fragile areas of natural beauty from further ravaging by no longer buying peat-based composts and limestone, and by making sure that your garden furniture and other wood products are from sustainable sources.

❀ Green gardening puts you in touch with nature and its cycles, aiding relaxation and giving you an outlet for and sanctuary from the frustrations of your busy day.

having a role to play. Native plants are now just as fashionable as exotics and are much more of a hit with the local wildlife. Unruly borders and meadows filled with wildflowers are just as keenly cultivated as any neatly tended bed of roses. The modern gardener accepts nature and works with it, and in so doing produces naturally healthy plants in an efficient and safe way.

Whether your gardening aspirations stop with a cheeseplant in the corner of your living room, or stretch as far as a vegetable patch, some fruit trees and perhaps a chicken or two roaming about, this eco-friendly method offers you the chance to get truly close to the natural world and to put something back into your environment.

With domestic gardens making up many millions of hectares of land worldwide, the combined efforts of green gardeners can produce the largest nature reserve on the planet – and you will have your very own slice of Eden on your doorstep.

Getting started tips

* Join an organic organization – they offer support such as advice helplines and mail-order services for organic gardening products (see Resources, pages 248–9).

* If you do not have a garden but are keen to get growing, find out about allotments or community gardening in your area, including school or charity gardening projects.

* Visit organic gardens or farms for inspiration. Your local gardening organization might have details of gardens in your area that are open for visits. Alternatively, contact an organic certifier (government agricultural departments should be able to provide contact details) to find out about local organic farmers who would be happy to show you around and pass on tips.

* Decide what you want from your garden before you start. A chill-out zone with minimal work? Enough vegetables to provide you with salads throughout the summer and a soup or two in the winter? Flowers and a lawn for the children to play on? Or maybe a place for entertaining on summer evenings? A garden can be many things, and they can all be green.

* Look around you. You will fare better if you create a garden in accordance with the local conditions for light, soil and weather. This goes for the type of plants you grow, too. It is easier to grow plants that are indigenous to your area; you should require less artificial aids and such plants will benefit the local wildlife.

* Assemble a few basic bits of kit: a water barrel, a compost bin or similar, and tools for weeding (these should be from recycled or sustainably produced sources).

* Get going with your compost first, since healthy soil is the root of successful green gardening.

GREEN GARDENING – DOS AND DON'TS

DO:

✔ Set up your own composting system or use locally produced organic compost – as much as 40 per cent of household waste can be composted.

✔ Grow plants that are native to your area and suitable for your garden's conditions – both climate and soil type.

✔ Grow traditional varieties of plants – newer hybridized crop varieties can provide little by way of food for birds, butterflies and other wildlife and are often lacking in taste, whereas older varieties are under threat of extinction.

✔ Use natural methods for reducing pest problems and boosting soil health.

✔ Recycle wherever and whatever possible.

✔ Set up a water-collecting system.

✔ Learn to be a little untidy – too much order in a garden is unnatural, makes useful bugs and animals homeless, and removes valuable food for birds and other types of wildlife.

✔ Buy local, buy sustainable and buy natural.

DON'T:

✗ Buy seeds, plants or bulbs that have been harvested from the wild – many areas of natural beauty are being devastated by commercial plant and seed collectors who are stripping the land.

✗ Use peat-based growing media or sphagnum moss as lining for hanging baskets – peat bogs are being mined out of existence in order to meet the demands of gardeners.

✗ Buy timber products without certification that the wood is from a sustainable source (see page 50).

✗ Rely on chemicals for pest control and to maintain soil health.

✗ Burn leaves in autumn – this contributes to pollution and wastes a valuable natural resource.

✗ Use sprinklers and neglect to collect rainwater in a water butt, also waste water in your house.

✗ Use a patio heater.

✗ Throw things away – there are uses for many household objects in and around the garden.

The basics

Green gardening is based on organic principles: minimizing pollution, promoting sustainability, working with nature and natural cycles. On a practical level, this means not using chemical fertilizers and pesticides, recycling and creating diversity in the garden. But it is about more than a collection of do's and don'ts. This kind of gardening is essentially a "state of mind"; it requires the gardener to think in a sustainable way and to work in harmony with nature. It does not matter how large or small the space you have available for your gardening aspirations – whether it is a tiny window ledge or several acres – nor how much time you would like to spend achieving your aims, these principles can work in any situation for every type of gardener. By adopting them, you stand to gain in so many ways.

Without toxic chemicals, your garden will be a safer place for you, your family and your pets to relax in. The food you grow will be safer to eat and your garden will attract and support a greater diversity of wildlife. You will be doing your bit for the global environment by saving water, planting traditional seed varieties that are under threat and reducing demand for peat and wood from threatened forests. Household waste will be reduced and you will save money by using natural resources. Above all, it is fun and satisfying to nurture a garden using age-old methods and your own creative ideas.

So how do you get started? There are a few basics that you will need to master, beginning with composting.

Front gardens (yards)

A crucial part of green gardening is making sure that you preserve the garden you have and keep it green, especially your front garden (yard). In some regions of England a third of front gardens have been paved over and in London front gardens covering an area 31 sq km (12 sq miles) have been lost to driveways. The loss of front gardens can have a devastating impact for the following reasons:

✳ **They provide valuable space for wildlife. Research has shown that even tiny front yards or green verges are vital for urban wildlife and can house more than 700 different species of insect.**

✳ **Front gardens reduce the chances of flash flooding as water is absorbed into soil whereas water runs off concrete, tarmac and paved areas into the already overstretched and old drainage system. This run-off picks up pollutants along the way and either makes its way into our rivers via storm drains or goes into the sewerage system.**

✳ **A greater amount of paving contributes to the "heat island effect" where an urban area becomes much warmer than its surroundings. Green spaces tend to regulate temperature whereas hard surfaces contribute to hotter temperatures, which in turn can lead people into using energy-guzzling air conditioning, especially at night when heat is released from paved surfaces.**

* Street trees and grass verges are also lost since they are commonly removed to accommodate dropped kerbs (curbs). Without the trees and plants, dust is no longer absorbed and there is nowhere for birds to nest and insects to feed.

* Research has shown that when entire roads pave over their gardens house prices can fall. Leafy streets attract buyers and make the area more desirable. Indeed a well-kept garden can boost a house's property value by 10 per cent. Plus paving can cause costly subsidence as it reduces or stops rainfall getting into the ground, causing the soil to shrink, especially if it is predominantly clay. Garden walls, paths and houses may develop severe cracks.

If you do decide that you need to park outside your house, there are still plenty of ways to keep the front garden green and reduce the impact paving has on the environment. In the UK, the Royal Horticultural Society makes these suggestions:

* Use materials for your drive that allow rainwater to penetrate the ground below such as brick pavers and gravel – especially gravel made with a by-product of the ceramics industry and not that taken from sea or river beds; or grass use pavers made from recycled plastic.

* Create just two paved tracks for the car wheels then cover the rest of the area with a permeable plastic membrane topped with gravel. This will suppress weeds but allow you to plant through the membrane by cutting a hole.

* Have a hedge instead of a wall either side of your drive entrance. The hedge will filter some of the dust from the street, absorb traffic noise and provide a wildlife refuge.

* If the car is moved fairly regularly, then there are plants you can grow that will tolerate being parked over. These need to be low-growing so the car does not brush them and tough enough to withstand the occasional running over. Try creeping jenny, bugle and thymes. Leave planting pockets in the paving or gravel to ensure there is soil for them to grow in, rather than hardcore or a bed of concrete.

* Install plant pots and containers on the sides of the driveway and plant climbers up walls.

Composting

Nothing excites a green gardener more than composting. It is the ultimate form of recycling, turning household waste such as old newspapers and vegetable peelings into valuable organic matter that will reinvigorate the soil and in turn aid the cultivation of plants. And, if you then grow your own fruit or vegetables using this compost, then the whole reuse cycle is complete.

TOP COMPOSTING TIPS

* Always protect the compost heap from rain with a waterproof cover.
* Make sure you can remove the bottom layer easily.
* Turn the heap every few months to introduce air into the mix.
* Dampen any dry material such as straw or autumn leaves first to aid its decomposition.
* Shred items like leaves, newspapers, cardboard and weeds to speed up their decomposition.
* Mix fresh grass mowings and fruit and vegetable leftovers with dry material to stop the pile becoming too sodden.
* Make sure you have broad mixture of materials in the pile and layer them evenly.

Such is the value of composting in terms of savings on waste disposal and benefits to agriculture that many local authorities will provide you with composting bins and give help and guidance on composting. Even if you have no intention of gardening, you could seek out a local composting project that will accept your household waste, since much of it could be turned into fertile soil instead of contributing to the problem of polluting landfill gases.

But composting does more than just save on waste-disposal costs. Garden compost improves soil structure in many ways – helping sandy soils retain water, contributing to drainage in clay soils and inoculating the soil with healthy microbes, some of which help plants take up more nutrients from the soil and also help improve their resistance to pests and diseases. No matter what soil you have to play with, it will always benefit from compost and you can also use the compost to make up your own growing media.

Setting up a composting system is relatively straightforward. You can choose between buying a composting bin – preferably made from recycled plastic – or make your own by wiring together four wooden pallets and lining them with cardboard, or drilling holes in an old plastic or galvanized dustbin (trash can), if you have a spare one. Whatever your choice of container, it should be covered, with either a lid or some old carpet, to keep out the rain and keep heat in. It is also best sited near your kitchen so you have no excuse when it comes to depositing your kitchen waste on the heap.

Once you have allocated a site for the compost heap or bin, you are ready to embark upon what many in gardening liken to alchemy. There is no shortage of composting "experts" who will be only too ready to blind you with science on their particular tried-and-tested method. However, the basic principles are simple. You need to provide food, air and water in order for billions of microbes (fungi, bacteria and so on), worms and insects to turn your waste into compost.

The food you add should be a mixture of high-carbon and high-nitrogen materials. Wood, paper and leaves are high in carbon but left alone would decay too slowly, and may deplete nitrogen in the soil. Grass clippings and fruit and vegetable waste, which are rich in nitrogen, break down much more easily but can create slimy, smelly compost heaps. A suitable mixture might include: dry, dead plant material such as straw, autumn leaves and wood chips – usually moistened first; fresh plant material such as green leaves, fruit and vegetable scraps from the kitchen, tea bags and coffee grounds; and fresh horse manure (ideally from organically fed horses). You can also add newspapers in small amounts and cardboard cereal boxes. (See boxes opposite and right for further suggestions.)

The ideal method for making compost is to make a heap in one go, but to do this you need to collect bags of waste for several weeks or months. If you add material gradually, it may take at least eight to 12 months before it is ready to use, whereas in summer a newly constructed, complete heap would take around two months to turn to compost. A gradual heap may also not reach high enough temperatures to kill off weeds or diseases.

* **To avoid attracting flies and insects to kitchen waste, make a hole in the centre of your compost pile and bury the waste.**
* **For best results, mix equal quantities of materials high in nitrogen (such as clover, fresh grass clippings and livestock manure) and those high in carbon (such as dried leaves and twigs).**
* **If you want a quick start to your composting you can purchase compost activators or accelerators containing organic material designed to kick-start your compost.**
* **If you have large quantities of leaves, it may be worth composting them separately in a wire mesh container or in plastic sacks.**
* **Check on any local or state regulations for composting in built-up urban areas – some communities may require rodent-proof bins.**

With either method, it is a good idea to layer the different materials, spreading them evenly and adding water if the material is dry, before covering the heap. Make sure your compost heap does not become too dry or wet. Soggy compost smells bad and takes a long time to break down; dry compost is also slow to decompose as microbes prefer damp conditions. To speed up decomposition, turn the compost with a fork every six to eight weeks.

MAKING COMPOST

THINGS THAT CAN GO IN:

✔ **Urine:** dilute it with water first.
✔ **Chicken manure:** ideally from organically reared chickens.
✔ **Comfrey:** rich in many nutrients, especially potash, but contains almost no fibre.
✔ **Lawn clippings:** but mix them with dry material first, such as damp straw, weeds or leaves, as grass clippings can be too soggy on their own.
✔ **Kitchen waste:** including tea bags, coffee grounds, fruit and vegetable trimmings.
✔ **Farmyard manure:** again ideally from horses or cows bred on organic farms.
✔ **Seaweed:** a great source of trace elements.
✔ **Garden waste:** chop it first to help the decomposing process.
✔ **Weeds:** especially stinging nettles which are high in nitrogen (treat in the same way as lawn clippings), but they should be young weeds that have not formed seeds.
✔ **Bracken:** but avoid handling when it is producing spores as it is carcinogenic.
✔ **Straw:** should be damp and ideally already partly rotted.
✔ **Woody prunings:** shred them first.
✔ **Newspaper, cardboard:** use sparingly, shredded or torn up and dampened, and avoid materials with coloured inks.

ITEMS TO AVOID:

✗ **Cat litter or dog faeces:** both of these can carry disease.
✗ **Cooked food, meat and fish scraps:** they smell as they rot and may attract rats and other pests.
✗ **Diseased plant material:** diseases can spread through the compost.
✗ **Perennial weeds and weeds in seed:** they may continue growing in the compost, especially if it is not hot enough to destroy the seeds.
✗ **Plastic, tin, glass and other synthetic materials:** they do not decompose.

Maintaining a high temperature is important to kill off weeds and diseases – your pile should be at least 50°C (122°F) (often not possible if composting gradually). If you are using a compost bin it should be at least 1 m³ (3 yd³) in size in order to achieve high temperatures and you can also help by lining the bin with dry autumn leaves or hay.

The compost is ready to use when it is a dark colour, smells earthy and the original ingredients have almost gone. Remaining straw, twigs and sticks can be picked or sieved out. The final result can be used on gardens, lawns and houseplants. Dig it into the soil or leave it on top for the worms to do the work for you. It is best applied in spring when the weather should be more conducive to its staying in the soil – heavy rain may wash the compost away before the worms can do their bit.

But if you are new to gardening and all this talk of creating your own compost has put you off making a start on your own garden, take heart – there are various green options that do not require you to devote a part of your garden to a decomposing pile of waste. Your local authority may well be running a community composting scheme or composting green waste from its parks and gardens, which it will deliver to you for a small fee, for example.

Growing media

Homemade compost can be used to make your own potting compost or growing media but it does take some time and effort. The quickest – but more expensive – option is to buy your growing media and there is now a wide range available that satisfies the demands of the green gardener.

The key thing to avoid when buying a potting compost is peat (see pages 184–5), but there are many good peat-free options, including those made using coir and added nutrients such as seaweed extract.

As with all things, be sure to check with the suppliers what is actually in their composts – manure should ideally come from an organically reared animal, for example. Beware also of the term "organic" when it is applied to growing media. Check with an organic certifier to see if they approve the compost for use in organic growing systems.

Other green soil helpers

In addition to the positive effects of compost, the green gardener has a wide variety of other soil-enhancing products at his or her fingertips.

GREEN MANURES

These are plants that are grown to enrich and protect the soil. They reduce the harmful effects of wind and rain, discourage weeds and can provide nutrients when dug back into the soil. The idea is to grow them on bare soil in winter or between different crops of vegetables in the summer. The types of plant used, quickly produce a mass of weed-smothering foliage. They include: alfalfa, mustard, buckwheat, clover, fenugreek, field beans, annual ryegrass and phacelia.

THE PEAT ISSUE

Each year in the UK, around 2.5 million m³ (over 8 million ft³) of peat are sold to commercial and amateur gardeners as a soil improver or growing medium, but at great cost to the fragile environments from which peat is taken. Peat deposits are also found in Ireland, Netherlands, Scandinavia, Russia, Germany, Canada, and more.

Peat is an organic material that forms in the waterlogged, sterile, acidic conditions of bogs and fens. Peatbogs are important sites for wildlife, supporting a wide variety of birds, invertebrates, birds and plants. They also help reduce the amount of carbon dioxide released into the atmosphere by dead plants, since plants do not decompose in peat bogs – instead, the organic matter slowly accumulates as peat because of the lack of oxygen in the bog. In the UK, the National Trust estimates that British peatbogs are storing the carbon equivalent to about 20 years' worth of national industrial emissions and that globally, peat stores twice as much carbon as forests.

In the UK over 94 per cent of the 69,700 hectares (172,000 acres) of peatbogs have been damaged or destroyed mostly to keep up with demand from gardeners. This destruction not only threatens wildlife but also worsens global warming since carbon, removed from the atmosphere over thousands of years, is released when bogs are drained and peat starts to decompose.

WHAT CAN YOU DO?

* Don't buy any form of peat for your garden. There are plenty of alternatives that can be bought, such as peat-free "multipurpose composts" that include coir-based mixtures, or use a version produced by you.
* Peat is actually a poor soil improver as it is low in nutrients. Instead, use home-produced compost, leafmould, bark products, manure and so on.
* As a mulch peat tends to dry out and blow away. Try peat-free mulches instead such as: bark products, cocoa shells, pebbles, cardboard and so on.
* Use pine needles or composted heather or braken to replace peat when you want to increase the acidity of your soil.
* Peat has been used to fill in planting pits for bare-rooted trees and shrubs but it has been shown that it is better to improve the soil of the planting area before planting rather than using a fill.
* Always check any container-grown plants you are buying are not in a peat-based medium.

But you should note that seed germination may be inhibited by decaying green manure, so you should leave a gap of at least one month between digging the green manure in and sowing seed.

LEAF MOULD

This can be used as a mulch (see page 186), but it is also invaluable for digging into the soil or in a seed-sowing or potting compost. Since leaves need more light and less air to rot down than other compostable materials, it is best to compost them in their own container. You can make this using four wooden stakes at least 1 m (1 yd) high, driven into the ground with chicken wire stapled around the outside. Be warned: it can take up to three years before you get good compost from leaf mould, but it is well worth the wait. If you need more leaves, ask your local authority if they could donate some from their autumn sweepings – or collect them yourself

MANURE

Although manure is likely to contain hormones, pesticides and other nasty elements if it comes from a conventional rather than an organic farm, it is thought that if it is stacked for at least a year these contaminants will not present a problem.

SPENT MUSHROOM COMPOST

Again, this will need to be left for at least a year to make sure any chemicals used in mushroom-growing leach out. Don't use it on acid-loving plants, but it is good for improving heavy clay soils.

WORMS, WONDERFUL WORMS

If you really have very little space, you may still find some room for a worm composter. Worms will eat their own weight of waste each day, producing rich liquid and dark spongy compost as a result. You can buy the whole thing or make your own worm bin and either collect or buy in the worms. The best time to start your worm bin is late spring or summer when the worms are more active.

FERTILIZERS

Occasionally, through a lack of readily available compost or severe deficiencies in your soil, you may need to resort to a fertilizer. But even then, there is no need to reach for the synthetic chemicals. There is a wide range of organic fertilizers on sale in both garden centres and by mail order, including: seaweed meal, fish bone and blood, gypsum for heavy clay soils, and hoof and horn. Animal-free products are also available if this is an issue.

Liquid fertilizers or feeds are often used in container gardening and for the green gardener there is a choice of fish emulsion, liquid manure and comfrey liquid (which is highly recommended for tomatoes and peppers). Seaweed extract is also sold as a soil and plant tonic. You can make your own comfrey liquid by growing the plant, soaking the cut leaves in a container with a tight-fitting lid for four to six weeks, and then straining.

FOOD DIGESTERS

Although you should never put cooked food in your normal compost bin, it can still be recycled using a food digester. All food, including fish, cooked meat and bones, can be placed in a food digester, where it will be broken down using natural bacteria and the sun's heat into water, carbon dioxide and a small amount of residue. Digesters, which should be rodent-proof, need to have their base below ground level since over 90 per cent of the waste will be absorbed by the soil as water. Once the digester is full – roughly every two years – the residue can be removed and dug into the ground. They should be placed in a sunny part of your garden.

Another option for cooked food waste is to use a specially designed "hot" composter, which can cope with cooked food provided it is mixed with garden waste. It comprises a closed, hot composting container, with an insulating jacket to ensure compost can be created all year round.

MULCHES

A mulch is a layer of material spread around plants on the surface of the soil to protect it from erosion, reduce water loss and smother weed growth. Some mulches are also biodegradable and therefore able to improve soil structure as they decompose. These organic mulches, which include grass clippings, compost, leaves, bark chippings, straw and manure, are preferable to inorganic mulches like black polythene, carpet or woven plastic. There are also purpose-made mulching fabrics available, including flax or hemp fibre matting.

If you use grass clippings, it is best to dry them out in the sun first before applying a layer 5–7 cm (2–3 in) deep.Otherwise they can be too slimy and may suffocate plant roots. Sheets of newspaper may be placed on the ground, covered lightly with grass clippings or another mulch to anchor them, but take care on a windy day! It is best to shred autumn leaves with a lawnmower or shredder first and then compost them over winter before using them as a mulch.

THE BENEFITS OF MULCHING

* It protects the soil from the elements, preventing it from erosion and compacting in heavy rain and drying out in windy, hot conditions.

* Mulching helps maintain a stable soil temperature.

* Weeds are prevented from growing up and establishing themselves.

* It can help keep fruit and vegetables clean and does the same for your feet when you are tramping around your beds in wet weather.

* Mulching can help feed the soil.

Water

No garden can survive without water, but gardeners are some of the worst offenders when it comes to wasting water. For example, in half an hour, a garden sprinkler uses as much water as a family of four does in a day, about 600 ml (1 pint) for every two seconds it is in operation, or 650 litres (172 gallons) per hour. The average gardener uses 10 litres (2½ gallons) of water daily on the garden, but on hot, dry summer evenings this can go up to as much as 50 per cent of the total domestic water supply used each day by the household – an average of 150 litres (40 gallons).

- Water plants only in the evening or early in the morning when the water will not simply evaporate in hot sunshine.

- Don't use a sprinkler or hose pipe – water the garden with a watering can instead.

- Where possible, don't water lawns, as overwatering can weaken your lawn by encouraging roots to seek the surface – any brown patches will soon disappear when the rain arrives.

- Collect rainwater by installing a water butt (made from recycled plastic) with a system of pipes that collects run-off rainwater from flat roofs and gutters. Cover the butt to prevent insects taking up residence and contaminating the water; also to prevent evaporation.

- Use an efficient irrigation system, such as a porous soaker hose allowing seepage along its length, or trickle-and-drip systems that deliver small amounts of water directly to the soil, reducing evaporation from plant leaves. Consult suppliers of such systems for advice on setting one up and the type of system best suited to your needs.)

- Grow plants that are adapted to dry conditions if lack of water is a problem in your area, such as: alyssum, aubretia, catmint, sedum, yucca, Spanish broom, yarrow, nasturtium, Californian poppy, moss rose, juniper, artemisia, lavender, sage, iris, thyme, crocus, New Zealand flax, rosemary and evening primrose.

- Investigate Xeriscaping – landscaping in a way that does not require irrigation, which is promoted in areas that do not have easily accessible supplies of fresh water. Xeriscape can reduce landscape water use by 60 per cent or more.

- Grow indigenous plants, since they will be best suited to your local natural conditions and should require less additional watering (although this will also depend on the soil you are growing them in).

- Use mulching to prevent water loss through evaporation and wind.

- Add garden compost to the soil to encourage it to retain water.

- Plant carefully: some plants can shade others and terracing helps keep water from eroding the soil.

- Make sure any water feature in your garden, such as a fountain, recirculates the water.

- Install windbreaks, hedges and fences to reduce the drying effect of the wind.

- Create a mini-wetland in your garden to temporarily store, filter and clean run-off water from your roof and lawn; also water from your bath and washing-up (provided you use biodegradable washing products).

- Save as much water from home use as possible – the water left over from watering your houseplants, water to rinse the dishes, bathwater and so on – and use it on the garden. The average bath contains 80 litres (21 gallons) of water, so make use of it by investing in a bathwater diverter, which makes sure this water does not disappear down the plug hole. It is a good idea to filter the water by tying finely meshed cloth at the end of your hose, and do not let it touch above-ground edible fruit, vegetables and foliage, especially those that are likely to be eaten raw, such as spring onions (scallions) and lettuces.

RAINWATER HARVESTING

Harvesting rainwater simply means the collection of water that would otherwise have gone into the drains or the ground, usually by diverting water from gutters. The quantity of water you can collect depends on the amount of rainfall in your region and the size of the area from which you will be collecting the rain. Large surfaces such as roofs or driveways are ideal for rainwater harvesting and can provide up to 100,000 litres (26,417 gallons) of water per year from a medium-sized area.

Various options are available, including installing a water butt that takes water from a drainpipe to more advanced commercial systems that include a filter and a means of storage (usually a large underground tank). Stored rainwater is not suitable for drinking, but through a separate pipe network it can be used to supply toilets, outside taps (faucets) and washing machines. Some systems use a control unit to monitor the water level in the tank. A good-quality system might not save you much cash, but it will be preserving a precious commodity.

Pest control

For many people, the most worrying aspect of going green in a garden is how to cope with unwanted visitors, be they weeds, insects or animals. For the regular gardener the response is usually a highly toxic one – applying herbicides, insecticides and traps liberally throughout the garden in a war against all unwelcome predators. These chemicals, which have mostly been available for the last 50 years, are harmful to other (beneficial) species, can leave toxic residues behind in the flowers, fruit or vegetables that are being grown and maycontaminate ground-water supplies. Still this hasn't stopped demand: the UK public spends around £50 million each year on pesticides such as slug pellets and weedkillers, while in the USA approximately $2.2 billion is spent on pesticides annually for home and garden use.

Clearly, there was a time when gardeners and farmers managed quite well without them, and the green gardener is living proof that this can still be the case. The green gardener seeks to minimize the need for intervention in the first place, but if it is necessary, ensures that any intervention causes the least disruption to the rest of the garden and the creatures within it as possible.

DISEASE AND INFESTATION

If you start off with the healthiest possible combination of soil, plant and insect life in your garden then it is less likely to fall victim to disease and infestation. Just as if you eat properly, exercise and get enough rest and relaxation, so you are less likely to succumb to illness.

In practice you need to take the following measures when establishing your garden:

+ Choose the healthiest plants available to you. If you are growing your own from seed, make sure they are well looked after at every stage of growth, that is, kept in good soil with plenty of space for root growth.

+ Keep the soil in tip-top condition by using compost, mulches, manures and so on.

+ Pick plants that will thrive in the available conditions and that are most resistant to pests and diseases.

+ Avoid overcrowding, since pests and diseases can take hold in cramped conditions.

+ Mix and match your plants so that your garden is balanced and no pest can dominate.

+ Rotate your planting, giving the soil a break and making sure that no pest or soil-borne disease can take hold in one place for years on end.

+ Get rid of the diseased part of a plant as soon as you spot it, remembering not to add it to your compost, and likewise crack down on a pest the minute you see one.

+ Proper watering can limit the spread of some diseases; trickle irrigation, which takes water directly to the soil, may be particularly helpful.

+ Use traps and barriers such as cloches, fences and enviromesh sheets to protect plants – many different varieties are available from organic gardening catalogues. Sticky traps also help you assess the level of infestation.

+ Encourage natural predators by planting companion species next to your crops. They attract insects that will dine out on the pests ravaging your plants.

+ Create a suitable habitat for frogs and toads, which eat slugs and snails.

+ Sow plants at times when pests and diseases are not such a problem.

+ Deter pests with repellents – some, available by mail order, use natural substances, such as a slug and snail repellent with a yucca extract and a cat repellent containing natural essential aromatic oils.

+ Know your enemy – the more you understand about a pest the better able you will be to outfox it and you may also discover that it is part and parcel of the bigger picture in your garden. For example, the caterpillar eating your plant may turn into the butterfly you have been trying to attract to your garden with another plant nearby. A pest may be attracted to your plant only when it is a seedling, so protection may be necessary only in the early stages.

+ Be ever-vigilant – the earlier you spot a problem, the easier it is to tackle it.

If you have tried all of the above and you are convinced you have an infestation that is beyond reasonable levels, then you may need to bring out some bigger guns, but there is still no need to reach for synthetic chemicals.

The first option is to use biological controls, usually available by mail order. These are living organisms that you introduce into your garden specifically because they feed on the pest you are having problems with, but they are safe for humans, pets and beneficial creatures. So, for example, you can buy microscopic nematodes that seek out and kill slugs, or delphastus, a relative of the ladybird, which can control severe white-fly infestations.

The main downside of these controls is that many of them require warm soil in which to survive and some are suitable for use only in the controlled and relatively compact environment of a greenhouse. They also need to be used as soon as you spot a pest problem, must be applied on the day of delivery and are sensitive to any sprays, including organic ones.

If you are still convinced you have a problem and nothing else has worked, then the green gardener can turn to sprays and powders as a last resort, but not conventional highly toxic brands. It is better to make use of those sprays approved for use in organic agriculture, which are generally of plant origin and biodegradable. These include: derris, a liquid or powder made from a number of tropical plants, which kills

PEST-CONTROL TIPS

* Don't forget your hands! Many insects can be removed by hand and dropped into soapy water or vegetable oil.
* Make protective cloches out of old plastic bottles – cut the tops off and sink them into the ground around your seedlings.
* Scare birds, rabbits and deer away by stringing up old CDs above your crops – the shiny surfaces will deter birds, but remember many birds are useful pest-eaters and should be enticed into your garden.
* Use old dry Christmas holly around the edges of freshly sown peas to deter mice.
* Soap is worth a try – a squirt of soapy water can kill aphids.
* Slug beaters include saucers of old beer or milk in the ground, which attract slugs, who then drown. Some gardeners suggest that human hair bordering their plants dissuades slugs from an attack and crushed egg shells, coarse sand, bark chips, soot and sawdust sprinkled round plants can stop slugs in their tracks as they dislike a gritty surface. You could try piling comfrey leaves in the centre of the bed you are about to sow – slugs love comfrey, although only in spring for some reason, and will be drawn to the pile. Leave it for several days then blitz the pile and remove the slugs that have collected there. After a few more days you can remove the leaves and compost them, sow your plants and surround them with a continuous ring of comfrey leaves to keep the slugs at bay. This will only work in dry weather.
* Create your own foul liquid of dead slug remains by plucking as many slugs out of your garden as possible (go hunting at night for the richest pickings). Leave them to decompose in a bucket of rainwater for a few weeks and then pour the contents in areas where slugs congregate – this is said to be the ultimate deterrent, but is for the non-squeamish only!
* Start plants that are particularly attractive to pests when they are young, such as cucumbers and pumpkins, indoors where they are protected.
* Garlic grown near roses is supposed to keep them clear of green fly, and a solution of bicarbonate of soda can control some fungal diseases on roses.
* Try out some of the natural insect-deterrent sprays recommended by gardeners over the years, such as those made from bracken, elder, rhubarb, nettle, seaweed and horsetail tea. You can find out how to prepare them by going to the website www.organic.mcmail.com/hints.htm.

aphids, spider mites, thrips, caterpillars and sawfly; pyrethrum, made from a certain type of chrysanthemum which kills aphids; and sulphur, which controls powdery mildew on fruit, flowers and vegetables.

Although effective, these and other treatments may also kill beneficial insects, damage other plants and kill fish, so they come at an environmental cost – hence their being last on our list.

WEEDS

If you are intent on creating a green Eden in your backyard it is important to reappraise the humble weed, since an environmentally friendly garden will never be weed-free. Many weeds are useful as lures for beneficial insects that prey on those eating your crops, others help enrich the soil and other plants by storing nitrogen in their roots, and most add to the diverse mixture of plants in your garden that make it so attractive to wildlife.

However, none of us want to see our lovingly planted beds overrun by couch grass or clover, so keeping weeds at tolerable levels is important even for the green gardener. But this does not mean that it is all right to douse the area liberally with chemical weedkillers, since this would contaminate the garden, leaving it dangerous for children, animals and other plants.

The aim of the green gardener should be to remove weeds in a way that does not disturb any other species in the garden and to reuse them in some way. Weeds can be invaluable for starting off a compost heap, for example, especially nettles and chickweed. Many can

be eaten in salads or soups, some can be drunk as teas and others have medicinal properties. You can even use weeds as feed if you keep chickens or rabbits. Cut weeds may also be dug into your soil to provide valuable nutrients, provided the roots of perennial weeds are removed and they are not in seed – this is best done in dry weather when they are less likely to recolonize your garden.

Hand weeding is obviously the first choice for many green gardeners and this can be made easier by using traditional weeding tools such as a kirpi, a specially shaped hoeing blade that is widely used in India and is available from mail-order catalogues. Care should be taken to avoid disturbing the root systems of your plants, so hoeing should always be a surface activity only. Unfortunately, for long-established perennial weeds with long, deep tap roots, such as buttercups, or an invasive creeping root system, like bind weed, hoeing doesn't help and heavy spadework is needed.

Mulching is another green way of controlling weed growth – by smothering them, preventing light and oxygen reaching the weeds. The best mulches are those that break down over time, enriching the soil as they do so. Examples include leaf mould, grass clippings, straw and bark chips. However, you will need to top up these mulches as they decay and persistent weeds may still find a way through them. Other more weed-resistant mulch options include flax matting, black plastic (go for recycled, if possible), carpet, recycled glass chippings, newspaper or cardboard. These are often covered in a layer of loose mulch to improve their appearance (see Mulches, page 186).

The final method available to the green gardener – a flame gun that burns back weeds – should really only be turned to as a last resort, since it uses paraffin or propane gas, which are pollutants. It is, however, still a greener option than chemicals and is a useful method for clearing a large garden, an allotment or paths and driveways in one hit.

What to grow

If creativity is missing in your life then get gardening! Whatever size canvas you have to work with, you can create the most wonderful sights, smells, textures and tastes by working with nature.

The first thing to consider is the environment in which you are hoping to create your green paradise. You should be trying to achieve a perfect balance between the conditions in your garden – the soil type, the amount of sunshine, wind and rain it receives – and your aims for the garden. In so doing you should have a garden that requires minimum intervention of any kind, be it heavy watering or pest control. A green gardener does not attempt to grow plants that need a lot of water in a dry, wind-swept garden or in a large, heavy container on a balcony, for example.

To assess the capabilities of your garden, observe it at different times of the day: notice where the sun reaches at certain points in the day, where the heaviest frosts are, where the drainage is at its poorest and where the wind hits.

To find out the type of soil you are dealing with, take some in your hand and rub it between your fingers. If it is sticky and rolls into a ball, it is clay soil; if it is crumbly and dry and looks grey, it is chalky; if is gritty and will not form into a ball it is sandy soil; and if it is smooth and silky, it is silt. It is also useful to determine the acid/alkaline balance of your soil by using a pH testing kit, available from garden centres. Some plants prefer one soil over another; for example, roses dislike sandy soils, and rhododendrons and azaleas love an acidic soil. Also, if you are in an urban environment with a garden close to a busy road, you may want to have your soil tested for lead content by the local environmental department. Should contamination be high and you want to grow edibles, then don't despair – container gardening is a good option, or you can build some raised beds with clean topsoil.

Once you know the capabilities of your garden, you must then consider how much time and effort you are willing to put into your garden and how much space you have in which to achieve your aims. If you have limited time, then growing fruit and vegetables may not be the thing for you, but tending to a few herbs in a window box and growing perennials and self-sowing annuals in your beds should be perfectly possible, and just as pleasing to the local wildlife.

Don't listen to those who say green gardening is more labour intensive than any other type of gardening. If you have a perfect balance of nature in your garden then you may actually find you have more time than conventional gardeners, as the frogs are eating your slugs and the mulch is smothering your weeds.

Having only a small space in which to garden is also not as limiting as many believe it to be. There are a wide variety of miniature fruit and vegetable plants that may be grown in containers, herbs take up very little space and a natural sanctuary can be made out of even the smallest, concrete-filled backyard, flat roof or balcony.

However, for the green gardener there are other considerations when it comes to choosing what to grow. The things to avoid are high-maintenance exotic plants that are not suited to your climate, have been transported for miles to reach your garden centre and are not attractive to local wildlife. It is also best to avoid buying large, established plants, as again they will have taken more energy in transportation and may have been chemically treated. Ideally, you should grow from seed

and the seeds should be organic or untreated, since conventional seeds are often given a chemical coating to combat fungus or disease.

Once your garden is established, you can harvest seeds from your own plants and plant them again. Tomatoes, marrows, pumpkins, melons, aubergines (eggplant) and green peppers (capsicums), for example, all have seeds that are easy to collect and can be sown again. Flower seeds, too, may be harvested by tying a paper bag over the seed head as it is ripening and shaking the seeds out when the head is dry. Seeds should be separated out from any dead plant material, dried and stored in labelled packets in a cool, airy drawer, before sowing the following year.

When buying plants, look beyond the standard varieties of fruits and vegetables used by commercial farmers. Instead, opt for tastier, traditional varieties that are no longer commonly grown and do your bit towards maintaining genetic diversity in our environment. Since these varieties were established before the advent of chemical fertilizers and pesticides they should also thrive in the organic conditions in your garden.

Beware of plants harvested from the wild. Stealing bulbs not only destroys the delicate eco-structure of the habitats from which they are taken, but the bulbs could easily be diseased. However, it is important that we continue to plant wild species of plants, provided they come from reputable sources. These species are disappearing from their natural habitats at an alarming rate, so it is important to do our bit towards biodiversity. Always buy your bulbs from a trusted source and enquire about where they have come from.

Containers

If you have a flat roof, balcony, small backyard or just a few window ledges, then container gardening is for you. No matter how small the available space, there is nearly always a container that will fit and an abundant choice of plants to grow in them. It's not just pelargoniums and pansies – herbs, dwarf vegetables and some fruits can all be grown in this way and often more easily than in beds, since soil conditions and pest control are far easier to manage in a small defined area.

Lack of shade and protection from wind are possible problems on balconies, roofs and ledges, so it is best to choose low-growing plants and/or plants that will thrive in the sun, such as Mediterranean herbs, vines, tomatoes, shallots and peppers (capsicums). Wooden trellises can also act as windbreaks.

Another consideration in these areas is the weight of your container – growing a miniature fruit tree may prove too much for your balcony to bear. But you can still cultivate some herbs in a small pot.

GREEN TIPS FOR CONTAINER GARDENING

* Avoid buying new, plastic containers and try to make your own using old car tyres, a tree stump, an old sink, a terracotta pot, ceramic bowls, a toilet cistern or an old wheelbarrow. Be sure to drill holes in the bottom for drainage.

* You can "age" containers by coating them in yogurt to promote the growth of lichen.

* Look for organic growing bags instead of the conventional ones. These should contain organic materials, peat from sustainable sources only (if at all), and are reputed to require less feeding and watering. Or try making your own using a sealed strong plastic bag filled with homemade compost, with composted bark instead of peat.

* Growing bags can be recycled. You can use them for potting bulbs or growing hardy annual flowers once your tomatoes and cucumbers have had their go. Or use the contents as mulch, add it to the soil on seedbeds or in seed trays, or add it to your compost heap.

* Avoid using sphagnum moss as a liner in your hanging baskets. Try lining them with recycled wool, coconut fibre or hemp fibre instead of moss. These are often biodegradable, from sustainable sources and hold water well, so reducing the need for watering.

* Be adventurous. Try baby tomatoes; herbs such as sage, chives, parsley and thyme; or strawberries in your hanging baskets. Fig trees, peach trees, dwarf apple trees and grapevines can all be grown in large tubs or pots, while lettuces, oriental greens, chard, spinach and trailing cucumber will thrive on ledges.

* Remember to use your homemade compost in containers. It will enrich the soil and also help it retain moisture – a particular problem with container gardening.

* Use a container to make a water feature – attracting useful garden helpers such as frogs and toads and providing valuable water for birds and insects (see pages 202–4).

Herbs

Herbs are pretty much the ideal plant – they smell wonderful, taste fantastic, look great and are a living medicine chest. On top of all this, they are pretty easy to grow, can be grown in the smallest of spaces and are a hit with bees, butterflies, hover flies and other garden helpers.

Growing your own herbs is worthwhile for those concerned about the environment. Store-bought herbs may look healthy but they are often the product of environmentally damaging and toxic growing practices. Dried herbs may have been irradiated or fumigated while fresh herbs may have been bombarded with herbicides and insecticides, with a top dressing of etherol – a ripening agent.

With the demand for year-round herbs increasing, they are now often grown in energy-guzzling glasshouses, using chemically enhanced, soil-free growing media, or flown in from sunnier climes. They may be sold in individual pots, which look natural and long lasting, but all too often disappoint, with the herb fading fast, or in plastic packs gas-flushed with nitrogen and carbon dioxide to extend their shelf life.

Nothing can compare with the simple pleasure of reaching out of your window and grabbing a handful of fresh mint to throw into your bowl of steaming buttered new potatoes or some basil leaves to scatter on freshly cooked pasta. And by indulging yourself like this you will be saving energy, reducing waste and benefiting your health.

HERB GROWING TIPS

* Most herbs suit containers of all types – from bay trees in large tubs to creeping thyme in a hanging basket – but they nearly all of them require good drainage and some sunshine.

* Growing from seed is the best method – look for the increasing variety of certified organic seeds now available.

* Try growing culinary varieties, such as basil, parsley, chives and rosemary in a window box, and fragrant varieties, such as peppermint, lemon verbena or sweet myrtle, in boxes on the indoor ledges to scent your house.

* Some herbs are best suited to growing in their own pots rather than being mixed into a window box, since the more rampant ones, such as mint and tarragon, can swamp the others.

* If you use a lot of one particular herb, such as basil, then grow several close together and pick from a different plant each time – that way they will have time to recover.

* Other herbs are useful in the fight against pests. For example, the liquid produced from steeping camomile flowers in boiling water for ten minutes is reputed to have insecticidal properties.

* Apart from many culinary uses, herbs are also very handy in other areas of our lives and make valuable green alternatives to many conventional products. Some can deter insects (see below) and household pests, aid house cleaning and decorating, be used in beauty preparations, and help make an effective first-aid kit (see pages 109–11, 119 and 146–150).

* Herbs can also be grown in beds and borders, acting as ground cover around larger plants.

* Many herbs are good companion plants, benefiting the growth of nearby plants. For example, garlic and chives sees off green fly from roses, nasturtium deters woolly aphids on apple trees and French marigold gets rid of white fly from tomatoes and repels eel worm.

Vegetables

Containers will not really allow you to grow serious amounts of vegetables, especially root crops, so if you have some beds and borders available make use of them by growing your own vegetables. With the addition of some compost, weeding and watering, you should be able to cultivate most vegetables, so the first step is to decide what you want to grow.

This decision should first and foremost be based on what you like to eat, since there is little point in growing hundreds of radishes if you don't actually like them. Bear in mind also that some of the easiest vegetables to grow include: beetroot, broad (fava) beans, ruby chard, courgettes (zucchini), lettuces, leeks, onions or shallots, potatoes and, yes, radishes.

Most vegetables can now be grown from organic seeds, either sown directly in your bed or started out in pots or trays indoors. Biodegradable pots made from coir and other fibres are best for both the plant and the environment, since they can be planted directly into the soil, where they will break down, without disturbing the plant's roots. Alternatively, make your own pots from newspaper, which act in the same way (avoid paper with coloured inks and glossy pages) – you can buy kits to do this. Trays, too, can be made from biodegradable paper or recycled plastic, or use empty egg boxes and yogurt pots.

Once seedlings appear or are planted out in your beds or borders, protect them from the elements and any predators by covering them with a cloche. Again, look for those made from recycled plastic or make your own from old plastic bottles. Beware of the sun though; seedlings can die pretty quickly if left under a plastic cloche in the hot sun all day.

Remember to mark what you planted where and to use the basics of green gardening – adding compost to the soil, chemical-free pest control and crop rotation – and you should soon have a harvest to be proud of. Start small and have fun – you may not be self-sufficient in one year, but you will be well on your way to having enough delicious produce for a good dinner party.

Fruits

Plucking fresh fruits from your garden is not only the preserve of those lucky enough to live in sunny climates and you don't have to limit your fruit-growing ambitions to a few apple trees and some strawberry beds. A wide variety of fruits can be grown by a patient green gardener, as long as the basics are there – a fertile soil, in as sunny and protected a spot as possible.

You could try apples, cherries, plums and pears or raspberries and of course strawberries. Organic varieties of blackcurrants, redcurrants, whitecurrants and gooseberries are also available.

It is easy to see why green gardeners would want to grow their own fruits. Many fruits in our stores have come under chemical bombardment from conventional growers, both pre- and post-harvest – some have their skins waxed and most of them are picked under-ripe in order to aid transportation. It is also getting harder and harder to find many truly tasty varieties of fruit. Although there are thousands of recorded varieties of apple, for example, only a limited number are used for the bulk of commercial production. Many commercial growers have decided to phase out some of the more interesting, but less predictable varieties in favour of the hardier, thick-skinned, but less juicy fruits that will travel well.

Apart from avoiding inferior fruit, growing your own is very cost-effective. Most soft fruit plants continue to produce fruit for 20 years; apple trees can keep going for 50 years and cherry trees even longer.

Lawns

A velvety carpet of close-cropped lush grass, free of brown spots and weeds, is high on the list of priorities for many a home gardener. It makes a great soft surface on which children can play safely and an inviting spot for an afternoon snooze in the summer. But maintaining an immaculate lawn can be exceptionally damaging to the environment. For example, a sprinkler can use about 650 litres (172 gallons) of water in an hour; a petrol-driven lawnmower, when used for an hour, causes as much pollution as driving a large car for 80 km (50 miles), and chemical fertilizers and herbicides contaminate water supplies and are even trodden into the home.

According to the Pesticide Action Network of North America, of the 30 commonly used lawn pesticides in the US, 19 are carcinogens, 13 linked with birth defects, 21 with reproductive effects, 15 with neurotoxicity, 26 with liver or kidney damage, 27 are irritants, and 11 can disrupt the hormone system.

The first thing to do is to put aside any preconceived notions of what is a perfect lawn. Learning to live with some dandelions and buttercups in your lawn, allowing it to go brown during dry summers and letting it grow just a little bit longer than normal are all good green practices. The following tips should also prove useful

SEEDING

The cheapest and greenest lawn will be one grown from seed. There are a wide variety of seed blends available for lawns, some suited for shady conditions under trees and others for grazing animals, for example. Choose one to suit your needs, such as a hard-wearing mixture containing perennial rye grass, which will be easier to maintain.

WATERING

You do not need to water your lawn – too much water can weaken it by encouraging roots to seek the surface rather than dig deep for water supplies. And grass is a remarkably good survivor of drought – brown patches will soon go green again when rain arrives. Spiking the lawn with a fork or with spiked boots will help it to absorb dew and rainfall.

MOWING

Allow the grass to grow to at least 4 cm (1½ in) before cutting it and don't cut it too short – about 2½ cm (1 in) is ideal – close cropping weakens the grass and this will reduce unnecessary mowing. The greenest mower is a hand-pushed model, giving you a good workout as a bonus. Petrol mowers pollute the air with emissions and, like electric mowers, waste energy. Leave the mowings to lie on the lawn where they replenish the soil, unless they are very long or it is cold and damp, in which case add them to your compost heap (see box, page 182).

FEEDING

Use only organic fertilizers or natural fertilizers like calcified seaweed, if absolutely necessary. In preference, you can sprinkle sifted compost on the lawn in mid-spring, ideally after rain. Brushing worm castings on the lawn on a dry day and raking in spring and autumn are also good ways to help the condition of the lawn.

WEEDING

If weeds are starting to take over, hand weeding is the answer. Use a kitchen knife to dig out dandelions, plantain and dock, removing as much of the roots as possible. However, if the grass is flourishing it should overcome weeds so moss and persistent weed problems are probably a sign that there are other problems, such as water logging, too much shade or high acidity.

The ultimate green lawn is one that has been allowed to go wild. (For more on creating a wildflower lawn or meadow, see page 206.) Another green option is to have a herb lawn using low-growing varieties of camomile or thyme. Popular in medieval gardens, herb lawns release fantastic fragrances as you walk on them and they do not need mowing, but they are not hard-wearing enough for ball games!

Trees

If you have the space then no green garden should be without some trees. They provide a home to wildlife, help clean the air, provide shelter from the wind and sun for you and your garden, and they can reduce your heating and cooling costs if sited near enough to the home.

Obviously you should choose your tree and its site carefully – a large, deep-rooting tree planted too close to a garden wall or house could spell disaster some years down the line.

Generally it is best to select a native species – it is more likely to support a variety of insect species and to

harbour birds. Be careful though not to choose a species that is already overplanted in your area, as this will not aid natural diversity and could add to the conditions necessary to allow a single pest to dominate, such as was the case with Dutch elm disease in the USA some years ago.

The ideal time of year to plant most trees is either at the end of summer or at the end of winter, when the ground is not too cold and the weather not too hot. Mulching around the tree base and providing protection around the trunk from rabbits and lawnmowers are also good ideas.

Creating a wildlife haven

A green gardener does not have to be obsessed with the size of his or her marrows. You can do as much for your environment by providing a sanctuary for local wildlife.

In fact, given the rate at which our meadows, forests and hedgerows are disappearing, doing your bit to help redress the balance is about as environmentally friendly as you can get. There are plenty of minor changes that you can make to your garden that will encourage more birds, bees and butterflies to pay a visit, but planting the most wildlife-friendly plants and trees will count for nothing if you continue to use toxic chemicals, such as slug pellets and weed killers, in your garden. You also need to make sure you are maximizing the conditions for wildlife with what you have in your garden already. Are you leaving seed food for birds? Or are you keeping such a "tidy ship" that there is precious little in the way of food or shelter for any wildlife in your garden?

Once you have made sure that your gardening practices are as wildlife-friendly as possible then it is time to consider ways in which you can go further, such as those outlined below:

ATTRACTING BIRDS

Birds are at the sharp end of industrial farming practices – the National Audubon Society has revealed that populations of some of America's most common birds have plummeted over the past 40 years, with some down by as much as 80 per cent, while in Europe farmland birds have declined by almost 50 per cent in the past 25 years. But it is not just commercial growers who have contributed to their decline. Gardeners, too, with their fondness for slug pellets and the like, have done their bit to decimate bird populations. Therefore green gardening is your chance to reverse this sad decline.

Providing food and water for birds is the first priority. Obviously you can put up a bird table or a squirrel-proof bird feeder in your garden (well away from prowling cats), but, best of all, you can make sure there is plenty for birds to eat naturally in your garden. As well as ensuring a variety of fruits and seeds are available all year round, you can encourage earthworms to the surface by spreading leaves on your beds. Provide water in the form of a pond (prevent it from icing over in winter by placing a rubber ball in it) or in a water dish left out for the purpose.

You can also help provide birds with suitable nesting sites – many have been lost with the removal of trees in towns and the loss of hedgerows generally. Lots of birds like dense and bushy plants such as pyracantha, trees obviously are home to many others and if all else fails, you can buy or make a nesting box and attach it to a tree or on a high wall. Make sure wooden boxes are made from sustainably produced wood (see page 50), or opt for "nests" made from seagrass, fern or coir, available through some mail-order catalogues (see Resources, page 248–9).

Finally, if you own a cat that likes to hunt birds, make sure it has a bell on its collar to warn any unsuspecting bird of its presence.

BRINGING IN BUTTERFLIES

In almost every country worldwide butterfly species are diminishing as a direct result of the destruction of their favourite habitats. Obviously all butterflies were once caterpillars, so a level of caterpillar activity should be tolerated in our gardens if we are to preserve our butterfly population.

Adult butterflies require food in liquid form, like nectar from flowers and the juices of extra-ripe fruit, so plant nectar-rich flowers, such as buddleia and fruits in your garden. They also need water, so if you do not have a pond or water feature, put out a shallow dish of water or leave some in the hollow of a rock in your garden.

Providing a basking site, where butterflies can warm up from the chill of an early morning, will also help them. You can do this by adding a light-coloured rock or garden sculpture to your garden which will absorb the sun's heat and to which butterflies will be attracted.

ENCOURAGING BEES

Bees are vital to the environmental food chain, pollinating many plants and producing delicious and healthy honey as a bonus. About 30 per cent of our overall diet is estimated to come as a result of a pollinating visit by a bee to flowering fruit trees or vegetable plant, so you can see how important they are.

By encouraging bees to come into your garden you may end up increasing the quality and quantity of your own fruit and vegetables. Bees love nectar and are drawn to white, blue and yellow-flowering plants. But new plant varieties are threatening their survival, especially that of the long-tongued bumblebees. They need access to deep flowers with an abundant supply of nectar throughout the spring, summer and autumn months in order to survive. However, many hybrids of traditional flowers often have no nectar, no spurs on which the nectar collects or they are in a form which helps honeybees get to the nectar that only bumblebees could reach in the past. Plus some exotic nectar-rich plants in our gardens are of little value to our bees as they are adapted to other pollinators like humming birds, with their specially designed long beaks (see page 204).

To attract bees, plant traditional cottage garden plant varieties. Bumblebees like common and musk mallows, woundworts, purple loosestrife, knapweed and meadow clary. Other bee favourites include: aubretia, polyanthus, yellow alyssum, borage, hyssop, honeysuckle, red clover, larkspur, snapdragon, nasturtium, lemon balm, sage, lavender, thyme, buddleia, Michaelmas daisies and sedum.

You can also help provide shelter for bees in your garden by drilling holes in a block of untreated wood and hanging it under the eaves of your house or garden shed, protected from direct sun and rain.

ATTRACTING FROGS AND TOADS

Toads and frogs are a real asset, as they munch their way through slugs and snails. A pond of some sort is needed (see pages 206–8), especially one with gently sloping sides, but they also hibernate out of water, under rocks or logs, so leaving the garden a little untidy should help.

BATS

A bat can eat half its own weight in insects in a single night, so they are pretty useful creatures to have around. They feed on night-flying insects such as mosquitoes, moths and beetles, and a single brown bat can catch up to 600 mosquitoes in an hour. To encourage these night prowlers to stay on your patch and do their good work, you should put up a smallish untreated wooden box at least 4 m (13 ft) high in a position that gets the sun most of the day. A pond would also help.

HUMMING BIRDS

If you are lucky enough to live in an area that receives these delightful summer visitors, you should do what you can to encourage them into your garden.

Like bees (see page 203), humming birds thrive on nectar, so plant a variety of good nectar-rich sources, such as bee balm, trumpet vine, any of the many varieties of honeysuckle, annual nasturtium, morning glory and delphiniums.

WILDLIFE TIPS

- Build a pond or provide clean, fresh water every few days in a saucer or hollow of a rock.

- Plant native plants.

- Choose plants that flower and bear fruit at different times of the year.

- Leave some "mess" in your garden such as dead, dying and hollow trees, and fallen fruit.

- Do not use chemical pesticides or herbicides.

Green roofs

The potential for greening your surroundings is not just limited to your backyard, garden, patio or window sills. You could convert a rooftop or wall into a green area.

Green roofs can be split into two categories – intensive, roof gardens which require a lot of maintenance as with a normal garden, and extensive roofs which support low-growing, tough drought-resistant vegetation which are both lightweight and require little maintenance. Extensive roofs do not require much, if any, additional structural support from a building and can be fitted onto existing buildings as well as created on new ones.

Green roofs are common in Germany, Austria and Switzerland. In Germany, it is a legal requirement in many large cities to include green roofs on new, flat-roofed buildings. In the US, they are also becoming popular, particularly in cities like Chicago and also Portland, Oregon and Seattle, Washington. The UK lags behind since there is no government policy, grants or standards for green roofs, so most are one-off projects rather than regional initiatives. This is set to change as a national green roof organization, Livingroofs.org, has been created and an independent research and demonstration body has also been set up, called the Green Roof Centre.

If you are keen to create a green roof on either the roof of your house, garage, garden shed or an outbuilding, there are advice sheets on creating one yourself from green roof organizations or you can hire a specialist designer. Either way, you should always consult a structural engineer to approve the plans.

A living wall is a vertical garden – where plants are rooted in a fibrous material that is then anchored to a wall. They can give the same benefits as green roofs in terms of insulating a property, provide a home for wildlife and reduce the possibility of flooding. Again a specialist will be required to advise on installation and maintenance.

The benefits of green roofs include:

- **Reducing the potential for flooding by limiting run-off from roofs by at least 50 per cent, and more usually by 60–70 per cent.**

- **Boosting biodiversity – they provide a home for a variety of species including rare invertebrates and ground-nesting birds such as skylarks.**

- **Roof life is at least doubled with the addition of a green roof as it protects the waterproofing from the effects of ultra-violet light and the weather, especially frost, thereby reducing the need to replace or repair the roof.**

Creating a wildflower meadow

The astonishing devastation of meadowland all over the countryside has led to the extinction and near extinction of many species of birds, insects and plants. So if you have access to a piece of land, however small, one of the most ecologically friendly things you could do with it is transform it into a wildflower meadow.

If you have a lawn already, you can create your meadow by inserting pot-grown wildflowers or small nursery-grown wildflower seedlings as plugs directly into the turf. The good news is that a wildflower meadow will need mowing only a couple of times a year, but you must clear the grass cuttings to prevent them from suffocating new growth.

You can also create a new meadow from scratch using wildflower mixtures or wild flower and grass mixtures – you can even buy mixes aimed at particular wildlife such as a "Bats in the Garden Mix" or "Wild Bird Mix". Make sure the soil is not too rich and that it is clear of weeds, then mix the seeds with dry silver sand to aid thin and even sowing.

As well as a beautiful meadow that sways gently in the summer breeze, you will attract a wide range of wildlife – and the birds will really appreciate it.

Ponds in the garden

Few people consider their garden to be complete without a water feature and it is not just because it is of value to the flora and fauna. Water is innately soothing and the sound of running water could be all that you need to shake off the tensions of the day and relax.

There are two options available to you if you are keen to introduce a pond into your garden: you can either dig a big hole and line it, or use a container such as a glazed pot or wooden barrel. If you are using a liner, then try to find one made from recycled plastic.

POND TIPS

* Build the soil up slightly around the pond to make
sure water drains away from it, not into it.
(Make sure that any drainage from the pond is away
from your house.)
* There will be less maintenance if your pond is not under trees.
Most aquatic plants grow better in full sun and you will reduce
the problem of leaves collecting in the pond (covering the surface
with a net in the autumn will also help).
* Let the pond sit for a few days before adding fish and plants.
This allows chlorine to evaporate from the water.
* Consider a mix of emergent, submergent and floating species of plant.
* In tiny ponds floating species of plants such as duckweed,
water lettuce and water hyacinth may be adequate
to maintain clear water.
* Avoid electricity-gobbling special effects such as fountains,
waterfalls and so on, although you can now buy or make
solar fountains, which will work on sunny days and
bright cloudy days.

MORE POND TIPS

* Don't waste electricity heating your pond in winter – fish
will survive provided the surface does not freeze over and
gases can escape. Placing a rubber ball in the water will ensure it will
not freeze over completely.
* A "balanced" pond will have algae at acceptable levels but scavengers, such
as snails, will help clean up wastes from the bottom of the pond. Avoid chemical
controls: if you have a real problem, try eco-friendly products such as pond pads,
which use barley straw as a natural agent for controlling algae in ponds.
* Locate the pond where it is least likely to attract unattended children.
When children are around, always be extremely vigilant!
* Most people surround their ponds with rockeries in order to make them
look more natural and provide places for frogs to hibernate. Try to use
local rocks, thus avoiding the environmental costs of transportation.
It would be even better to use reclaimed rocks – those being
removed from a building site, rather than those
sourced from a quarry.

Community gardening

If you don't have the space to fulfil your gardening ambitions or you have some spare time that you'd like to invest in greening your local area, community gardening is a great way to extend the benefits of green growing to those around you. There are various options and many different organizations to help you get involved. Community gardening projects are neighbourhood-based initiatives which stimulate social interaction and enable you to grow your own plants and/or food locally.

Allotments

A type of community garden popular in the UK, allotments are usually allocated by the governing council or local authority for a very small annual rent. There may also be privately run sites: there may be a waiting list for a plot – they have become incredibly popular – but you might be able to find someone who wants to share their plot with you while you wait. A normal plot size in the UK is usually 9 x 6 m (30 x 20 ft). Facilities vary on-site, so check if water is available, whether there is an on-site shop and whether vandalism is a problem.

Parks and green spaces

For many people their only chance to access green space is by visiting their local park or woodland. They are vital resources for communities but they do also

need community support. Contact your local council to find out if there is a support group – often called a "friends" group – that you can join. A friends group should give you ample opportunity to get your hands dirty as well as a chance to meet your neighbours. Alternatively, you could set up a friends group if there is a green space that you know about that could do with some tender, loving care. Local government and other organizations provide advice on how to go about setting up a group, fund raising and other issues for those interested in helping to protect and maintain a community green space.

School gardens

Schools provide great locations for gardens – giving children the chance to learn about the environment, experiment with growing food and perhaps find a tranquil space away from the rigours of the playground. Research has shown that schools which have created outdoor learning areas reported that 73 per cent of their pupils had shown behavioural improvement, while 85 per cent said that the gardens had increased healthy active play.

There are plenty of organizations who can give assistance to schools that are interested in creating gardens, for example, in the UK the national school grounds charity, Learning through Landscapes. Schools are also great places to introduce children to the concepts of water conservation through the use of water butts, composting, and recycling.

GARDEN ACCESSORIES

Not all kinds of patios, fencing and garden furniture are created equal when it comes to the environment – some are definitely greener than others. But it is still early days in terms of how much information you can find on the environmental impact and sustainability of garden products. The best advice is to question your local garden centre, do-it-yourself chain or manufacturer to find out where the product comes from, how it is produced and how much energy has been used in order for it to reach you. They might not have the answers readily available, but without public pressure they may never bother to find out.

Patios and terraces

There is life beyond a lawn, and it used to be crazy paving, but these days people are opting for more natural-looking patio surfaces in their gardens than concrete. But choosing the most eco-friendly hard surface for your garden is a tricky business. Concrete is best avoided anyway since cement is a key ingredient and the cement industry accounts for over 5 per cent of global carbon dioxide emissions. But there can be problems with using stone instead. Imports of natural stone account for around 10 per cent of the UK market for home paving and are expected to account for 20 per cent within 10 years, but Indian sandstone is being mined often by children as young as six, working long hours in inhumane conditions. Stone quarries in China also have dubious records with regard to the environment and working conditions. It is vital that you seek a supplier who can prove their stone is ethically sourced. In the UK,check to see if they have signed up to the Ethical Trading Initiative (www.ethicaltrade.org).

Still the environmental cost is also high: polluted groundwater, the spoiling of the landscape by illegal dumping and the energy consumed to transport the stone halfway across the world to our gardens. And even if you find ethically sourced, imported stone, one company has calculated that it generates 84 per cent more carbon dioxide than its other products, such as a reconstituted concrete which looks like Yorkstone – so it's not a straightforward business (this same company offers customers a carbon calculator service in order to help them choose the least carbon demanding product).

Another issue to consider when creating a terrace or paved area is whether it will worsen any drainage problems in your lawn – especially if you live in a high-rainfall area. Use of permeable paving that allows water to drain away through gaps, and other measures, will ensure that run-off is reduced. Look out for specialists in Sustainable Urban Drainage (SUDS), who can advise you on a complete system for your garden, or contact your local department of public utilities for information on water management.

Decking was the garden design hit of the 1990s, but just because it is wooden does not mean it is necessarily green. The wood could be from poorly managed forests or have been treated with toxic chemicals (see box, page 51), so get as much information as possible before

you buy. Instead of buying new, you could try using reclaimed wood to give a unique look to your patio. Old railway sleepers are also useful for bed edging.

You can also buy secondhand for your patio if you use bricks or paving – reclaimed bricks and paving are available from some builder's merchants.

Whatever your choice of surface, remember the principles of green gardening and learn to live with a few "imperfections', such as moss. Do not use chemicals to blitz all plant life growing between the cracks in your paving. If things are really getting out of control, try the traditional tried-and-tested method of weeding by hand.

Fences, walls and hedges

No matter how small or large your garden, it is likely to be bordered by fencing, wall or hedge.

The ideal green boundary is a hedge – a living fence. Hedges have become rare commodities in today's countryside, with large commercial farms having ripped out many of them to make way for larger fields and to allow farm vehicles access.

Hedges are hugely valuable as a home to birds, animals and insects, as well as providing a safe habitat for wildflowers and other plants, but on a practical gardening level, they also act as far more effective windbreaks than fences. Wind tends to

bounce up and over when it hits a solid boundary such as a fence, and swirling on the leeward side often damages plants. This can also create the conditions that lead to fences being blown down. Hedges, on the other hand, filter and slow wind down and every 30 cm (1 ft) of hedge height offers 3 m (10 ft) of shelter.

So you will be helping both the conditions in your garden and the environment as a whole by keeping any existing hedges and planting others if you have a suitable space. This need not be at the edge of your property – hedges can also be used to segregate different areas in the garden, such as a lawn from a vegetable patch.

If you are not convinced of the merits of hedges over fences then choose your fencing carefully (see Woody Issues, pages 214–5). If you prefer walls, then make sure they are built using reclaimed bricks or stone, if at all possible, or, failing that, select a stone that is local to your area. If you are painting or staining fences or walls then remember to choose natural organic products that do not use petrochemicals.

Finally, use the walls and fences as vertical canvases on which to continue your garden by fixing trellises on them and growing climbing plants such as vines, clematis, honeysuckle or wisteria. Western red cedar wood is commonly used to make trellises, but the Canadian forests from which the wood comes have not been well managed so avoid this wood unless it has the Forest Stewardship Council (FSC) mark (see page 50).

HELPFUL HEDGE TIPS

❖ As with all planting in your garden, keep it local – there are locally distinctive hedgerow types so find out which ones predominate in your area before deciding which to grow.

❖ Consider which hedges attract the most wildlife – oak, blackthorn (sloe) and hawthorn, for example – and help further by planting wildflowers and grasses at the foot of the hedge.

❖ Remember you don't have to plant just one variety – you could mix the all-green varieties of holly or privet with variegated species. Hedges can also provide colour in the garden – try planting flowering shrubs such as spiraea, barberry or escallonia in informal hedges.

❖ Low-growing hedges can be used for ornamental effect between borders, and can also appeal to other senses – try aromatic varieties such as lavender and rosemary.

❖ Avoid the infamous fast-growing Leyland cypress, which monopolizes soil nutrients over a wide distance and can reach a height of 135 m (443 ft). Opt for hawthorn, yew and beech if you want a quick-growing hedge.

❖ Don't be overzealous with the trimmer (use garden shears instead) and avoid shaping the hedge into an upright rectangle, as this can lead to top-heavy growth with gaps below. Training the hedge into an "A" shape (when seen from the side) makes sure the lower levels get as much light as the top and gives a much stronger and healthier structure that makes a better wind- and weatherbreak.

❖ If your hedge has become thin and gappy, it can be partially revived by the seemingly drastic technique of cutting it almost right down to the ground (with a sloping cut). New growth will usually appear by the next spring, which, with new planting to fill any large gaps, will give a reasonable hedgerow within three to four years.

Garden furniture

There is no point having a gorgeous green garden if you do not spend any relaxing time in it – which is where garden furniture comes in. But before you rush off to get your picnic table and sun loungers, take time to consider what materials have been used to make them.

If you are buying hardwood tables and chairs, for example, then be sure of the timber's origins, especially if they are made from teak, iroko or nyatoh – again look out for the FSC mark (see page 50).

If plastic furniture appeals to you, check the recycled content. There are now many suppliers of recycled plastic furniture. Cast-iron furniture is also popular in gardens, but it is important to check what paint has been used to coat it. Is it lead-free? Does it contain solvents? And also, how far has the furniture travelled from manufacturer to retailer?

Woody issues

When choosing wood to use in your garden, be it for decking, trellises, fences, furniture or a shed, there are some key issues to be aware of.

The first is the kind of wood being used and how it has been produced. Garden furniture in particular has been made using wood from some of the most vulnerable forests in the world, the tropical rainforests; wood from poorly managed western red cedar forests in Canada is also commonly found in garden products. It is important to find out if the wood has come from a sustainable source.

The most reliable way of checking out the wood you buy is to look for products that carry the Forest Stewardship Council (FSC) mark (see page 50). This is an independent guarantee that the forest or woodland of origin is managed according to agreed social and environmental principles and criteria.

Plenty of retailers make green claims for their wood furniture but the FSC scheme is the only credible certification for wood products.

The second major issue of concern when it comes to wood in your garden is the use of wood preservatives, such as creosote. Used to prevent rot and decay by bacterial and fungal agents, preservatives are commonly applied to fence posts, compost boxes, bed edging, fence panels and sheds.

The most dangerous preservative for the environment is creosote, which leaches into the soil, gives off vapours for seven years and is harmful to people and animals. CCA-treated timber – sometimes called "tanalized" timber or "pressure-treated" timber – can also pose a risk to the environment since it uses incredibly toxic chemicals such as copper arsenate. These chemicals are meant to stay in the wood once dry, but American researchers have found traces of arsenic in the soil and on the hands of children who have been playing on equipment made from this timber. There may be a danger to you if you fail to use gloves when handling the wood and a mask when sawing it, and certainly this wood should never be burned.

There are other preservatives available, such as those based on boron and acetypetacs zinc and copper, which are all said to have a low toxicity to plants, humans and animals. There are also an increasing number of plant-based preservatives on the market, although these will not necessarily have been endorsed by organic gardening groups. But even these preservatives should be used only if essential. It is better for you and the environment if you avoid the need for any preservatives by taking the following steps:

* Set wooden posts in concrete or use metal "shoes" for fence posts as the main area of decay is likely to be where the wood meets the soil and air.

* Oil wood that is in contact with the soil – linseed is easy to apply and allows the wood to breathe, avoiding trapped moisture.

* Choose the right wood for the job – without preservatives, oak, sweet chestnut and western red cedar will last 20 years in contact with the soil, and untreated pine and larch will last five and ten years respectively. Heart wood and well-seasoned wood is more resistant to decay.

* Consider whether you need to use preservatives at all – most wood will not decay for years anyway and does it matter if wood used on bed edges and compost boxes eventually decays?

* Most wood sold for outdoor use in garden centres and large do-it-yourself stores will have already been treated so if you want to avoid them opt for wood sold for indoor use or visit your local sawmill and ask for untreated wood.

* If you want a green easy life, avoid wood altogether and choose "wood alternative" instead. Made from recycled plastics, this synthetic wood is now used to make fence posts, panels, trellises, bed-edging boards and boards used in garden benches. With no need for preservatives, stains or paints, this option could be the easiest and greenest going and should be available from a large do-it-yourself store or garden centre.

The happy gardener

It is no good creating a green garden paradise if your mosquito bites are so bad you dare not enter it. And slapping chemical insect repellent all over yourself is not the answer, considering the lengths you have gone to avoid chemicals in the rest of your garden. So have the following natural products handy before you go out into the garden to make sure you are as happy in it as all those insects.

CITRONELLA OIL

This essential oil repels mosquitoes, but smells pleasantly lemony to humans. It can be applied directly to the skin if diluted in a carrier oil, can be added to a vaporizer, and is often found added to outdoor candles. Lavender oil can also be used in this way, or you could try washing the skin in a pennyroyal or elderflower infusion.

TEA TREE OIL

A fantastic all-rounder for any gardener, this essential oil is antibacterial, antiviral and antifungal. It can soothe an insect bite, sting, cut or graze and prevent it becoming infected.

ALOE VERA

This plant has a huge number of uses, but it is good for gardeners since it soothes sunburn and can also help heal cuts. Have a go at growing the plant yourself – it thrives in hot, sunny conditions so you may have more luck on an indoor window ledge – or buy an aloe vera preparation.

HOMEOPATHIC REMEDIES

Keeping a homeopathic first-aid kit can be helpful to a gardener. Try pyrethrum tincture for bee stings, arnica or ledum tinctures for wasp stings, and a mixture of hypericum and calendula tinctures for gnat bites. For skin that has come into contact with poison ivy, bathe it with milk and take anacardium 6c every 15 minutes. Ask a registered homeopath for more information on specific remedies.

SUN PROTECTION

No one should need reminding of the dangers of prolonged exposure to direct sunlight and gardeners are especially at risk. Always cover up as much as possible (even if working in the shade), wear a hat that shades the back of your neck, and wear sunscreen. Choose a sunscreen with a sun protection factor (SPF) of at least 15, which protects against UVA and UVB rays, and look out for those that contain certified organic ingredients or that are available through health-food stores, as they are likely to have fewer petrochemicals in them. You could also try taking 30 mg of beta carotene daily during the summer as this has been shown to give greater protection against the dangers of radiation on the skin.

GARDEN TOOLS AND EQUIPMENT

First, try to get by with as few tools as possible by
making do with what you have around you. An old kitchen
fork or spoon can be used to separate and lift seedlings, while
a pencil or ice cream stick are also good for lifting seedlings and
creating small holes in which to plant them. For larger tools look out
for them at car-boot (garage) sales or on websites such as Freecycle or
Efreeko, which allow people to give away unwanted items.

When it comes to machines, always opt for the ones requiring manpower
alone. Conventional push lawnmowers are now lighter than in the past.
Avoid a petrol-powered lawnmower, hedge trimmer, brush cutter,
blower/vac or chainsaw, which can produce 100 times the pollution
of a modern car when measured in terms of emissions per unit of
fuel consumed. Electricity is a more environmentally friendly
power choice, especially if using rechargeable batteries. But
if petrol (gasoline) power is unavoidable, look out for
new ultra-low emission engines that can cut
emissions by up to 80 per cent over
traditional models.

The green barbecue

As soon as the evenings become lighter and warmer, the urge to cook and eat outdoors gets stronger, and by the middle of summer the barbecue season will be in full swing. They are a great way to get you and your friends out in the garden, but are barbecues environmentally friendly?

Just as with patio heaters (which can release 7 kg (14 lb) of carbon dioxide in just a couple of hours), some of the latest top-of-the-range barbecues are among the least eco-friendly garden accessories. So, the first consideration is the kind of barbecue you plan to use. Probably the best type is home-built, using old bricks or an old tin drum, but if you have to buy one then make sure that any wood used as shelves and knobs is from a sustainably managed source.

When it comes to what you burn in the barbecue, most people opt for charcoal – indeed 50 per cent of UK barbecues are fed on wood charcoal – but it has an uncertain environmental record. Ideally, charcoal should be produced from old wood that is a by-product of good forestry, that is, the thinnings, but there have been concerns that in some countries trees are being felled for the sole purpose of making charcoal. There are also worries that some countries are destroying environmentally sensitive mangrove forests in tropical coastal areas in order to produce charcoal. One hectare of forest could produce 150,000 kg (330,688 lb) of timber but just one-tenth of that in charcoal. Just 3 per cent of charcoal bought is "sustainable" and up to 90 per cent of the 40,000 tonnes of charcoal burnt in the UK each year is sourced from abroad.

Given the question marks over the sustainable nature of charcoal, production overseas and the amount of polluting air miles notched up to bring in this kind of charcoal, it would be best to buy your charcoal locally, where it is likely to have come from managed coppiced woodland.

It is, however, important to avoid using briquettes in your barbecue. In the US, 63 per cent of barbecues are fired with briquettes, consisting of waste timber and sawdust, mixed with cornflower (cornstarch) to bind plus a hydrocarbon solvent, similar to lighter fluid, to start easily. But according to the US Environmental Protection Agency, charcoal briquettes release 105 times more carbon monoxide per unit of energy than propane and a lot of toxic volatile organic compounds. But propane or liquid petroleum gas is not the answer either since it is a fossil fuel and a net contributor to atmospheric carbon dioxide levels.

The way you light your barbecue is also a factor. Lighter fluid or self-lighting briquettes will give off volatile organic compounds emitted when burnt, which are not great for your health. If you are using charcoal, use a chimney starter instead. It consists of a metal cylinder with a grate near the bottom – unlit charcoal is put inside the cylinder and newspaper is placed under the grate and lit. The charcoal at the bottom of the cylinder lights first and the "chimney effect" ignites the remaining charcoal above.

Look out for natural firelighters which can be bought online, such as Fairtrade fire sticks from Guatemala that are 80 per cent resin but dry to the touch and make ideal natural fire lighters. You could also try Swedish Fire Steels. Developed by the Swedish defence department, they produce a spark up to 3,000 °C (5,430 °F) in the wet or cold, by moving a striker across the steel. They are ideal for starting barbecues provided you have some kindling to hand to get the fire going.

Whatever you do, make sure you're not tempted to buy one of those heavily packaged disposable barbecues from your local supermarket or garage as they cannot be recycled or composted. For a longer-lasting alternative, try a bucket barbecue; this is a galvanized bucket with air holes in the sides and bottom, a wooden handle and removable grill top.

Remember, too, that you can use charcoal ash (but not briquette ash) as a fertilizer and it will raise the pH of acidic soils, but it is very alkaline and should be applied sparingly. You can also sprinkle a little of the ash around your plants to keep slugs at bay.

Lastly, be aware of some health risks associated with barbecues. Smoke from both charcoal and wood produces not only hydrocarbons but also tiny soot particles that pollute the air and can aggravate heart and lung problems. A study in Texas found that microscopic bits of polyunsaturated fatty acids released into the atmosphere from cooking meat on backyard barbecues were helping to pollute the air in Houston.

Meat cooked on a barbecue can form two kinds of potentially cancer-causing compounds: polycyclic aromatic hydrocarbons (PAHs) and heterocyclic amines (HCAs). According to the American Cancer Society, PAHs form when fat from meat drips onto the charcoal; they can then rise with the smoke and collect on the food above. They may also form directly on the food as it is charred – the hotter the temperature and the longer the meat cooks, the more HCAs are formed.

The atmospheric garden

All five senses can be stimulated in a garden – you can relax as you watch and listen to bees buzzing around heavily scented honeysuckle, while lying on soft grass, munching a home-grown apple. Paying attention to the sensory effects of your garden will bring rich rewards, so try some of the following:

WATER

For many people, the key to relaxation is water – be it the sound of crashing waves or a long hot soak in the bath – so bring water into your garden with a pond. It does not have to be a big lake; you can start small by making a mini water feature in a container on your patio. (See Pond Tips, pages 207–8.)

LIGHT

A garden at night is a special place, often unrecognizable from its daytime guise. Many different animals and insects come out in the evening and the cool air is often filled with the scents of various flowers that have opened during the day. Lighting your garden by night will help you make the most of it – allowing you to see it an entirely different way and making it a warm and welcoming place for evening entertaining.

But this does not mean you should call in the electrician immediately. Give the latest in solar-powered lighting a try – solar globe lights will give up to 20 hours of light when fully charged, switch on automatically at dusk, and best of all can even be used floating in your pond. Or consider soft lighting from candles and oil burners. Large garden flares can last for many hours and many candles have the added bonus of deterring insects with the addition of citronella oil. Look, too, for recycled glass lanterns or put tea lights in old glasses and position these around your garden. But bear in mind that light pollution is a growing problem. In the UK, between 1993 and

2000 light pollution increased 24 per cent nationally and the amount of truly dark night sky fell from 15 to 11 per cent. Not only is this a waste of energy and sad for those of us who enjoy star gazing, it is also having a detrimental effect on many birds and animals. Stray light at night can confuse their natural patterns and affect their breeding cycles. While the problem is mostly due to badly designed street and road lighting, security lights, and floodlights, you should ensure that you are not contributing to it by making sure you use low-intensity lights that are directed downwards. And try to keep an area of your garden as dark as nature intended for the sake of local wildlife.

SCENT

Choosing your plants carefully can help make your garden more than just a visual experience. Plant according to scent, especially in areas where you are likely to brush past plants, such as raised beds abutting a path. Herbs grown near a kitchen or by your outdoor dining table will arouse the tastebuds with their scent and a summer's day will be that much sweeter with the smell of jasmine, sweet william and phlox filling the air. Look out too for plants that release their scent in the evening, such as tobacco plants.

SOUND

Encouraging wildlife into your garden will provide you with the perfect soundtrack to relax to – birds, bees, frogs and grasshoppers all contribute to a soothing garden symphony. But you can add your own sounds with running water in your pond (you can buy solar-powered pond fountains) and wind chimes made out of old wood. Just sit back, close your eyes and unwind.

GREEN FOOD AND DRINK

If you wish to live a truly green life you cannot afford to ignore what you eat. Much of the planet is used to grow food, be it wheat on the American prairies, rice from the fields of China or bananas from a Caribbean island. So many countries give over most of their land to food production that the type of agriculture that is practised is vital for biodiversity and environmental conservation. By opting for "green" food you could be making a difference to the ecology of many countries – your decision has a global impact.

Conventional farming practices do not have a good record when it comes to protecting the environment and they are costing us all dear as a consequence. But the good news is that it is relatively simple to make a green choice when it comes to food – go organic. Whether you grow your own or buy it in, you will know that organic food has been produced in a way that nurtures rather than exploits the environment. And by buying only certified organic produce you know that there is a legal system ensuring that producers' green credentials are as good as they say they are.

The organic difference

The aim of organic farming is to work with nature to create the healthiest conditions in which to grow food, without the need for artificial inputs such as fertilizers, pesticides, antibiotics or growth-promoting hormones. The emphasis in organic farming is about achieving a natural balance with the environment in which a farm exists and to be as self-sustaining as possible.

The following are the key differences between organic and conventional farming:

SOIL HEALTH

To maximize the chances of producing healthy crops, organic farmers pay a great deal of attention to the health of their soil. Techniques for soil improvement include crop and animal rotation, planting soil-enriching plants or green manures, and adding manure and home-made compost. By doing this, organic farmers avoid the need for artificial nitrate fertilizers and they make sure the soil can support a rich variety of life. This is important, since it has been estimated that it takes 500 years to form 2.5 cm (1 in) of topsoil; keeping it in good condition and preventing its erosion is therefore vital for the environment.

ORGANIC DEMAND

- **There has been a dramatic increase in sales of organic food and drink. Global sales were valued at £19.3 billion (about $27 billion) in 2006 with Europe being the largest market by value for organic foods and North America the second largest. The UK organic market is now the third largest in Europe, after Germany and Italy.**
- **Organic food purchases are still only a small proportion of all food sales – they make up around 4.5 per cent of total food sales in Denmark, Austria and Switzerland, 3 per cent in Germany, 1.6 per cent the UK and 2.5 per cent of total US food sales.**
- **In terms of land use, in 2005, there were just over 6.5 million ha (16 million acres) of organic farmland in the EU, approximately 4 per cent of the total agricultural land area.**

Conventional farming, on the other hand, often makes heavy use of artificial fertilizers – two-thirds of which leach away from the land and end up contaminating our water supplies with excess nitrogen. Water companies are having to introduce more and more treatment programmes costing millions to tackle this contamination.

SELF-SUSTAINING

Organic farmers aim to be self-sustaining. For example, they keep livestock alongside crops, thereby providing valuable manure for the land and organic animal feed. They rotate crops and pastures, preventing disease and soil imbalances. Growing plants known to attract pest-eating insects beside a valuable crop – companion planting – is another way in which they work with nature

Conventional farmers are more likely to buy in their animal feed, ship out their manure and look outside the farm for solutions to pest problems and soil fertility, ignoring the answers in their own backyard. Overall, organic farms are likely to use far less energy and non-renewable resources (such as diesel fuel) than conventional farms. Studies have found that organic farming typically uses 27 per cent less energy than non-organic farming.

CONSERVATION

Organic standards demand that farmers conserve natural wildlife habitats such as grassland, hay meadows and moorland. They also ensure that old farm buildings are protected, existing ponds maintained, and old hedgerows and stone walls are looked after. In addition to conserving habitats, organic farmers are encouraged to contribute further to the environment by planting native trees, creating ponds, and nurturing wildflowers and grasses in wide borders between cultivated fields.

Conventional farming has, in recent times, meant intensive farming, whereby the larger the scale of a farm, the cheaper it has been to produce the crop. However, the cost to the environment of this kind of farming has been heavy. For example, in the last 50 years, half the UK's natural woodlands and 40 per cent of its hedgerows have been destroyed as farmers expand their cultivated land.

The loss of wildlife as a result of this habitat destruction has been enormous – huge numbers of species of birds, bees, butterflies, wildflowers and insects are disappearing fast because of this kind of agriculture. But recent research by the British Trust for Ornithology and other organizations has found that the organic farms in lowland England with cereal crops are supporting: 32 per cent more birds and 35 per cent more bats, as well as 109 per cent more wild plants within the cropped area. Plus, there was a far greater diversity of wild plant species, with 85 per cent more species in the organic field cropped areas.

AVOIDING SYNTHETIC CHEMICALS

One of the biggest differences between conventional and organic farming systems is the former's reliance on synthetic chemicals – either pre- or post-harvest. There is no place in organic farming for synthetic chemical pesticides. Instead, organic farmers concentrate on improving soil health, planting disease-resistant varieties, inspecting their crops frequently, rotating crops, and encouraging natural predators with companion planting and by creating ponds, hedgerows and so on.

Occasionally, even organic farmers have such a severe pest problem that they turn to insecticidal sprays, but these must be approved by organic certifiers and are based on natural compounds, which biodegrade quickly. Mainstream farming has, in contrast, come to depend on highly toxic synthetic pesticides. The result of all this spraying has not been a decrease in the loss of crops to insects; in fact the global loss has almost doubled in the last 50 years as insects, diseases and weeds have developed more and more resistance to these products.

These pesticides have also contributed to the disappearance of many farmland birds as the bugs they feed on are wiped out or poison the birds that eat them. Wildflowers have also been devastated by mass spraying of land, as have the insects and butterflies that feed on them. Land and water pollution is another by-product of this.

Of major concern is the fact that many countries with the most fragile and threatened eco-structures are becoming the biggest users of pesticides and they are often the least careful in terms safe usage and disposal of these chemicals.

Post-harvest chemicals are also popular with conventional growers since they extend food shelf life. For example, methyl bromide is applied to strawberries and to sterilize grain after harvesting. Other foods likely to have been sprayed in this way are bananas, citrus fruits, grapes, apples, pears and cherries – even potatoes can be sprayed with a toxic fungicide to inhibit sprouting.

Apart from their possible impact on human health, some of these chemicals are highly damaging to the environment. Methyl bromide is thought to be 60 times more damaging to the ozone layer than the more commonly known CFCs, and 50–90 per cent of the substance enters the atmosphere when sprayed on crops.

BIODIVERSITY

Encouraging natural biodiversity is an inherent aim of organic farming, not only in the greater environment in which the farm exists, but also in terms of the kind of crops and livestock that are being farmed. Organic farmers often grow unusual varieties of fruits and vegetables that are fast disappearing from our countryside, and they are also more likely to rear traditional breeds of livestock, since these will be best suited to the local conditions.

Variety has all but disappeared from conventional farming, with farmers relying on just a few types of seed and animal, bred specifically to meet their needs – yield and size – and not that of consumers – which is taste. In France, the Golden Delicious apple accounts for nearly 75 per cent of all apples grown. In the UK there are 2,300 known varieties of apple but just two – the Cox and the Bramley – now dominate; and of 550 different sorts of pear, three varieties are generally available. Virtually half of Britain's pear orchards and nearly two-thirds of its apple orchards have been destroyed since 1970. These orchards were wildlife havens for many plants and bats, hares, badgers, owls and woodpeckers.

On the livestock front, the world is losing at least two breeds of animal every week. One thousand different breeds of domestic animal have become extinct during the past century and one-third of surviving breeds are endangered, according to the United Nations Food and Agriculture Agency (FAO). They blame this on the success of breeders in the developed world in exporting animals that have been bred to produce more and better meat or milk. The poultry and pig industries are highlighted as being reliant on only a handful of specialized breeds.

The impact on the environment of monoculture or "genetic erosion" is severe. We are endangering thousands of other species that rely on these plants and animals, losing plants that may well prove of medicinal use in years to come and creating an environment in which disease and pests run rife.

GENETIC MODIFICATION

The only way to be sure your food has not been genetically modified (GM) – whereby a gene or genes from one species is inserted into another – is to buy organic food. Worldwide organic standards prevent genetic modification

or the use of GM ingredients for many reasons, including the unknown impact of this technology on the environment. Although, to the dismay of many, the European Union has passed a new law which allows organic food containing up to 0.9 per cent of GM content to be classed – and labelled – as organic, and consumers would not be notified of any GM presence below this 0.9 per cent threshold. This is to allow for accidental contamination from GM crops grown adjacent to organic ones. The UK's organic organizations have promised to maintain their higher standard of a lower 0.1 per cent threshold for GM content.

The use of GM seed encourages farmers to depend on a single seed supplier and reduces the chances of a variety of seeds being sown, thereby further threatening natural biodiversity. But despite the fact that research concerning the impact of genetic modification on the environment and human health is still pretty thin on the ground, GM crops are already being cultivated and eaten in many places around the world. In the USA, in particular, conventional farmers have greeted genetic modification with enthusiasm and many thousands of acres of land have been dedicated to the cultivation of GM soya and maize. This has led to the widespread introduction of GM ingredients in food production – up to 90 per cent of processed food may already contain GM material.

GENETIC MODIFICATION: THE FACTS

Genetically modified (GM) crops have been engineered to be resistant to herbicides, to produce toxins to kill pests, or to provide higher yields. There are approximately 100 million hectares (247 million acres) of GM crops being grown around the world by about 10 million farmers. But three quarters of the world's GM crops are now grown in the US and Canada – the main GM crop in the US is soya and maize, and in Canada it is oilseed rape.

In 2004, the British government announced that no GM crops would be grown commercially in the country for the "foreseeable future" due to public protests but today there is pressure to adopt GM technology as it grows. Only one GM crop, a form of maize, is approved for use in Europe, and that is only grown in Spain.

WHAT ARE THE PROBLEMS?

Those developing GM crops claim they are vital for the development of higher-yield and hardier food for the world's increasing population and that they will help produce crops that can be used as biofuels in the fight against climate change. But concerns remain about their impact on health and the environment. These include:

- Increasing use of pesticides. Pesticide and herbicide tolerance could mean that farmers spray their crops more liberally. Research from the US has shown, for example, increased herbicide use on GM maize.

- Cross-contamination. There are concerns that organic crops could become contaminated with GM material and GM material might also contaminate protected landscapes. A 2003 government report on cross-pollination of certain crops and wild plants revealed significant contamination and once widely released it would be almost impossible to reverse this process. Researchers have found that pollen from oilseed rape can travel up to 4 km (2.4 m) and can escape from fields even when they are surround by barrier crops.

- Health risks. Antibiotic-resistant genes can cross from our food to our stomach, possibly making antibiotics ineffective and other health concerns include a higher risk of allergies through the accidental transfer of allergenic genes – an allergenic Brazil-nut gene has been transferred into a transgenic soybean variety; its presence was discovered during the testing phase.

- Threat to biodiversity. A loss of weeds altogether in crops of herbicide resistant crops will reduce the ability of wildlife to exist in our fields and genetically modified organizms (GMOs) could compete or breed with wild species posing a threat to crop biodiversity, especially if grown in areas that are centres of origin of that crop.

- Genes can mutate. It is not yet known whether artificial insertion of genes could destabilize an organism, encouraging mutations.

- Greater impact on birds and insects. Widespread use of GM crops could lead to the development of resistance in insect populations exposed to the GM crops and birds feeding on them.

- Mixing of GM products. Unauthorized GM products have appeared in the food chain. For example, last year long-grain rice sold in the UK was found to be contaminated with a GM strain grown in the US.

- Loss of farmers' access to plant material. Biotechnology research is carried out predominantly by the private sector and there are concerns about market dominance in the agricultural sector by a few powerful companies. This could have a negative impact on small-scale farmers all over the world. Farmers fear that they might even have to pay for crop varieties bred from genetic material that originally came from their own fields.

- Impact of "terminator" technologies. Although these are still under development and have not yet been commercialized, they would, if applied, prevent a crop from being grown the following year from its own seed. This means that farmers could not save seeds for planting the next season.

HOW CAN I AVOID GM FOODS?
In the US, GM foods and products are currently not labelled and roughly 70 per cent of the foods in supermarkets have GM ingredients. The European Union products have to be labelled as GM if they are from a GM source, but products produced with GM technology (cheese produced with GM enzymes, for example) do not have to be labelled and products such as meat, milk and eggs from animals fed on GM animal feed also don't need to be labelled. Japan, China, Russia,

Australia and New Zealand are among other countries that have strict labelling requirements.

The only reasonably sure way to avoid GM foods is to buy organically certified foods. Organic standards prohibit the use of GM ingredients or GM feed. But be aware that there is still a very slight risk that some GM contamination may occur even in organic food. In Europe, provided contamination is less than 0.9 per cent and the contaminant is a GMO that has an EU authorization, a product can still be certified organic.

LOCAL AND SEASONAL
Although not actually written into the legal standards that govern organic food, the majority of organic growers support local food initiatives, which encourage consumers to buy their food locally and seasonally. The organic community supports local food initiatives such as farmers markets, where farmers sell their own produce usually in monthly gatherings held in local towns and cities; box schemes, whereby mostly organic fruit and vegetables that have just been harvested are delivered to your door for a fixed fee; and small independent stores such as healthfood stores or organic fruit and vegetable stores.

As these are often run by the farmers themselves they reinforce the link between grower and consumer that has been lost over the years in developed countries and which many believe has led to the mistrust and divisions between town and country.

Buying local produce also avoids the costs of pollution associated with conventional food production and distribution. Conventional farmers and retailers appear to pay little heed to the environmental cost of shipping crops around the world and growing strawberries in mid-winter. As a result, air transport – now the fastest-growing source of carbon dioxide emissions – is used for an increasing number of food imports. Further pollution is generated when the food is then brought to a central depot before being trucked out to the individual supermarkets, and then driven home by a customer.

Also, food that has travelled long distances tends to require more packaging in order to protect it on its journey, resulting in the waste of huge amounts of plastic, cardboard and glass.

BETTER FOR HEALTH

By eating organic your chances of avoiding any synthetic chemical residues in your food are higher. These chemicals are increasingly being linked with damage to the nervous system, birth defects, cancer, dropping fertility levels, and other human ailments. Most governments do set minimum acceptable levels allowed in food but few take into account the effect of eating a variety of these residues – the "cocktail effect" – or adjust these levels when considering children's intake.

And most of these residues do not wash off easily since many are designed to withstand rain, and some are designed to actually enter the plant, ruling out peeling as a way of getting rid of them.

Pesticides do not just threaten your health; they are also incredibly dangerous for farm workers worldwide.

It has been reported that 40,000 people are killed every year due to pesticide exposure and the World Health Organization found that up to 30 per cent of Latin American farm workers it tested showed signs of exposure to organophosphates, chemicals linked with serious health damage.

Organic crops are also believed to be healthier in terms of their chemical structure. Research in Germany, Denmark and Switzerland has found that organic produce has higher nutrient levels when compared with conventional produce.

If you eat organic you are also less likely to be eating food that contains antibiotic residues, since organic farmers are not allowed to routinely give their animals antibiotics as a preventative medical measure or in the form of growth promoters. The use of antibiotics has increased by 1,500 per cent in the past 30 years, and 65 per cent of all antibiotics are used in conventional farming. It is widely believed that this overuse of antibiotics in farming has led to worrying levels of antibiotic-resistance in humans, leaving us with fewer weapons against infection, and the rise of drug-resistant superbugs such as MRSA.

Lastly, organic food can help reduce the problems associated with food safety such as bovine spongiform encephalopathy (BSE). There has not been a case in any herd in full organic management prior to 1985. Given that organic standards do not permit the use of animalbased products in feed, the BSE crisis in Europe, with its huge cost to the taxpayer, could probably have been avoided altogether if organic farming had been the norm.

PESTICIDES AND HEALTH

✚ Around 31,000 tonnes of chemicals are used in farming in the UK each year and research has found that 40 per cent of the fruit, vegetable and bread samples tested in the UK contained pesticides. In the US, consumers can experience up to 70 daily exposures to residues through their diets, according the Pesticides Action Network North America. Even worse, British government tests have found that 70 per cent of samples of free school fruit and vegetables given to children contained pesticide residues and 1.7 per cent had residues above the legally permitted limits.

✚ For many years, these pesticides have been linked with an array of health problems, especially for those people living close to the spray zones in fields. Only recently in the UK, the Royal Commission on Environmental Pollution (RCEP) called for more precaution in the face of the uncertainty over possible risks to health and recommended buffer (no-spray) zones around homes and schools.

✚ Question marks remain over whether pesticide exposure is directly linked to a range of illnesses including cancer, leukaemia and Parkinson's disease. For example, a study has found that high levels of exposure increased the risk of contracting Parkinson's disease by 39 per cent, while even low levels raised it by 9 per cent.

✚ Many pesticides have neurotoxic, carcinogenic and hormone-disrupting capabilities and studies have shown that very low doses of pesticide can disrupt hormone systems at much lower levels than previously thought safe.

✚ Another problem with assessing the risks to public health from crop-spraying is that it is currently based on an assumption that you will only be exposed to a single pesticide at any time. But pesticides are rarely used individually and are often used in mixtures. The long-term effects of this "cocktail" of chemicals have not been fully assessed, although one study at Liverpool University in the UK found that combinations of different pesticides proved far more toxic to human cells than similar quantities applied individually.

IMPROVED ANIMAL WELFARE

Strict animal welfare conditions are included in organic standards, such as the requirement that animals have free access to fields or outdoor areas; that they have ample natural bedding, such as straw; and plenty of space in indoor areas such that they are able to express their natural behaviour patterns. So you will never find caged battery hens in organic farming.

All organically reared animals must be fed natural organic feedstuff, and graze on organic pastures such as herb- and clover-rich grass. They are not pumped full of antibiotics and growth promoters – instead, through a mixture of good husbandry and natural and homeopathic remedies, animals are healthier and require less medication.

Some certifying bodies also specify the maximum time any animal can spend travelling to an abattoir – the Soil Association in the UK, for example, requires that this is no more than eight hours – and they encourage the use of local abattoirs.

TASTIER

While this is purely subjective, organic food is often the tastiest option. This is because organic farmers often grow traditional, uncommon varieties of fruit and vegetables that have been selected for their taste rather than their suitability for transportation or yield. Also, if you buy your organic produce from a local source, such as at a farmers' market, it is likely to be fresher, which always makes for a better taste. And since organic fresh produce is not sprayed with post-harvest chemicals to prevent decay, you will not be fooled into buying an apple that has been hanging around for some time in the belief that it was picked that morning.

Frequently asked questions

How can I tell whether something is organic?

Organic is a legal definition when applied to food, so for a food to be labelled or sold as organic it must have been produced according to national organic farming and processing standards, and this is true worldwide. If you want to be sure that the food you are buying is organic, then look out for either of these on a label or, if buying unpackaged products, ask the retailer for proof.

Are all organic foods healthy?

Yes and no. Organic foods are less likely to contain chemical and antibiotic residues (see page 233), and they are not allowed to contain hydrogenated fats, artificial additives, flavourings or preservatives, so in this respect they are healthier. However, they are not "health foods". You can buy organic ice cream, biscuits (cookies) and chocolate, for example, none of which should be eaten to excess if you are concerned about your health. But organic foods are definitely healthier for the environment.

With organic food being transported long-distance via air freight, how green can it be?

Organic imports feature heavily in many countries around the world, and there are clearly environmental costs in transporting food internationally or within a vast country like the USA. However, the environmental benefits of organic farming are so great that anyone serious about green living should buy organic. In addition, the more people who buy organic, the more likely it is that farmers will convert their farms to organic production and that governments will help by subsidizing these farmers during the conversion process (up to three years).

Do buy as much of your produce locally as you can and eat seasonally. The organic community encourages both.

Are organic foods also fairly traded?

The term "organic" does not automatically mean that a product is fairly traded as well. There is a separate mark to look out for – the Fairtrade mark – if you want to be absolutely certain that workers are paid a fair wage, work in safe and humane conditions and are given training. At present this is given only to coffees, teas, bananas, cocoa, orange juice, chocolate and honey, and exists in only 18 countries worldwide. See Fairtrade Labelling Organizations International (FLO) at www.fairtrade.net.

Organic agriculture is rarely at odds with the principles of Fairtrade, since by avoiding the use of synthetic chemicals, for example, workers are already being given a healthier working environment. And organic producers have traditionally had a strong ethical basis which has seen them provide long-term contracts at fixed fair prices to suppliers, along the same lines as those that exist in fair trading.

So it is likely that, if you are buying organic, workers will benefit. However, with larger, less ethically conscious companies getting in on the organic act, this may not always be the case, so keep a look out for goods that are labelled as both organic and Fairtrade.

Why is organic food more expensive?

The price of organic food is coming down, but it does cost a bit more than conventional produce. This is mostly because it costs more to produce – manual labour is required for weeding and spreading compost, fewer animals are squashed into one shed and better-quality feed is given to these animals, for example. It is also costly to get your food certified as organic and to keep testing it to ensure that it is free from genetically modified organisms (GMOs) – pollution from GM crops has already occurred.

However, the price of your weekly shop is not the entire cost to you and your family. The true cost of the food you eat should reflect the amount you pay in tax and water bills, since it falls to governments and utilities to clean up the environment, to tackle food scares and to subsidize threatened rural communities that often result from conventional agriculture. Taking the environmental, social and health costs of conventional food into account makes organic food a bit of a bargain.

Why does organic fresh produce often look worse than conventional produce?

If you mean a carrot that is not perfectly straight or an apple that does not gleam, then it is probably because organic produce is not manipulated in order to look good. In the organic world, food is judged as much on content as looks, so apples are not routinely waxed, for example.

Requiring your produce to conform to supermodel good looks comes at a cost. Supermarkets apply such strict rules regarding physical attributes that tonnes of produce fail to make the grade each year and are left to rot.

SUPERBUGS

❋ There is widespread use of antibiotics in conventional farming. The US Centers for Disease Control and Prevention estimates that 22.6 million kg (50 million lb) of antibiotics is produced each year in the US and about 40 per cent of that is used in livestock, mostly for growth promotion. Most intensively reared farm animals are fed antibiotics on a daily basis, as growth promoters, as a preventative measure or to treat illness, according to the Soil Association.

❋ This use of antibiotics is thought to be linked to the onslaught of antibiotic-resistant superbugs such as MRSA and the new superbug – a strain of E.coli. This new strain emerged in the UK in 2003 and has spread rapidly; approximately 30,000 people are now being infected in the UK annually. The elderly are most at risk from the bug and people who contract urinary tract infections caused by this type of E. coli have a 30 per cent risk of dying.

❋ Despite the British government agreeing to reduce the use of farm antibiotics, there has been no significant change in the farm use of antibiotics since 1999, according to the Soil Association. In fact, use of two groups of antibiotic potentially linked to these bugs has increased each year.

❋ Antibiotics are permitted in organic farming, but are limited to clearly defined situations and complementary therapies and trace elements must be used instead where these are effective. After the use of antibiotics, all organic farmers must observe significantly longer withdrawal periods than required by medicinal legislation before meat, milk or eggs may be sold for human consumption. This is to further reduce the chance of antibiotic residues in food and to allow any resistant bacteria to decline. The number of antibiotic treatments permitted for individual animals is also limited, and any animals that receive more treatments than allowed lose their organic status.

Food and drink

When buying food and drink a vital consideration is the distance it has travelled to reach your kitchen – calculated as "food miles". These are notched up in several ways – air or sea travel for food imports such as green beans from Kenya, the transportation of food for packaging and distribution to supermarkets, and the distance traveled by you to do your shopping.

The average distance that food travels to reach our plate has doubled over the past 20 years. In the UK, the government estimates that transporting food to and around the country produced 19 million tonnes of CO_2 in 2002, of which 10 million tones were emitted in the UK; that is 1.8 per cent of total UK CO_2 emissions. It believes the overall social and environmental cost of food transport is £9 billion (about $12.8 billion) with impacts on road congestion, accidents, climate change, noise and air pollution.

Clearly, buying food that has been grown locally is a good way to mitigate these costs but be aware that some foods that appear to be from local suppliers might have toured the country between distribution and packaging depots before arriving back in your local supermarket. So it is a good idea to buy from a smaller, local store, famer's market or box scheme that doesn't rely on huge distribution networks.

You could also consider joining the Slow Food movement (see Resources, page 249). This is a non-profit, eco-gastronomic organization that was "founded to counteract fast food and fast life, the

disappearance of local food traditions and people's dwindling interest in the food they eat, where it comes from, how it tastes and how our food choices affect the rest of the world". It has over 80,000 members worldwide and national branches which coordinate Slow Food events and projects.

FRUIT AND VEGETABLES

Eaten raw and often unpeeled, fruit and vegetables grown with the use of pesticides and subject to post-harvest treatment pose a particular threat to our health from chemical residues. For example, an independent working party in the UK has found one in three pieces of fruit and vegetables tested at random contained such residues and almost 2 per cent of the samples tested had higher levels than those permitted by law. The highest in terms of detectable residues were: celery – 72 per cent; lettuces – 56 per cent and apples – 47 per cent.

Apples can be sprayed with pesticides up to 35 times before they reach your local supermarket and the average pear is sprayed more than 13 times. Given that children, with their less developed immune systems, drink 16 times more apple juice than the average adult, then you can see the impact non-organic apples could be having on your family.

In addition, with so many fruits and vegetables coming from overseas, where different rules apply as to the use of pesticides and other chemicals, it is hard to know what has been used.

Fruit and vegetables are sometimes the subject of other environmentally-wasteful agricultural practices. Some are being picked when they are under-ripe to aid transportation, and then being ripened in chambers pumped full of ethylene gas. Others are grown in heated, lit glasshouses so they can be produced year round and of course they appear increasingly on the list of the geneticists, looking to modify fruit in particular to make it less susceptible to disease and to ripen slowly.

The lack of choice in varieties is another problem (see Biodiversity, pages 225–6). Organic farmers are more likely to pick traditional varieties since they often offer better resistance to disease or are juicier than the mainstream ones. So supporting local organic fruit growers is essential.

DAIRY PRODUCE

Organic milk, cheese, yogurt and butter all originate from cows who graze on organic pastures, who will not have been routinely given antibiotics, and whose welfare is high on the list of priorities for the farmer. The benefit for you is that they are less likely to contain unwanted pesticide or antibiotic residues.

By choosing organic dairy produce you will also be assured that the genetically modified hormone, BST or rBGH, has not been used on the dairy herd. The hormone is injected into one-third of American dairy cows to increase milk production, but it causes a five-fold increase in a protein that has been linked with breast cancer.

CHOCOLATE

The cocoa plant is one of the most heavily sprayed crops in the world and intensive cocoa production is the cause of much soil erosion and deforestation in tropical countries. By going organic, you will be supporting a safer working environment for plantation workers and getting a healthier product, since organic chocolate contains up to twice the amount of cocoa solids as conventional brands and no hydrogenated fats, refined white sugar or artificial flavourings.

BABY FOOD

A child's immune system does not fully develop until about the age of five, so bombarding children with pesticide-drenched food does not give them the best start in life. They are also far more likely to be eating food that contains residues – milk, fruit and vegetables – and are thus five times more likely to be consuming residues than an adult. And most government safety limits on pesticide residues are based on levels considered safe for adults.

CHILDREN'S FOOD

- Concern about the impact of food on children's health is common, especially given the obesity statistics. It is expected that almost half of all children in the UK will be dangerously overweight by 2050 unless drastic action is taken. In the US one-third of children and teens, ages 2 to 19, are overweight or at risk of becoming (2004 statistics) while the US Surgeon General's office also warns that 70 percent of overweight teens will grow into overweight or obese adults.

- The use of additives in conventional, processed food has been a particular worry for many parents, who suspect that they are linked to their children's behavioural issues and a 2007 UK Food Standards Agency (FSA) study has confirmed this. It found that 300 random children behaved impulsively and lost concentration after a drink containing additives and certain mixtures of artificial food colours, alongside sodium benzoate, a preservative used in ice cream and confectionery. This research confirms earlier work on the negative impact of the "cocktail effect" of additives on children's behaviour.

- Most of the 290 additives allowed in non-organic food are prohibited in organic food, including all artificial colours or flavours. Organic food also cannot contain a host of ingredients that researchers say may be harmful to our health such as aspartame, hydrogenated fat, phosphoric acid, sulphur dioxide, monosodium glutamate, or artificial flavourings and colourings. .

- According to the US Food and Drug Administration, some additives are linked to allergies; for example the colour FD&C Yellow 5 (tartrazine) may prompt itching or hives in some people.

MEAT AND FISH

It is better for the animals as well as you if you opt
for organic meat. Organic livestock are kept in more
humane conditions, fed GM-free feed and not dosed
with antibiotics. But you may have a problem sourcing
organic meat and it is considerably more expensive. This
is because organic livestock farmers are dependent on
supplies of organic feed, but UK self-sufficiency in organic
cereals fell below 50 per cent during 2006, increasing the
need for imported organic grains. The cost of livestock
feed, whether for organic or non organic farmers, is also
rising as a result of recent poor global harvests, increasing
diversion of cereals into biofuel production and rapidly
rising demand, particularly from China and India.

Organic fish, too, are better cared for. Farmed fish such
as trout and salmon are not kept in over-crowded tanks
and not fed artificial colourings to turn their flesh pink;
no routine medication is allowed and the fish are killed
as humanely as possible. Organic standards also do not
allow genetically modified fish – GM salmon are being
trialled in conventional fisheries.

The environmental hazards of conventional fish farming,
such as pollution of surrounding waters, are also avoided.
Such pollution is mainly due to the use of chemical
pesticides to control infestations such as sea lice, and
other chemicals used to clean cages and prevent weed
build-up. Fish waste and excess feed can also build up
beneath cages, reducing oxygen levels in water and
leading to dangerous algae blooms. Intensively farmed
fish are also fed fish meal in pellets, often derived from
threatened species of fish – these pellets are now being
blamed for contaminating salmon with toxic chemicals,
since they concentrate the trace amounts present in the
fish from polluted oceans.

Many species of ocean fish are clearly endangered
because of overfishing and the toxic effects of pesticides
and other pollutants that run into the sea or are dumped
there deliberately. There is, however, a certification
scheme for sustainable fisheries run by the Marine
Stewardship Council, so look out for its logo on fish
products (see box opposite and Resources page 249).

SOYA AND MAIZE (CORN)

In reality this is most processed foods since soya and maize
(corn) are on the ingredients list of up to 90 per cent of
manufactured foods. They are not always in forms that
you would immediately recognize either; for example,
they are commonly used in anti-caking agents, colourings,
emulsifiers, flavourings and food supplements.

The main reason you should opt for organic is the GM
issue. Both GM soya and maize have been enthusiastically
planted by American farmers and they meet much of the
Western world's demand. Most countries have limited
labelling, but if you are lucky you may be able to tell whether
GM ingredients feature in your food. However, the surest
way to avoid them, and the health and environmental risks
that may come with them, is to eat organic.

You will also avoid many processing aids altogether, since
organic standards restrict the number that can be used
and requires as much transparency as possible on labelling
with regard to ingredients and processing methods.

THE FISH CRISIS

The situation for fish in our oceans is dire: 52 per cent
of fish stocks are being fished at their maximum biological
capacity, 24 per cent are overexploited, depleted or recovering
from depletion and 21 per cent are moderately exploited. Only 3 per
cent of the world's fish stocks are underexploited. This overfishing is
driven by demand. Over the last 30 years, demand for seafood products has
doubled and is anticipated to grow at 1.5 per cent per year through 2020.
In an attempt to provide a sustainable solution to this problem, the Marine
Stewardship Council (MSC) was set up in 1997. It has established the only
internationally recognized set of environmental principles for measuring fisheries
to assess if they are well managed and sustainable. Fisheries are assessed on three
principles: the condition of the fish stocks, the impact of the fishery on the marine
environment including other non-target fish species, marine mammals and sea
birds; and the fishery management systems.

Over 45 fisheries are either certified or being assessed by the MSC which
represents over 3.5 million tonnes of seafood. Global sales of the 850
MSC-labelled products have more than tripled since 2004, but MSC
certification may not be enough. It still only covers 7 per cent of
world fish catches, and there has been some criticism that it is not
rigorous enough in its assessements. However, on balance
MSC-certified fish products are likely to be the most eco-
friendly option so look out for the logo. You can
also find out who stocks MSC-certified fish
by looking on the website.

TEA AND COFFEE

Tea and coffee plantations have suffered a similar fate to cocoa plantations. Drenched in pesticides, they have become larger and larger, with an increase in the resulting deforestation and soil erosion. But it is not just conventional tea that has environmental consequences; herbal teas may also have a poor environmental record, since herbs are commonly grown in glasshouses, in soil-free substrates, with heavy use of chemicals before and after harvest.

WINE AND BEER

You may not realize how far from its traditional image modern winemaking has come. Once again, the chemicals are out in force in most vineyards and there is little by way of other vegetation left for the local wildlife. Chemicals also feature in the winemaking process, with high levels of sulphur often finding their way into the finished product – these have been linked with allergies and headaches. Here, too, the geneticists are busy – genetically modified vines are on their way.

Organic wines are, needless to say, produced in an entirely more environmentally-friendly manner, with grasses and wildflowers cropping up beneath the vines. Lower levels of sulphur are specified in organic standards and chemicals are less likely in all stages of winemaking.

It is worth seeking out organic beers as well – conventional beers are produced using hops that are likely to have been sprayed with over 15 different pesticides around 12 times a year.

PALM OIL

- Palm oil is found in one in ten supermarket products, including chocolate, bread, crisps (potato chips), detergents and lipsticks, and demand for the oil continues to rise, particularly in the growing economies of China and India. Sales in Europe have also grown recently due to palm oil being a good substitute for partially hydrogenated soft oils as manufacturers seek to remove transfat acids from their products.
- The areas under palm oil cultivation have increased by about 43 per cent since the 1990s, most of which were in Malaysia and Indonesia – the world's largest producers of palm oil. But it is the most significant cause of rainforest loss in Malaysia and Indonesia. The development of palm oil plantations was responsible for 87 per cent of deforestation in Malaysia between 1985 and 2000.
- Palm oil plantations have led to destruction of forests, impacting on biodiversity, while the use of fire for preparation of land for oil palm planting has been reported to contribute to the problem of forest fires. Plantations are also associated with human rights violations and worker exploitation, according to Friends of the Earth. In Indonesia, the area of land occupied by palm oil plantations has doubled in the last ten years, threatening species, including the orangutan and Sumatran tiger, with extinction. The industry could drive the orangutan to extinction within 12 years.
- A global initiative on sustainable palm oil, the Roundtable on Sustainable Palm Oil (RSPO), was established in 2004 with the aim of promoting the growth and use of sustainable palm oil. It is working on a certification scheme and has agreed a set of criteria governing oil palm plantation development. All major UK supermarkets have signed up as well as some US brands such as Kelloggs.
- Without a certification scheme the only way to avoid driving palm oil growth is to try to avoid purchasing products using the oil. This is hard given that often it is labelled only generically as vegetable oil, so this might require you writing to manufacturers and stores to find out more.

Top tips for green eating

✔ Grow your own. There are no transportation costs for your food to reach you, no waste packaging, no polluting and dangerous pesticides, and if grown using your own compost, then it is the ultimate form of recycling.

✔ Buy local. Support outlets as close as possible to where your food is grown or made, such as farm shops, farmers' markets, box schemes, local grocers and healthfood stores. Your food will have travelled fewer miles to reach you, costing less in terms of pollution, and you will know that you are also getting food that you can trust. In addition, these outlets are likely to be small businesses in need of your support.

✔ Buy certified organic produce. That way you know your food has been produced with the utmost care and attention being paid to its environmental impact and you will be sure that it has met stringent legal standards.

✔ Buy unusual varieties. You will be encouraging biodiversity and signalling to retailers and growers that there is a market for more than just Granny Smiths and Golden Delicious, for example.

✔ Buy loose. Avoid all the packaging that comes with your food by buying it loose – and not just fruit and vegetables. Look for bulk bins of rice, beans and pulses, dried herbs and spices, nuts and grains, most commonly found in healthfood stores. If you cannot find it loose, then choose a brand with as little packaging as possible, preferably one that uses recycled and biodegradable packaging materials.

✔ Wise up on labels. Learn to spot ingredients that are likely to have been genetically modified, look for organic certifying marks or numbers, and for country of origin and local producer information. Avoid generic, mass-produced, poorly labelled, non-organic products.

✔ Buy and eat seasonally. In doing so you will be sending a message to retailers and growers that it is not necessary to fly strawberries around the world in winter and you will be discouraging the use of energy-guzzling hothouses to grow summer fruits in winter.

✔ Keep processing to a minimum. Look for food as close to its natural state as possible, without the addition of colourings, preservatives, flavour enhancers, bulking agents and so on, which has not been through many stages of manufacture. And at home, eat as much raw food and do as much home cooking as possible rather than buying pre-prepared and cooked food. (For more on the greenest methods of cooking, see pages 82–4).

✔ Eat low on the food chain. It takes less input and energy to produce grains, fruit and vegetables than it does meat and fish, and of the meats it takes less grain and water to produce pork or chicken than it does beef, for example. By mainly eating a meat-free diet you are opting for the most energy-efficient diet.

✔ Support your local and national organic and green organizations. They are working to guarantee you a supply of good-quality food produced in a sustainable way and will keep you updated on availability, campaigns and threats to your right to choose.

RESOURCES

This section is an invaluable resource for green companies, manufacturers, campaigning and information groups. You will find suppliers of many of the products mentioned throughout the book in the following pages, along with further information on how to get more involved in a green lifestyle.

Green consumerism is a great way to flex your consumer spending power but it is not always the most environmentally friendly option. Before you buy something new, make sure you can't mend, upgrade or update the thing you are replacing.

Organizations like Freecycle are brilliant for circulating unwanted items and prevent waste ending up in landfill sites. Remember, the item you are getting rid of may be exactly what someone else is looking for, so make good use of these networks.

Chapter 1: Back to Basics

Big Green Switch
Tips on switching to a greener lifestyle.
www.biggreenswitch.co.uk

Building For Health Materials Center
A central supplier for healthy, environmentally-sound building materials, appliances and home comforts.
www.buildingforhealth.com

Cornish Organic Wool
For a range of organic wools and knitting kits.
www.cornishorganicwool.co.uk

Ecocentric
A green interiors website hosted by environmentally aware designer Oliver Heath. It sells everything from eco-friendly wallpaper and paints to LED lighting.
www.ecocentric.co.uk

Ecos Paints
For a range of anti-formaldehyde and ELR-neutralizing paint, as well as wall insulating paint.
www.ecospaints.com.

Ecotricity
Green energy supplier in the UK
www.ecotricity.co.uk

Energy Saving Trust

A non-profit organization funded by the UK government and the private sector to address climate change issues.
www.energysavingtrust.org.uk

Farrow & Ball

For environmentally-friendly paints made without the use of ammonia or formaldehyde.
www.farrow-ball.com

Good Energy

Supplier of renewable electricity to homes and business.
www.good-energy.co.uk

Green Building Store

For products that promote energy efficient, sustainable and healthy buildings.
www.greenbuildingstore.co.uk

Green Glass

Website selling a range of recycled glass products such as drinking glasses and jewellery.
www.greenglass.co.uk

Green Home

A store for green home products.
www.greenhome.com

National Grid

Green energy options for US consumers.
www.nationalgrid.com

The Natural Store

For a range of silk-filled duvets and other home supplies.
www.thenaturalstore.co.uk

Onya Bags

These very lightweight, reusable bags fold up into a pouch which can be clipped onto a key ring or bag.
www.onyabags.co.uk

Patagonia

Produces fleece made from recycled plastic bottles.
www.patagonia.co.uk

Recycle Now

General information about recycling a range of materials.
www.recyclenow.com

Renewable Energy Association

Renewable energy trade association in the UK.
www.r-p-a.org.uk

Seasalt

For organically certified organic clothing.
www.seasaltcornwall.co.uk

Think cans

Information about cash for cans and drinks can recycling.
www.thinkcans.com

Timber-framed double glazing

For more information on timber-framed windows visit www.greenbuildingstore.co.uk or the British Wood-working Federation at www.bwf.org.uk

TRAID - Textile Recycling for Aid and International Development
Operates textile recycling banks across the UK. It diverts clothing from ending up on landfill by repairing and customizing items before selling them, raising funds for overseas development and environmental projects.
www.traid.org.uk

Urbaneliving
For a range of natural, handmade wall coverings and wallpapers, as well as fungicide-free wallpaper paste.
www.urbaneliving.co.uk

US Department of Energy Efficiency and Renewable Energy
Gives advice on energy saving.
www.eere.energy.gov

Waste Online
An online document library.
www.wasteonline.org.uk

Chapter 2: The Green House

Campaign for Safe Cosmetics
A coalition that campaigns for the health and beauty industry to phase out the use of chemicals linked to cancer, birth defects and other health problems and replace them with safer alternatives.
www.safecosmetics.org

Energy Star
A joint programme of the US Environmental Protection Agency and the US Department of Energy to provide energy-efficient products and practices.
www.energystar.gov

Environmental Working Group
An organization that works to protect public health and the environment.
www.ewg.org

Green Fibres
A wide range of certified organic bed linen and mattresses.
www.greenfibres.co.uk

Guide to Less Toxic Products
Information about health risks of common products.
www.lesstoxicguide.ca

ISP Services
For green ISP services.
www.greenisp.net
www.phonecoop.coop
www.gn.apc.org

National Association of Diaper Services
The international professional trade association
for the nappy (diaper) service industry.
www.diapernet.org

The Natural Collection
For a range of recycled office equipment including pens
and pencils, mousemats made from recycled tyres and
recycled printing paper and notebooks.
www.naturalcollection.com

Nigel's Eco Store
Sells a range of LED lighting ideal for home office
environments.
www.nigelsecostore.com

Oxfam International
International charity which recycles mobile (cell) phones
and ink cartridges.
www.oxfam.org

Raft
A range of beds and other furniture made from
reclaimed hardwood.
www.raftltd.co.uk

Recycle Your Jeans
Turn your old denim jeans into brand new sandals.
www.recycleyourjeans.com

Skin Deep
A cosmetic safety database.
www.cosmeticsdatabase.com

The Solar Cooking Archive
For information on solar cooking.
www.solarcooking.org

There Must be a Better Way
For natural nail varnishes and acetate-free removers,
as well as certified organic cuticle oil products from
Sante and Zebra Prescot brands.
www.theremustbeabetterway.co.uk

UK Craft Fairs
Learn how to make your own vegetable dyes.
www.ukcraftfairs.com

Warren Evans
For handmade organic mattresses and beds.
www.warrenevans.com

The Water Guide
Provides water-saving tips.
www.water-guide.org.uk

WaterSense
The USA's EPA website on water saving.
www.epa.gov/watersense/

Women's Environmental Network
Educates and informs, and runs the Real Nappy Project.
www.wen.org.uk

World Wildlife Fund
For climate change and a guide to toxic chemicals.
www.worldwildlife.org

Chapter 3 :
Green Growing and Eating

BTCV
Supports volunteering opportunities in the
countryside and outdoors.
www.btcv.org

Campaign to Protect Rural England
Campaigns on light pollution and landscape issues.
www.cpre.org.uk

Community Composting Network
Supports community composting projects.
www.communitycompost.org

The Composting Association
Promotes composting.
www.compost.org.uk

Environment Agency
Information on your local environment and guides on
rainwater harvesting and sustainable urban drainage.
www.environment-agency.gov.uk

Food Alliance
For certified farms, ranches and food producers in the US
that practice sustainable agricultural and food handling.
www.foodalliance.org

Food Commission
Campaigning for safer healthier food in the UK.
www.foodcomm.org.uk

Gene Watch
Monitors genetic technologies – public interest,
environmental protection and animal welfare perspectives.
www.genewatch.org

The Green Roof Centre
An independent research and demonstration
hub on green roofs.
www.thegreenroofcentre.co.uk

Green Roofs for Healthy Cities
Promotes green roofs in North America.
www.greenroofs.com

Green Space
A registered charity which works to improve parks
and green spaces, providing advice and a directory
of community and friends groups.
www.green-space.org.uk

It's Your Space
A website containing advice for people wanting to
transform a local green space.
www.itsyourspace.org.uk

Learning through Landscapes
A national school grounds charity, able to provide
advice on school gardens in the UK.
www.ltl.org.uk

Living Roofs
For independent advice on green roofs.
www.livingroofs.org

Marine Conservation Society
A UK charity that campaigns for clean seas and beaches, sustainable fisheries and protection for all marine life.
www.mcsuk.org

Marine Stewardship Council
Certifies sustainable fisheries.
www.msc.org

National Coalition for Pesticide-Free Lawns
Useful information about pesticides and the alternatives.
www.beyondpesticides.org

The National Society of Allotment and Leisure Gardeners
For allotment holders and vegetable growers in the UK.
www.nsalg.demon.co.uk

Natural England
Provides information on wildlife gardening.
www.naturalengland.org.uk

Organic Trade Association
For organic facts, food safety and standards in the US.
www.ota.com

Pesticide Action Network North America
Works to reduce the use of hazardous pesticides .
www.panna.org

Project for Public Spaces
For creating and sustaining public places and gardens.
www.pps.org

Roundtable on Sustainable Palm Oil
Promotes a sustainable palm oil industry.
www.rspo.org

Royal Horticultural Society
The UK's leading gardening charity dedicated to promoting good gardening and advancing horticulture. For advice on green gardening and school gardens.
www.rhs.org.uk

Royal Society for the Protection of Birds
Provides advice on gardening for birds and other wildlife.
www.rspb.org.uk

Scottish Allotments and Gardens Society
An allotment body for Scotland.
www.sags.org.uk

Shoppers Guide to Pesticides in Produce
A guide to the pesticides in your food.
www.foodnews.org

Slow Food
A movement to promote locally grown food.
www.slowfood.com

The Wildlife Trusts
For advice on gardening for wildlife.
www.wildlifetrusts.org

Woodland Trust
For advice on trees and community woodlands.
www.woodlandtrust.org.uk

Index